ASIA'S INVESTMENT PROPHETS

ASIA'S INVESTMENT PROPHETS

TOP MONEY MANAGERS AND THEIR SECRETS OF SUCCESS

CLAIRE BARNES

C
CENTURY
BUSINESS
BOOKS

To Rosalind and Jonathan

Claire Barnes has asserted her rights under the Copyright, Designs
and Patents Act 1988, to be identified as the author of this work.

First published by Century Ltd
Random House, 20 Vauxhall Bridge Road, London SW1V 2SA

Random House Australia (Pty) Limited
16 Dalmore Drive, Scoresby
Victoria 3179, Australia

Random House New Zealand Limited
18 Poland Road, Glenfield
Auckland 10, New Zealand

Random House South Africa (Pty) Limited
Box 2263, Rosebank 2121, South Africa

Reprinted 1995

Random House UK Limited Reg. No. 954009

Papers used by Random House UK Limited are natural,
recyclable products made from wood grown in sustainable forests.
The manufacturing processes conform to the environmental
regulations of the country of origin.

Companies, institutions and other organizations wishing to make bulk
purchases of any business books published by Random House should contact
their local bookstore or Random House direct:
Special Sales Director
Random House, 20 Vauxhall Bridge Road, London SW1V 2SA
Tel 0171 973 9000   Fax 0171 828 6681

ISBN 0 7126 7767 4

Phototypeset by Intype, London
Printed and bound in Great Britain by
Mackays of Chatham PLC, Chatham, Kent

Contents

Acknowledgments

One of the first things I discovered in writing this book is that there was little point in seeking observations about fund managers from most stockbrokers. My thanks to Nick Ruffer for the perceptive comment that all fund managers are wonderful, especially those who give him the most commission.

Thanks also to Richard Armstrong, Adam le Mesurier, Nick George, David Shairp, and Alan Hargreaves, for more practical insights; to Jenny Crivelli for her help in Australia; to Priscilla Coker for invaluable advice and practical assistance in the US; and to Jonathan Compton, who remains devastatingly perspicacious on all aspects of the investment business, especially after a good bottle of claret.

Roger Edgley, who not only contributed valuable insights but also carries the responsibility for persuading me to write this book, has moved to the buy side himself, going from Hong Kong to Chicago to join Wanger Asset Management. Had he done so earlier, his focus on superior businesses would probably have secured him a place in the profiles.

Most importantly, my thanks to all the investment managers who gave up their time and assisted my thinking, including all of those profiled, and a great many more. The list includes some outstanding individuals whom I would very much like to have included, but who preferred to avoid the limelight.

In Asia: Andrew Alexander, James Alexandroff, Renu Bhatia, Diahann Brown, Dan Carroll, Chin Ean Wah, Bill Ebsworth, Gavin Graham, Ray Hood, Michael Kwee, George Long, Mark Mobius, David Paterson, John Quinn, Bruce Seton, Anil Thadani, Robert Thomas, Terry Thomas, and Elizabeth Tran.

In the UK: John Ager, Richard Chenevix-Trench, Tristan Clube,

Peter Curtin, Martin Dixon, Giulio Franzinetti, Jeremy Hosking, Jan Kingzett, Kathryn Langridge, Heather Manners, Peter Montgomery, Anthony Newsome, George Robinson, Martin Shenfield, Stephen Swift, George Veitch, Michael Watt, and Anne West.

In the USA: Marshall Auerback, Deepinder Bhatia, Andrew Economos, Tom Haslett, John Hickling, Laura Luckyn-Malone, Paul Matthews, Grace Pineda, Steve Silverman, and Bryan Sudweeks.

A number of other people in the industry provided invaluable assistance, and I should like to thank Stewart Aldcroft, Stephen Hill, Jo McBride, Carl Meerveld, Aligo Mok, Steve Petersohn, Grahame Stott, and Richard Thornton.

My thanks, also, to Elizabeth Hennessy and Simon King at Random House; to Claudia Cragg who effected the introductions; to my agent Patrick Walsh; and finally to my sister Anne, for help and encouragement when most needed.

ASIAN MARKETS

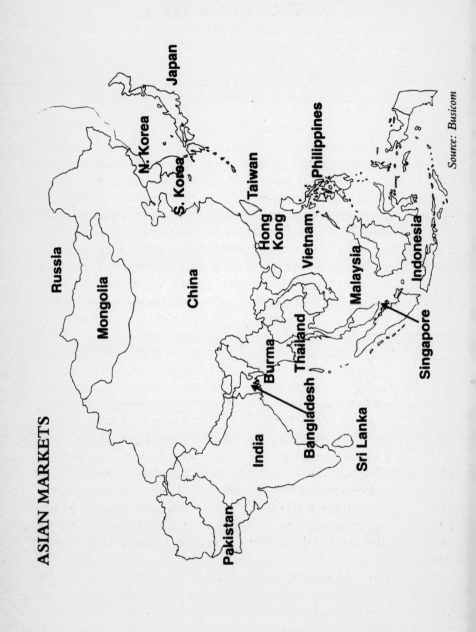

Source: Busicom

Introduction

In the single year of 1993, more investors were introduced to Asian markets than in any year previously. United States investors alone poured US$17 billion into Asian stock markets, a sum equivalent to the national product of a small country. About one third of this sum went into Japan, a highly developed stock market, although a depressed one — but the same again went into the tiny city-state of Hong Kong. Investors from continental Europe became noticeably more prominent in the markets of Hong Kong and South-East Asia. The British have been investing in the region since the nineteenth century, but in Britain too new funds were raised to capitalize on the booming Asian markets.

This book concentrates on the Asian markets other than Japan. Japan is so important that funds there are almost always run by specialists; and if you are running a Japanese fund it is unlikely that you will be able to spare enough time to develop a deep understanding of Thailand, let alone Bangladesh. The Asian markets excluding Japan (shortened by investment people to Asia-ex-Japan) accordingly constitute a major investment arena in their own right. The number of markets followed by foreigners has proliferated dramatically in recent years, from two or three in the early 1980s to fourteen now, and in many of these markets the number of companies in which foreigners are interested has also grown rapidly. In the interests of readability, this book will refer just to Asia, but will generally mean Asia-ex-Japan.

If you live in the United States or Western Europe, and you have any life insurance, or a pension entitlement, it is now likely that a portion of it is invested in Asia. Many individuals will now also have more direct exposure, through international growth mutual funds, or more targeted Asian vehicles.

In the United States especially, this is a relatively new development. Throughout the 1980s, it was expected that the US pension funds would increase their foreign exposure from previously minimal levels, but the predicted tidal wave of funds never materialized in great size. However, sometime during the decade, a critical mental shift took place. Previously, it had been felt that it was imprudent to invest overseas (distant markets were more volatile, and less information was available, so the risks were too high). Gradually, as the evidence piled up, it was accepted that it was imprudent *not* to invest overseas (especially in fast-growing countries where returns should be higher, and the risks would be reduced by diversification). The decision was taken at different times, but a bandwagon gradually began to roll. The maturing of a more than decade-long US bull market, a collapse in US interest rates, and a quest for growth outside an increasingly highly-rated US stock market, finally combined to start the surge.

Other factors contributed. Among the various categories of US investors, pension funds led the way into international markets, spurred on by the ageing of the US workforce and the relentless build-up of pension liabilities. The collapse of communism in Russia and Eastern Europe helped, both by reducing the perceived external dangers, and by highlighting the growth opportunities. It also caused US investors to re-evaluate China, despite the lack of political change there, on the theory that communism had failed totally as a basis for economic management, and that free market principles will inexorably replace command economics. In 1988 the US investor consensus on Hong Kong was sceptical as to the territory's continued economic and social viability. By 1993, this scepticism had given way to starry-eyed optimism over the business potential of China. Inevitably, reality eventually impinged on this new euphoria, which in turn gave way to a somewhat better informed caution, coupled with more measured long-term optimism.

Not only the former communist bloc was changing. The 1980s saw the emergence of almost worldwide consensus on the benefits of free market economics and sound monetary policy. The remarkable growth of the Asian Newly Industrializing Countries (NICs) provided a persuasive role model, and in particular convinced many developing countries of the merits of foreign investment. Direct investment was the initial focus, but as portfolio investment flows built up and the open stock markets were seen to be able to raise billions of dollars in new capital for industry, rival economies were jolted into action. The opening up of new markets, and improvements in stock-market infrastructure and regulation, attracted further attention and emerging market investment in a virtuous circle.

The resurgence of Latin America was critical. The economic transformation of an entire continent was too big to ignore, especially if it was happening on your doorstep. The importance of Mexico was helpful; it was close, many investors had already been there on holiday and, like Hong Kong, it proved visitor-friendly. To some extent, Latin America competes with Asia for funds, but in practice the excellent investment returns in both regions helped to build confidence in emerging markets as an asset class, and to attract a much-increased share of global portfolio flows. The Mexican currency crisis in early 1995 therefore reverberated as far afield as Thailand.

Within Asia, too, buoyant stock markets and slicker marketing caused a flood of investment into mutual funds in the early nineties. By late 1993, the computer systems at several of the major Hong Kong firms were suffering under the strain, and one leading company closed its doors to new customers. The inflows caused the established fund management companies to scramble for more staff, even while American investment houses were desperately trying to establish their first foothold in Asia.

This unprecedented hiring spree means that many of the fund managers investing in Asia are new to the game; average experience can be no more than a few years. Many are new to the industry and have yet to experience a full cycle; others have experience elsewhere, but are new to Asia.

Hence this book: the stock-market opportunities in Asia are too good to miss, but there are traps for the unwary. Many of the fund managers featured here are among the longest-established in the region, and have excellent track records. Their styles differ widely. How do these top players tackle the diverse regional markets? What are the main difficulties and pitfalls? And what separates these top performers from the crowd?

WHY ASIA?

The case for investing in Asia is extremely strong. Over the last ten years, many Asian countries have recorded real growth in gross domestic product averaging between 6 per cent and 9 per cent a year. China has averaged a double digit growth rate. Meanwhile, the high-income western economies have managed only 2–3 per cent a year. This growth differential is likely to continue for some years to come, as Asia is catching up from a low base.

The World Bank expects East-Asia-ex-Japan to achieve average growth of 7.3 per cent a year in the next decade, compared to 8 per cent in the ten years to 1992. This would translate into real per capita growth of about 6 per cent, enough to fuel a continuation of the rapid growth in demand for consumer goods. This growing affluence is visible everywhere.

When I first came to Hong Kong in 1981, peasants in traditional coolie hats could still be seen ploughing the rice paddies of the New Territories with the assistance of water buffalo. Tourists were taken to the Chinese border to peer across into a largely empty countryside. Within a few years, the rice had given way to containers, stacked three or four high – much more lucrative for the smallholders, who now have day jobs in offices in the new towns – and an entire city of skyscrapers had sprung up across the border in Shenzhen, looking remarkably similar to Hong Kong itself.

The cities of Asia now have six-lane highways choked with BMWs and Mercedes limousines. The roadside foodstalls of South-East Asia still exist, but in dwindling numbers: diners are forsaking the humidity in favour of fast food in air-conditioned complexes. Bangkok by the end of 1995 will have two of the five largest shopping malls in the world. McDonald's, Benetton and the Body Shop are flourishing Asia-wide. Mobile telephones are more popular in Asia than anywhere in the western world. The hotels and nightclubs of Asia are among the swankiest anywhere, and all of the highest spenders are Asian. In London, Asians have replaced Arabs in the minds of real-estate agents and Bond Street jewellers as the stereotypically super-rich.

Brand-consciousness is paramount. Plastic pens are anathema; the white snowflake of Mont Blanc is *de rigueur*. If you see an investment banker with a Swatch, he is British or American; if he is senior, his Chinese colleagues may be so embarrassed by this eccentricity that they club together to buy him a respectable Cartier. This is equal-opportunity brand snobbery: several new business empires have been built with the help of a plausible French or Italian name and expert marketing.

This conspicuous consumption may give the impression of frivolity, but underlying progress has been just as impressive. There are certainly still sweatshops, but there are also now hi-tech factories with state of the art technology. In South-East Asia this technology is mostly imported, but local managers apply it, although firms like Creative Technologies in Singapore (makers of the Soundblaster computer sound boards) are changing the stereotypes. Taiwan's electronics industry is in the world class; and Korea has in POSCO one of the largest and most efficient steel companies anywhere.

The operation of Asia's sophisticated new businesses and infrastructure has necessitated a remarkable upgrading of management and technical skills; and with it the growth of a huge middle class. Stockbroking firms have provided as vivid an impression of the change as other industries; the dusty Dickensian offices and handwritten ledgers which could be found only a few years ago in several of the South-East Asian markets have given way to lavish modern premises and sophisticated computer systems. (Anyone wanting a glimpse of the past may still obtain it in Bombay, where the brokers cluster in squalid office blocks close to the Exchange. This however is a function of Indian rent controls, which may mean they are paying US$5 per year for the whole office, compared with free market rents which, as a corollary, are among the highest in Asia. Do not make the mistake of assuming these people are poor. India's reformist government may move on to the property market soon, a move long overdue, so see this phenomenon while it lasts.)

High savings rates are a key part of the equation in East Asia, although conspicuously less so in the Indian subcontinent. As Peter Everington of Regent succinctly explains, the savings rate of a country corresponds to the ploughback rate of a company: 'High savings equals high investment equals high growth equals Asia.'

The less impressive savings rates of the Indian subcontinent and the Philippines are partly the result of very underdeveloped financial systems, which historically paid unattractive rates to depositors and consequently fail in their key role of mobilizing savings for productive investment. The story here is reform: privatization, deregulation, new sources of capital, and the release of potential. In the meantime, many private sector companies have been able to flourish at the expense of a labour-bloated public sector.

The productivity of the investments generated by those savings is also critical. Corruption and inefficient allocation of resources can blunt the effect. Many of the Asian countries are however investing very heavily in basic infrastructure, such as roads, power, and telecommunications. The liberating effect of these facilities on economic

Gross domestic savings as a percentage of GDP, 1992

Singapore	47
China	40
Indonesia	37
Malaysia	35
Thailand	35
Korea	35
Hong Kong	30
Taiwan	27
India	22
Philippines	18
Sri Lanka	15
Pakistan	14
Bangladesh	6
United States	15
United Kingdom	14

Source: World Bank, BZW

activity can be dramatic, especially when the country is starting from a low base. The impact of an adequate power supply in Manila, of working international telephone lines in Bombay, and of decent roads in the Pearl River delta, is to accelerate economic development remarkably.

Trickle-down investment is another major factor. As Japanese labour costs rose, the first beneficiaries were Korea, Taiwan, Hong Kong and Singapore. As labour costs in these countries rose, investment spilled into Malaysia and Thailand, Indonesia and China. Now Vietnam, Myanmar, and the Indian subcontinent are amongst the new contenders. Over time, the quality and complexity of production in each of these countries has risen, starting with low cost assembly operations and moving quickly upscale.

Intra-regional trade is becoming more important. The US is still the most important market for many of the regional economies, but Japan is typically in second place. The Asian model of export-led growth was tested in recent years by recession in the west. In the event, Asian exports soared further. This was due to an increase in global market share, which may not be indefinitely repeatable, and to increased regional trade, which is.

Meanwhile, the Asian countries furthest up the ladder (Japan, followed by the four NICs, Korea, Taiwan, Hong Kong and Singapore, and then by countries like Malaysia and Thailand) are well placed both to assist and to take advantage of the opportunities in the emerging economies just beginning the climb. The pace of change is accelerating, as countries no longer have to invent new systems and technologies, but instead apply template solutions honed by experience.

The accelerating pace of economic development

Years taken to double per capita output

UK	1780–1838	58
USA	1839–1886	47
Japan	1885–1919	34
	(and less after WWII)	
Brazil	1961–79	18
S. Korea	1966–77	11
China	1977–87	10

Source: *Foreign & Colonial Emerging Markets*

The later a city or country joins the industrialization process, the faster it can move, given the will to do so. Vietnam, with its highly literate and determined workforce and generally pragmatic economic policies, may well be the fastest growing country in Asia over the next twenty years – if its control-oriented bureaucrats do not stymie the process. North Korea or Myanmar could emerge as strong contenders for the mantle, given their lower and later starting base, depending how their presently-unstable internal politics play out.

The emerging ladder-climbers in Asia, which are also the key to the future growth of the more established economies, are no small, marginal markets: they are the biggest in the world. China had a population of 1.2 billion in 1992, 21 per cent of the world total. The four most dynamic markets of the Indian subcontinent – India, Pakistan, Bangladesh, and Sri Lanka – were together about the same size. Indonesia had 184 million people, more than three times the population of the United Kingdom; and the Philippines 64 million. The three countries of Indochina – Vietnam, Cambodia, and Laos – had 82 million, and Myanmar 44 million. These are only the countries which are already clearly on the move, and they contain half the world's people.[1]

Because the Asian industrializing experience is so recent, it falls within the personal experience of many of the region's entrepreneurs. A Malaysian industrialist recently returned from his first visit to Vietnam, excited by the scale of the opportunity and the clarity of his business plan. 'I know *exactly* what to do,' he told me, 'Saigon is *exactly* like Kuala Lumpur thirty years ago!'

Such projections of course are not without risk. In the 1950s, the Philippines was generally agreed to have the best prospects in Asia. It had the highest standard of living, a literate English speaking population, American support and legal/accounting infrastructure, and abundant natural resources. Resource-poor Japan was the postwar basket case. Japan went on to achieve the first of the region's many economic miracles, and the Philippines became the sick man of Asia. Moreover, there are no stock markets yet in Vietnam or Myanmar. Country funds have been launched for both, but these are direct investment vehicles, and not for the fainthearted. Rapid growth is not necessarily accompanied by profits for foreigners in the early years, as the experience of pioneering foreign companies in China proves.

In these true-frontier markets, Asian companies nevertheless can often do better than western ones. For many positions the adaptable Malaysians have become the most sought-after expatriates in Asia. The British engineering group TI has recently concluded that it needs an Asian partner with Chinese-speaking staff and *guanxi* (connections), and has signed a joint venture agreement with Singapore's Sembawang Holdings. And Hong Kong maintains its traditional role as entrepot and service centre for Southern China. So it is reasonable to expect that the growth of Asia's newly emerging countries may be reflected to some extent in profits of other regional companies; and their home bases, after all, are not doing badly, having once again been able to learn from experience and avoid the more obvious mistakes of the west.

Asian stock markets have generated excellent returns for investors. The MSCI Pacific-ex-Japan Index returned 15.5 per annum in US dollar terms in the ten years to 1994 – enough to quadruple your money over the period – despite including the lower-growth Austra-

1 1992 World Bank data

8

lian and New Zealand markets. (The return rose to almost 20 per cent a year if gross dividends were reinvested.)[1]

The markets have also become bigger and more liquid, helped by privatizations and new other listings. While the range of companies available in the early eighties was quite narrow, it is now increasingly broad and representative. Capitalizations of the twelve Asian 'emerging' markets in the IFC (International Finance Corporation) database grew at a compound annual rate of 25 per cent between 1980 and 1993, to over US$1 trillion. The growth in Hong Kong and Singapore, which add another 50 per cent to the total capitalization, would have been similarly dramatic.

All of the individual markets have given investors a roller coaster ride: all have suffered crises from time to time. Many of the markets have been characterized by very long periods of steadily rising prices, punctuated by short, sharp setbacks. Expressing the same thing statistically, Bryan Sudweeks of Montgomery Asset Management points out that while the standard deviations of monthly returns for most Asian markets are in the 30–40 per cent range, the semi-standard deviations, which take into account only months when the markets fell, are typically 10–20 per cent. In other words, much of the volatility is in the investor's favour. Moreover, while common factors often drive several markets at a time – the health of the US market for Asian exports, for example, or waves of Japanese direct investment – the crises are often localized. For example, while the Hong Kong market tumbled in 1989 after the Tiananmen Square massacre, Thailand was extremely strong, and Singapore was also firm. When Thailand's market suffered from its own political bloodshed in 1992, Hong Kong in turn was buoyant.

Many investors have now come to the conclusion that they can afford to ignore politics, and treat any political setback as a buying opportunity. This may be a conditioned response, after a series of events in which this has been the correct reaction – several coups in Thailand, the Tiananmen Square massacre in China, the Gulf War, and the tensions in North Korea. Also, as one fund manager confessed, 'We can't even spell the names of most Malaysian politicians, let alone work out who's winning and losing.' More importantly, there is a broad consensus in Asia that economic growth is the priority goal, and political upheavals often have very limited economic consequences. Countries have been spurred on by their

1 Source: Micropal

competitors. To give just one example, when Thailand's economy surged in the mid-eighties, there was a noticeable sense in both Malaysia (which considered itself more advanced) and Indonesia (bigger and more powerful) that something should be done. This was essentially a matter of pride, but strategic imperatives have also been in play – for example, in India, which keeps a wary eye on the growing economic strength of its traditional rival, China.

This growth consensus is not totally universal. In all of the communist countries, there is some reactionary disapproval. Investors have been worrying for years about the possibility of instability in China after the death of Deng Xiaoping, who has been the principal propagator of the present growth and reform philosophy. Vietnam has a similar internal debate between different communist party factions; at present, like China, the country is aiming for economic growth while resisting political change. Myanmar is moving in the same direction. North Korea has never subscribed to the consensus, and at the time of writing is continuing its self-imposed isolation; economic hardship in recent years has been devastating, and the leadership is unpredictable. Islamic fundamentalism is sometimes suggested as another possible cause of breakdown in the growth consensus, but both Malaysia and Indonesia have considerable expertise in defusing religious tensions. Investors may have more cause to keep an eye on religious concerns in Pakistan and Bangladesh. At the micro-level, increasing environmental consciousness in many Asian countries is causing closer scrutiny of individual projects. Overall, however, the growth consensus remains firmly intact throughout most of Asia.

Within individual Asian countries, huge disparities of income still exist, and not all citizens have profited from the national economic gains. In most countries, however, a large number of people have benefited, and have an interest in continued growth. In many countries, land reform played a critical role in achieving this. In Korea, Taiwan, Hong Kong, Singapore and Malaysia, the benefits of economic growth have been very widespread. In Pakistan, the benefits have not spread far beyond the feudal landlords; power also remains very concentrated in the Philippines and Indonesia. At the time of writing, there are few signs of escalation in such tensions, but for the long-term investor it is often worth noting such distinctions.

WHICH MARKETS IN ASIA?

The number of stock markets of interest to foreigners has grown apace. In the early 1980s, there were only two markets attracting much interest: Hong Kong and Singapore. The Philippines had been popular in the eighties, but both the economy and the stock market suffered under the Marcos administration, and investors had given up visiting. The lights were out, as Anthony Newsome of Genesis recalls, both metaphorically and physically.

Foreigners were also interested in Malaysia, but did most of their trading through Singapore, as almost all stocks from both countries were listed there, and the Singaporean brokers were more used to international dealing. Malaysia and Singapore therefore tended to be regarded as a single unit. I remember great amusement in the small local investment community when a senior executive from one of the largest US investment banks, at the end of a trip to both Singapore and Malaysia in 1984, was reported to have given a dinner in Kuala Lumpur for the Malaysian prime minister and other dignitaries. He thanked them for their hospitality, and said how impressed the delegation had been 'by the cleanliness and efficiency of your capital, Singapore'. The prime minister left the dinner rather early. The story may have been apocryphal, but was not implausible, and certainly little was heard of that particular company in Malaysia for some years thereafter.

Thailand was the next market to attract foreign attention, followed by Korea and Taiwan, which in the event opened their doors only slowly to foreign investors. The ousting of President Marcos led to a recovery in the Philippines, and Indonesia's previously comatose market was revitalized from 1988–89 onwards. Malaysia withdrew its companies' listings in Singapore, and went on to become one of the region's most vibrant stock markets in its own right, with turn-over in 1993 at times exceeding that on the New York Stock Exchange. China introduced stock markets, tackling the additional non-trivial hurdle that it had to restructure its state owned enterprises into recognizable corporate entities before listing. The nineties have seen foreigners investing enthusiastically in Sri Lanka, and then in India, Pakistan and Bangladesh. By 1994, the Russian Far East became a target of the adventurous; by contrast with China, all companies were privatized in haste, and some of the structural details are still rather hazy.

The number of markets which may be routinely covered by an

Asian fund manager has therefore gone from two in the early eighties to four in the late eighties and as many as fourteen by 1994 – with many managers also fitting in excursions to Vietnam and Myanmar to keep an eye on the possible emerging markets of the future. Even Mongolia has attracted some attention, but has, like Vladivostok, to contend with the 'fun factor', or rather the perceived lack thereof. Countries wishing to be taken seriously are considerably advantaged if they have a pleasant climate, good food, sandy beaches, and other attractions.

At the same time the structure of many markets has evolved considerably. Malaysia has been transformed by the listing of the two big utility companies, Telekom and Tenaga. Telecommunications and property stocks, and the growing importance of the finance companies, have changed the profile of the Thai market. Foreigners investing in the Philippines used to buy only two stocks; now they have a choice of perhaps eight or ten which are reasonably liquid.

A flood of convertible bonds and other offshore instruments from most of the Asian markets, issued in the recent bull run to tap international funds and skirt local dealing constraints, have increased the choice. Warrants have long been popular in Asia, but the number in issue is now greater than ever before. Increasing numbers of funds are now looking at stock shorting possibilities, thanks to easier stock borrowing facilities provided by the US investment banks; and customized derivatives can be offered by the same US firms. Some regulatory authorities are beginning to look more sympathetically at the possibility of allowing short selling on their exchanges, recognizing that it might help to diminish the influence of the 'big hands' (local market manipulators). The range of instruments available to the fund manager in each market has therefore increased dramatically, as have the quantity and quality of information, although the latter still leave much to be desired.

WHICH FUND MANAGER IN ASIA?

The size of funds under management has swelled rapidly. It is not uncommon for individual unit trusts, after a period of success, to attract so much new money that they grow ten-fold within a couple of years. Some managers can adapt; others find their original trading style severely hampered by liquidity. This happens in western markets too, but to a much greater extent in Asia because of the growth and the market inefficiencies which can lead more often to spectacular performance, and because of the severity of the liquidity constraints in many markets.

Fund management companies, as a whole, have seen assets under management balloon, and this has sometimes placed strains on human and systems resources. Many investment institutions are moving from individual to team management, a tricky transition. Recruiting, training, and integrating the newcomers necessary to handle the expanding funds and growing number of markets is not always easy, especially in the frenetic job market of Hong Kong.

The mobility of individual fund managers between companies may make life hard for the retail investor. Some firms are more structured and better placed for the long term than others, and some funds are better structured than others for the investment objective at the time of purchase, but Asian markets are still sufficiently inefficient to mean that the identity of the individual manager is the key factor. A good manager at a good investment house is the best combination. If you decide to back a great individual at a bucket shop, ensure that you will know if he moves.

Continuity is much less than in the west. Few fund managers have been running individual funds for ten years; of the institutional equity managers featured here, only Charles Fowler can claim to have done so. Long-term track records for individuals, therefore, are often composite. If they are in marketing mode, they may show you a composite track record based on their best single funds of each period, rather than an average. If they are based in the United States and have switched jobs, they may be constrained from giving you any figures at all.

The diversity of parameters between funds makes it difficult, if not impossible, to compare track records directly between managers. How do you compare a track record built up successively in the Philippines and Malaysia with one dominated by Korea and Thailand?

Gearing also makes it difficult to compare performance. Even when investors are told of the financial gearing, they rarely have additional information on the use of warrants and other derivatives, or of average beta, which might provide a clue as to the real risk exposure of the fund.

Nevertheless, there are fund managers with track records long enough and consistent enough to stand out well above the pack. Several of the managers in this book have sustained annual growth of 30 per cent or more over long periods – five years, ten years, or more. Due to the magic of compounding, a 32 per cent annual return is enough to quadruple your money every four years. Such rates are exceptional, putting more than a couple of years together, and usually dependent on being in the right place at the right time.

Compound annual growth of 20–25 per cent over long periods, and averaged over *all* funds under management, rather than just the top performer selected for marketing purposes, has been more than respectable, even in Asia. Growth of 20 per cent a year is sufficient to triple your money every six years; growth of 25 per cent will do it in only five. Many of the managers in this book have historically achieved growth of this magnitude.

That does not, of course, mean that it is sustainable. The performance of individuals may slip; that of the whole region may slacken. Earnings growth in Asian markets has historically been reasonably well correlated, over long periods, with the nominal growth in gross national product. High as this economic growth may be, it is generally lower than the figures just mentioned. Part of the performance of Asian and other emerging markets over the early 1990's came from upward re-rating, and while this may be taken further it can not be extended indefinitely. Asian markets will probably continue to offer long-term returns well in excess of the developed world, but they may not be quite as high as in the recent past. Performance difficulties between managers, already wide, may widen.

On what will a manager's out-performance depend? In Asia, this is now a multi-billion dollar question. This book aims both to provide some insight into the thinking of key players, and to illuminate the differences between various types of funds. Readers may judge that the clearest investment philosophies and most distinctive styles are to be found amongst the hedge fund managers, grouped together in the middle of the book. This is no accident; all exceptional investors have the opportunity and the individuality to strike out with their own firms, and many do so. They may then limit their investor base, to allow greater flexibility or focus than they found possible in an institutional environment. However, not all investors can be clients of such firms, and not all would wish to give their managers such latitude. Institutional managers in Asian markets may contend with huge and volatile fund flows in illiquid markets, and with commercial pressures of constraining their judgment. How the best managers of multi-billion dollar funds cope with these difficulties is of practical importance to a far greater number.

The managers featured here operate with widely varying objectives and constraints, but include many of the finest investors I know. They are also amongst the bravest. Most have talked in great detail about specific examples of their investment thinking, which are much more enlightening than mere statements of principle, but expose them to far greater risk of embarrassment. Given the volatility of stockmarkets and the lead times of publishing, some of these views will have been proven wrong by the time this book reaches the shelves. Investment is a game of percentages and controlled risk-taking. The greatest investors make mistakes; the secret of continued greatness is to learn from each one. Readers are urged to step sympathetically around the banana skins.

Chapter 1

Institutional stockpicking

Peter Phillips and Fidelity

One of the most analytical stock-pickers in a large Hong Kong investment house is Peter Phillips of Fidelity. A slight and unassuming Australian with a boyish grin, he ran the Hong Kong/China fund for three to four years, and achieved outstandingly good returns with well-below-average volatility. He has now taken over Fidelity Funds South-East Asia.

Value investing works in Hong Kong, he is convinced, with Jardine Matheson an example of the opportunities created by fickle sentiment. Twice in the last four years it has traded at bargain levels. In 1991 it was regarded with general disdain, the consensus was disparaging of the management, and it was widely expected that the company would never do anything right. When the market's low expectations were exceeded, the stock soared. It ultimately went to a premium rating, only to be hammered again when it decided to delist from the Hong Kong market.

There may be an opportunity cost in waiting for the market to recognise cheap stocks. The Hong Kong television company TVB languished for years in the early 1990's, before suddenly bursting into life and rising six-fold in two years. Phillips 'would have a company like that in the portfolio, but initially a small percentage. You look for catalysts that might cause the value to be recognized.'

On the companies Phillips knows well, he can pull out a sheaf of handwritten notes from a pile close at hand. All his visit notes for the last few years in Hong Kong are kept in folders in his office, providing the immediacy which a library lacks. He never types up his notes, but just highlights key points with a coloured marker. He finds a note from August 1992, when he met TVB's financial controller and asked whether the station might be able to charge premium rates for advertising given the large unofficial audience over

16

the border in China. (Hong Kong has a population of less than six million; the neighbouring province of Guangdong more than ten times that. Cantonese is the first language of both.) The TVB man said this would be impossible. Phillips visited again four months later, and this time 'before the meeting even started, he produced a survey of Guangdong province showing the potential. By now the stock was already beginning to move.' The following month, Phillips visited his wife's cousin in Foshan, and found that he was watching the English-language news from Hong Kong, partly to improve his English and partly because he believed Hong Kong television more reliable than the government version. Another cousin commented that the guy in the Giordano advertisements was really cool . . . Phillips was by now convinced; the story stacked up.

THE LEVERAGED ATTRACTIONS OF THE MEDIA SECTOR

The media sector in general is a favourite. Phillips pulls out a little book of regional advertising statistics, to show how advertising expenditure is rising as a proportion of GDP in each country. In a growing economy, media companies are capable of strong growth and excellent cash generation. 'First you benefit from GDP growth; second, from the rise in advertising expenditure as a proportion of GDP; third, from the relative decline of billboard advertising in that total, and the rise of more sophisticated media, first newspapers and then television; and fourth, perhaps from margin expansion, if the particular company has attained a critical size.'

Phillips particularly likes newspapers, which tend to have very strong free cash flow, resulting in good dividends and self-financed expansion: if anything they may tend to build up excessive cash balances. *The South China Morning Post* had been an old favourite, but Murdoch's sale to Robert Kuok had caught Phillips by surprise, and he has reduced his holding while awaiting evidence of Kuok strategy. He had originally felt that the Post was a key part of Murdoch's strategy for Asia, and that Murdoch had demonstrated real commitment to developing the Asian business. This view had been confirmed by the move into Chinese language publishing (which the market had taken as a negative because of its short term costs), and by the negotiations for Shanghai magazines which were under way in September 1993, when Murdoch suddenly sold the

Post and bought the controlling stake in Star TV. 'Then the case fell apart.' The shares subsequently fell back, in a rising market. Phillips says ruefully that he has been proved spectacularly right on Murdoch's commitment to Asia, but picked the wrong vehicle.

Why then does he still hold some shares? With the Saturday paper thumping onto doorsteps with 150 pages of classified advertising, surely *Post* revenues could only go downhill from here? Phillips whips out his desk diary to show me the figures carefully pencilled in to the columns of the monthly planner; he has been counting the pages in the Saturday edition for the last three years, and his notes show the number of advertising pages to be up 10% for the year to date. He also likes the state-of-the-art plant in the New Territories, and thinks that Chinese publishers will soon be beating a path to the new facilities.

He is extremely enthusiastic about prospects for the entertainment industry in Asia, although there are limited ways to play this theme as yet, beyond the various Malaysian gambling companies which are gradually expanding in the region. He is fascinated by the Chinese national soccer league – not for the standard of the football, but as a social phenomenon: the extraordinary spectacle of Guangdong v Shanghai, sponsored by Marlboro, and broadcast region-wide by Star TV. The recent world cup in the US, broadcast live on Star and therefore screened in the early hours of the morning in Asia, generated tremendous interest in Hong Kong and Singapore, and even Bangkok's notorious traffic jams eased up noticeably.

Phillips sees 250–300 companies a year, and reckons that when he was covering Hong Kong this was more than anyone else on the buy side. Company visits are indispensable, he maintains, but it is rare to come out of a meeting definitely bullish or bearish. 'If you are, it probably means you are being lied to! Or given inside information, which we can't use.'

ASIA'S BIGGEST EMERGING MARKET

Taiwan is the largest emerging market in Asia, Phillips argues: big, illiquid, and poorly researched. With his responsibilities newly broadened to include that market, he is racing to get up to speed with Taiwanese companies, and has been averaging one trip a month. He is encouraged by the quality of the companies he is seeing; many have operations in China which seem more technology-driven and

18

less dependent on connections than their counterparts in Hong Kong, and appear to understate earnings to avoid tax. He is finding the companies more operations-focused, less status-conscious, and more often run by executives with strong engineering or technical qualifications. Head offices tend to be unostentatious; visitors may be served with paper cups. Broker research is poor and the earnings estimates very volatile; on the research note closest to hand, the current year profit estimate has been raised by 25% without explanation. For many years brokers' optimism has been repeatedly dashed; now, for a change, many forecasts are being upgraded.

Phillips likes a number of Taiwanese food companies, and is particularly impressed by Standard Foods, which was listed after a management buyout of the old Quaker Oats business, and appeals to the growing health-consciousness of young Taiwanese. Phillips finds the management convincing, and likes the fact that the chief executive has a PhD in food science. Gross margins are over 50%, the company is growing at not far short of 25% a year, and the shares are on a price-earnings ratio of 18.

Phillips is cautiously optimistic about the scope for superior stock selection in Taiwan. He has done reasonably well so far, he says, partly by avoiding the financial sector, without which values are reasonable. He is pleased that more foreigners are qualifying to participate in the market, and that more Euro-issues are coming out. 'Since locals are looking at price-earnings ratios in order to front-run the foreigners, this is good: one won't be left stranded like Robinson Crusoe.'

He feels that cross-border experience can be very helpful, allowing a fund manager to spot the potential for re-rating, by understanding how similar companies are evaluated in other markets. His example is TVB, where knowledge of the media industry in Australia gave him the confidence to hold on to the share after it doubled, on the basis that the rerating could run much further. However, he reckons that it is then essential to evaluate individual shares in the context of their own market – he would not, for example, observe that Hong Kong banks are more cheaply rated than Malaysian banks and conclude that they must necessarily therefore be a better buy.

International experience allows an investor to understand industries better, because different companies highlight different facets of the business, especially as they encounter different operating conditions; to spot anomalies, for example excessive depreciation charges which may be disguising the true level of profitability: and to identify possible turning points, whether in industry cycles or in valuation. We talk about the new breed of industry specialist analysts within broking firms, covering a single sector across the region. Specialist knowledge of individual industries may enable such analysts to ask better questions and produce superior analysis: Phillips quotes Andrew Harrington, the telecommunications analyst at Salomon, as an example. To turn that potential advantage of a superior perspective into reality, however, Phillips is convinced that the possible scenarios must then be evaluated in the context of the domestic stockmarket. An understanding of the local market is essential, in order to interpret correctly the implications for individual shares.

A SERVICE ORIENTATION

Phillips' portfolios show a bias towards the service sector. Biases can be dangerous, he comments, but less so if you are aware of them and regularly re-evaluate. He thinks that coming from Australia, a service economy, has helped him to appreciate the potential of service industries. The service sector is expanding rapidly in Asia as the local economies mature, and with the exception of the banks is generally not capital-intensive.

Life insurance is an example of a sector he likes. Premium income in Hong Kong has been growing at around 27% a year for the last decade – and this is one of the 'difficult' markets, because of the Chinese superstition that it is imprudent to tempt fate by providing for death.

National Mutual, however, has provided a recent bruising experience in Hong Kong. The company had been doing phenomenally well; it had hit the right note in its advertising, it acquired a suitably solid building, it was moving sensibly into China, and it was generally building up tremendous local consumer confidence. Then in 1994 it lost a large part of its sales force, and the managing director, to a tiny rival with giant ambitions and powerful local backing. The company was rocked to the core by the losses, and by the bitter recriminations. Phillips is currently out of the stock, while trying to work out the long-term implications of the crisis. 'That's why you need diversified portfolios of securities', he says philosophically; 'there are some hiccoughs in developed markets, but there are more here in Asia.'

Banking accounts for perhaps half of the service sector in many countries. As we talk in the third quarter of 1994, Phillips feels that the banking sector is still reasonably sound despite rising interest rates. Contrary to expectations, margins are generally holding up; banks now have plenty of equity, and provision levels are already high, while economic growth remains strong. Bank disclosure is improving, in Hong Kong especially, and this gives him an additional degree of comfort.

Corporate disclosure generally is improving across the region, he believes, although he remains very critical of many companies on this score. We pause to laugh at the day's remarkably frank announcement from Tsingtao Brewery. 'Mr Zhang Ya Dong resigned his posts as Chairman and General Manager of the Company. The positions he held proved to be hard work, and he found it difficult to adjust to the workload given the state of his physical health and limited energy. As party committee secretary, Mr Zhang will focus more on party business. The board accepted his resignation and decided that it should separate business policy decisions, everyday management, and party committee matters . . .'

Phillips became interested in economics and investment while at school in Australia, and went on to take the Securities Institute course during the last year of a degree in accounting. At this stage it was an academic interest – but he did sharpen his numeracy, in those days before computerisation, by working for a bookmaker every Saturday throughout his university course. He then joined Elders Finance, doing credit analysis for the merchant banking side and investment analysis for the pension fund, and went on to ANZ as an investment analyst. In 1986 he became the first person in Australia to take the American CFA (Chartered Financial Analyst) course. That first examination was in the teacher's house near his home in Melbourne; the system later became a little more formal. He joined Fidelity in 1987.

K. C. LEE

Fidelity has other characters in the Hong Kong office. One is K. C. Lee, a maverick in his early thirties with an owlish academic look, heightened by the sagging cardigan and slippers he invariably wears in the office. His office has an impressive hi-fi system, with classical music clearly the preference. He doesn't play it during office hours, he explains, but spends enough time there in the evenings and weekends that it is worthwhile being relaxed.

Like Phillips, Lee runs regional funds, but he emphasizes the more traditional markets of the region – Hong Kong, Singapore, Malaysia and Thailand – and the larger stocks within those markets. 'Institutional investors as a whole have lost money in emerging markets; in some cases these markets have been graveyards. If you look at indices and volumes, you find that most investors were able to get in only towards the very end. When a market is first discovered, there is very little volume, so prices go up very quickly. Higher prices attract new supply, including low quality issues. Foreign investors end up paying too much for high quality companies, and far too much for low quality companies. Then, a small amount of selling can push prices sharply lower.'

China is Lee's example of a stockmarket to avoid. 'In an emerging market, companies need a lot of capital to finance expansion. The debt markets are undeveloped, so equity is the principal source of funding. The supply is huge, almost infinite. Therefore there is a risk of multiple contraction. Therefore you need huge growth in earnings per share to justify the multiples, but most companies raising money from foreigners suffer massive earnings dilution.'

In selecting stocks, and even more importantly in avoiding them, K. C. Lee finds it helpful to think in terms of market capitalization and enterprise value. 'There are still a lot of concept stocks capitalised at ridiculous prices.' With the Thai company Telecom Asia, for example, the difference between the value of the business estimated before listing and the market capitalization after listing was almost US$ 15 billion. It was clear that it would get no significant new contracts in Thailand, and that contracts in China were unlikely to be large. Lee says; what could therefore justify a premium comparable to the entire capitalization of Hongkong Telecom?

Now, the capitalization of Thai securities companies is absurd, he feels. The capitalization of Finance One is almost half that of Morgan Stanley, he says, fumbling for an MSCI quarterly to prove his point. Finance One's capitalization is given as US$ 2.0 billion, and that of its competitor Phatra Thanakit as $1.6 billion, while Morgan Stanley is at $4.2 billion, and the US discount broker Charles Schwab at $1.4 billion. 'Is that reasonable? Are the franchises comparable?'

More positively, he likes Korea Electric Power Company, which has a capitalization only just larger than Malaysia's Tenaga, with comparable profits, but three to four times the generating capacity.

Profits are being depressed through excessive depreciation charges, he believes. Either KEPCO is very cheap, or Tenaga very expensive. But he is less optimistic than the consensus on Korea, because investors are ignoring the level of debt.

Lee monitors the ratio of turnover to market capitalization on a monthly basis to assess investor psychology. He believes this is more reliable in assessing the final stages of a bull market than valuation, since the markets have topped out at different PE levels in each cycle. In Hong Kong, he reckons that turnover of more than 5% per month spells danger, and that the warning bells were therefore ringing from October 1993 onwards, when the Hang Seng index was at 9,000. Thailand entered the danger zone at around the same time, and Malaysia a couple of months earlier. In late 1994, although markets appear to have stabilized, he believes they are still risky, because they have yet to fall to the levels at which these danger signs first appeared, and markets remain way above long-term trend lines. Investors have yet to give up, he says: there is still too much specu-lation, and too much overvaluation of concept stocks. Moreover, for turnover to be as high as it has been in Malaysia and Thailand, either brokers or bankers or both must have been imprudent: he expects more scandals and repercussions to emerge, and this may take time.

Many investors in the region are still paying too much attention to concepts, Lee argues, buying a story if they think the market will go for it. Cyclicality is not well understood; investors often pay high multiples right at the peak of the cycle. The worst examples, he says, are in Singapore, where almost all stocks are cyclical, and only one stock (Cerebos) has reported unbroken eps growth in each of the last ten years. He is frustrated when we speak: he can see many sectors at cyclical highs, but few at cyclical lows.

ALLAN LIU

I ask Allan Liu, the manager of the ASEAN fund, about the particu-lar perils of managing money in the ASEAN (Association of South East Asian Nations) markets. The greatest, he says, is that company managers probably incur no liability if they lie, and as an outsider it is quite easy to be cheated. Moral sanctions don't work, because historically the expansion of the markets has been such that there are always more investors to replace those who have blacklisted the company. However, there is a danger in becoming too prejudiced by past history: many businessmen with a poor track record have gone on to become great successes, and you cannot afford just to rule out their companies. 'If you miss a stock and it doubles or triples, then of course this is better than losing money, but there is a major opportunity cost.' So all decisions are taken case by case. The fund manager cannot afford to tick only to the safest companies, because he might miss out on the majority of the growth stocks; and he has to take a *relative* view on technical expertise, competence, and management reliability. Liu emphasizes company visiting, but his approach is clearly affected by the quality of businesses available in his markets. However, he tries to avoid purely political stocks. 'If you have a stock which has no expertise or means of delivery, but expects a contract because the controlling shareholder is a friend of someone . . . then you have to think twice.'

SYSTEMS EFFICIENCY

Fidelity's dealing operation was centralized in the early 1980's; it is perhaps surprising that fund managers at many large Asian institutions handled their own dealing for so long. Managers like Peter Phillips, who take a long-term analytical view of the market, are now freed of daily execution and reconciliation chores; fund managers to whom short-term market movements are important now rely on the in-house dealers for information, and such information is more efficiently disseminated; and the in-house dealers are better placed than the fund managers to keep on top of all the trading and settlement eccentricities of the fast-multiplying markets in which they deal. Brian Martin, who runs the Hong Kong dealing operation, makes the point that differences between dealing and settlement systems in the fifteen principal Asian markets are much greater than between the various European markets.

Phillips especially points to the centralization of dealing as a major benefit, along with information technology; improved software for harmonizing and comparing different portfolios, and various information sources networked onto individual PCs. He now studies the previous day's market movements and does all his administrative work in the first hour of the morning, hands the day's orders to the dealers, and is free for analytical work for the rest of the day.

A phenomenon of the last few years, Phillips comments, has been the explosion in the number of countries and industries and stocks to be covered. This puts particular strain on a bottom-up manager, and may in part account for the present fashion for emphasizing the big market calls. But the efficiency of the markets has not been increasing over the years, as the expansion of the markets has outpaced the number of strong professionals involved. There is a relatively small pool of good and experienced people, who move around from company to company, and from country to country, frequently being 'promoted' into sales or administration. This market inefficiency presents opportunities.

Fidelity is unusual among institutions in Asia, in that staying in fund management is the key career path. Bill Ebsworth, the chief investment officer, is however a former analyst and fund manager himself who now describes his role as similar to that of a soccer coach. He is now greatly boosting the number of portfolio managers and analysts to cope with this explosion of regional markets. In years gone by the assets under management in Asia were the funds raised in Asia, and resources accordingly were a fraction of those in Boston, but it clearly makes sense for a stock-picking group to make full use of personnel on the ground.

The number of analysts and fund managers based in the region has grown to twenty. Phillips feels that there is no question that a presence in Asia is essential for good stock selection. It may not be important for market timing, he concedes, but then he makes no attempt to call overall market movements.

The analytical process is described as 'training by osmosis'; senior managers from both Hong Kong and Boston visit companies alongside the specialist analysts. The flow of ideas has swelled in recent years with the build-up of personnel, assisted by the introduction of an electronic mail system (probably the norm in the United States, but still relatively new in Asia). The communication of ideas is inevitably somewhat haphazard, but nevertheless their sheer number represents a growing resource. Phillips stresses the efficiency of spreading the analytical workload among a number of like-minded individuals, and his ability to build on the stock selections of country specialists. This enables him to focus his own efforts on a universe of perhaps four hundred companies, out of the eleven thousand listed in Asia.

There is very little top-down analysis in the Fidelity investment process. Ebsworth notes that asking Asian companies how they are affected by macro-economic trends is often more enlightening than the government statistics. A classic example was the expansion of Hong Kong manufacturing industry across the border into China in the mid to late 80's, which was initially denied by the Hong Kong government because they had not noticed the phenomenon and did not have statistics to detect it. Only when the Hong Kong economy had been clearly hollowed out, leaving behind head offices and service industries, was this huge structural change officially acknowledged.

LOCAL UNDERSTANDING AND AN OPEN MIND

Ebsworth reckons that the principal mistake made by foreigners is to buy a stock because it looks cheap, without understanding the personalities involved. It is essential, he feels, to take the time to understand regional history, current social trends, and the background of the families involved – the owner-managers in this modern-day version of 18th century capitalism. Local newspapers are often poor, reporting random facts with no understanding of context. There is no substitute for being on the ground in the region and building up your own contacts. Ebsworth emphasizes the desirability of networking with your own contemporaries around the region: 'one day those guys will be the taipans and ministers.' (This is a real possibility. Journalist-academic James Clad tells the story of the TASS correspondent whom he knew a a friendless hack in Kuala Lumpur, and next encountered as the finance minister of one of the Central Asian states. The educated elite is still relatively small in many of these countries; your statistical chances of meeting the VIPs of the future are high.)

Phillips nevertheless observes that, although experience is usually an advantage, fresh thinking occasionally wins the day. Old Asia hands said Hong Kong banks would never abandon the practice of hidden reserves; newcomers took a fresh look and thought procedures might change. The banks eventually adopted full disclosure. The moral must be to understand as many as possible of the factors at play, and to keep questioning all of your assumptions.

Chapter 2

Level-headed calm

Adrian Cantwell of Global Asset Management

One of the most consistent of all the institutional managers in Asia is Adrian Cantwell of Global Asset Management. The interesting thing is that few of his contemporaries are quite sure why. He makes no claims to brilliance. He is not obsessed by investment. He spends weekends with his stunningly beautiful wife Elaine and their three small children, and is a relaxed and sociable figure. And yet over the last few years he has achieved remarkably good results.

What distinguishes him? He is very methodical. He knows his limitations – how much research he can read, how much can be expected from country visits, how confident one can be of stock selections and market selections. He is very focused: GAM's system requires him to spend practically no time on marketing, and he manages courteously but effectively to spend little time talking to brokers. He knows his objective, which is simple: it is to make money for the client, while avoiding losses and preserving the capital.

In this quest for absolute returns and lack of an index benchmark he is somewhat akin to a hedge fund manager, although his options are limited to equities and cash and the fees are considerably more modest. He is accordingly prepared to take moves much bolder than most of his equity competitors, and was 38 per cent liquid in the Singapore/Malaysia fund at the end of 1993.

In April that year he had visited Malaysia, and felt that everything still looked very positive: the private client sections of stockbroking firms were not full, the election story could run for a while (elections in Malaysia are thought to ensure a good market beforehand), and there was scope for many small over-valuation bubbles. By the time of his next visit in November, it was apparent that many of the stories were conceptual, and brokers were reaching out to 1996/97 to try to justify share recommendations. In all, 'Malaysia

27

was extraordinarily overvalued, and Singapore didn't look fantastic relative to cash.'

The much larger ASEAN (Association of South-East Asian Nations) fund however remained fully invested. (ASEAN is a misnomer: the fund invests in all Asia-Pacific markets except Japan and Australia, including New Zealand.) Cantwell says that, having realized the degree of overvaluation in Malaysia, Hong Kong, and Singapore, he has been kicking himself for not spotting the equivalent degree of overvaluation in other markets such as Thailand, Indonesia, and the Philippines. He was kidding himself that he could find value elsewhere.

Indonesia has been one of the drags on performance in 1994. He had taken it up to a very aggressive 22 per cent weighting in 1993 – a capitalization weight would have been around 5 per cent, and many regional funds of this size are permanently underweight in that market because of poor liquidity. By the end of the year he was thinking of selling out entirely, but was not quick enough to do so: he had cut back only to 18 per cent in early 1994 before the market fell away. By the fourth quarter of 1994 the weighting was a more moderate 10 per cent, and Cantwell was happy with this: earnings growth remains intact, and a 5 per cent cut in corporate taxes should provide a welcome boost in 1995.

Cantwell will talk candidly about the practical problems of information overload, which are common to all Asian managers – probably to all fund managers everywhere, but to a greater degree in Asian markets. The number of markets he follows has risen from eight to fifteen in the last two years, and privatizations and new listings have considerably increased the number of stocks in each market. He will readily admit that he cannot monitor everything all of the time. Yet he is convinced that one overstretched person can outperform a committee. 'I can make the decision to switch out of a Korean bank into a Singapore property company; as an investment decision, that's very valuable. Whereas, if you sat down a Korean expert, a Singapore expert, a Philippine expert and a Hong Kong expert, what sort of portfolio are you going to come up with? . . . That's one of our strengths; it's one person's brain.'

Within GAM, the Far East fund managers exchange ideas regularly, but have autonomy over their own portfolios. Cantwell tries to talk every day to Mike Bunker, the very highly regarded London-based leader of the Far East team, and sits across a desk from Marcus Pakenham, whose fund covers Korea and Greater China. Cantwell reckons that this arrangement enables them to make the most of the individuals' complementary strengths, while avoiding the weakness of a bureaucracy. There is no approved stock list, for example, at GAM, or any other attempt to enforce standardization.

AGGRESSIVE ALLOCATION AND ABSOLUTE RETURNS

Another advantage is the flexibility of asset allocation within the fund. 'There are fifteen markets, so even if you don't like three of them, probably there are three others which you like a lot. You can have zero weighting in the first three, and be massively overweight in the others. Like Indonesia, I've had New Zealand up to a 22 per cent weighting. Conventionally that would be considered aggressive, but we don't think of it as aggressive, we think, "Will we make money?" and "Do we risk losing money?" '

Cantwell says he adopts both a top-down and a bottom-up approach. 'You can be both at the same time, and you can be both at different times.' In practice, however, he is a firm believer in stockpicking, and tries to buy on a two year view. 'In the nature of equity markets, you normally make money in good companies. It may be true that Asian markets don't discount the future as far ahead as more developed markets . . . in January of any year, most people will be looking at the end of the year. I try to look further than that, and then buy and hold and wait.' Portfolio turnover is low. He subscribes to the maxim: 'More money is made by thinking than is ever made by buying and selling.'

Portfolio weightings seem to follow from intuition, and risk-spreading. 'Juggling these fifteen balls, which one is going to outperform the most, and over what time period, and how am I going to capture that? You can't go throwing 80 per cent of the money into this market for three months and that market for three months and expect to get it right, you have to have prudent diversification, a core.' The Hong Kong weighting of the fund under Cantwell's stewardship (a revealing word) has ranged from 12 per cent to 60 per cent, and is now in middle ground. The Thai weighting has ranged from 4 per cent to 36 per cent, and is now at the lower end of the range.

There are no rigid guidelines. 'Would I ever put 80 per cent into Hong Kong? I guess it's conceivable, although it's extraordinarily unlikely. If there was a political crisis and Hong Kong went back down to seven times earnings, that would signal the time to have the maximum amount of money in Hong Kong, irrespective of what any other market is doing – and Hong Kong is the most likely candidate for that.'

However, in late 1994 he is taking the Malaysian weighting in the main fund down to zero. It is already only 30 per cent of the Singapore/Malaysia fund, dramatically below its capitalization weighting. He thinks the market very fully priced, and although not necessarily predicting a decline he thinks he can do better elsewhere.

Assessing value, for Cantwell, is always subjective, and comes down to experience. 'Earnings per share are what drive the share price in Asia. I don't think it's right to go into dividend discount models or inverse yield ratios in what are still emerging markets. You are looking for the undervalued: a low PE relative to the historic trading range, plus good earnings growth. Whether that earnings growth is above average or average, doesn't really matter. Then you can catch that earnings growth, plus a re-rating at some point. And then you've got to be prepared to sell.'

He goes on, 'Hong Kong Telecom and Cathay are great examples of why you cannot afford to buy and hold, you've got to react.' Charts are produced. Telecom bottomed in 1981 at a PE of 5, after a period of flat earnings when the rest of the market was much more exciting. The low for the stock coincided with the turning point in the earnings relative, and earnings growth comfortably outpaced the market for the next ten years. By 1986, however, the stock had been hugely re-rated, briefly attaining a PE of 35. It then dipped sharply, spiking again to the same PE a year later before finally halving. It was a most unrewarding investment for four years from 1986, but 'in the early eighties we might have held it for five years – that's not short term,' he says.

'Cathay Pacific is a very well-managed company which it is right to own at certain times, but wrong, dead wrong, at others. It outperformed here (from '87 to '89) and has underperformed ever since. But look at the forecast earnings relatives; now these are beginning to turn up, so I suspect that the relative performance of the shares is going to be very good. This would be one of my favourites, on a two-to-three year view.'

Cantwell also likes Singapore Airlines, believing that the earnings potential for the airlines may now be hugely underestimated. He does not worry about domestic share prices, or the size of the premium on a foreign stock; he thinks only about the price which his fund has to pay, and the value which that represents. Likewise, he does not bother much with ratings relative to the market, or to a sector. He thinks more in absolute terms, relative to the company's own historic trading range.

He will stick with a company very doggedly if he still believes in the underlying story and the value has yet to be recognized. He held First Pacific through many years of lacklustre performance, and was finally rewarded when the share price burst into life. In late 1994, the shares are worth more than three times his average purchase price, and he still believes they can double again.

PAPER MOUNTAINS

Cantwell's office, and the shelves adjoining the dealing desk, are stacked high with piles of research: one pile for each country, in the main, but some countries need more than one. He tries to discourage brokers from sending so much, and is disparaging about its utility, but it does all get sifted – mostly into the unlikely-ever-to-read piles, but a small percentage makes it into a may-read pile. When he organizes a trip, that pile in turn is skimmed to produce a list of suggested names to visit. For a three-day visit he gives about twenty names to a broker, and asks him to fix what he can, so there is a random element in the outcome. Cantwell sees two or three hundred companies per year, a high figure comparable to that of the managers at Fidelity. He now tends to take three-day trips to one country at a time, which he finds much more effective than longer trips, after which 'the meetings tend to blur together'. Over the last four years, the maximum length of time he has spent in Hong Kong is three weeks.

Before each meeting he gathers two or three recent broker research notes – often the relevant pages of the reference compilations – and does about forty-five minutes' preparation. His line of questioning is structured, although the questions themselves are very general. What he is looking for in each meeting is an impression of the business, management style, management logic, and broad business direction. He does not have time to go into detailed numbers; but says ultimately numbers are created by people. 'If, later, they have a rights issue or buy a property, you may then have an idea why they may have done it and whether the decision is likely to be sensible, or whether the deal is a rip-off, and the company may have bought an inflated asset from the brother.' He avoids over-direct questions, and on profits for example tends to ask, 'This is the range the market is talking about; what do you think of market perceptions?' He tries to avoid questions which inspire defensiveness or bravado, and says the companies are often more helpful when they know that he is not an analyst, and doesn't have to fill in a box with a profit forecast.

Like Phillips, he takes legible handwritten notes, and may refer back to them years later. He says that handwritten notes, rather than typed impersonal ones, 'make the meeting come alive again. You remember, "when he said that he smiled", or "when he said that I didn't really trust him on that point".' He has started to do a greater number of repeat visits, rather than always visiting new companies.

He is worried about the growing number of investors and analysts seeking to interview companies, which is overburdening the managers whose job is to run the business, and that consequently access to the major shareholders may become more restricted. Corporate spokesmen 'may be able to tell you what the company does, what they intend to do, how many houses they will build, and what price they're going to sell them at, but they won't give you the feel of what the company is really about'. This of course must be the case in the US and the UK, but those are more mature capitalist systems: in Asia, the controlling shareholder is often all-important.

After a trip, Cantwell rarely takes immediate action. He has dealt on the car telephone after a meeting twice, he says: 'once in Malaysia in April 1993, after seeing TRI, which had just the night before been given the licence for the international gateway. The management were explaining that they had been up all night working on the plans. It was a great telecom story, plus these new deals . . .' He bought at M$4, even though the stock had already quadrupled in the space of a few months, and sold out later between $9 and $10. The stock surged on to $14, but has settled back to the price at which he sold it. Cantwell says he would probably buy it back at $10 in six months' time, since by then it will have another year's earnings in the bag since it was sold, or before that if it went to $8. There are earnings coming in, he says; it is just a question of valuation. The other occasion on which he dealt instantly was after a visit to an Indonesian packaging company; at the meeting 'it became clear that the company's growth plans were falling apart.'

Usually, however he returns to the office, and keeps a few of the more interesting visit notes aside to mull over. 'If you have the luxury of time in making investment decisions – if you have more time to look, to research, to let the short-term froth get blown out of a stock, and then buy when nobody else is looking – you will probably make better investments.'

WHEN NOT TO HOLD CASH

One of Cantwell's most memorable learning experiences, he remembers painfully, was when he was running the Singapore/Malaysia fund at a different company in 1986. The failure of Pan-Electric, following a period of major weakness in corporate profits and some other major scandals, led to the collapse of share prices in both markets in late 1985. In 1986, everything looked pretty black, and Cantwell had 70 per cent cash. 'Then the market turned, and it went up so quickly, one couldn't get back in. It hurt . . . What it made me focus on was, when is the right time to hold cash, and when is the wrong time? The right time to hold cash is when you think you are at or near the top of the market, but it is very obvious what my mistake was with the Singapore/Malaysia fund; the market had gone down a lot, and it wasn't right to consider that it was anywhere near the top, so I should have started to go fully invested. There is nothing wrong with being fully invested when the market has already fallen.'

Now, he is wary of Japan. 'Not many people switched into Japan ahead of its rise, they have all been chasing it up. Meanwhile you have a 40 per cent disparity in performance (with the yen rising, the Japanese market up, and other Asian markets down) and yet people still want to buy Japan. It's probably wrong. Is it going to go up that much more in the next six months? Pocket the gain. Meanwhile, the Asian markets are back to where they were in September 1993, and we have almost another year of earnings growth in the bag.'

I ask about the main differences between investing in Asia and in more developed markets. 'Throughout the whole of Asia, you are always at risk of the main shareholder acting to the disadvantage of minority shareholders. There are probably too many of these to say, "that was the one that taught me that lesson". We are still learning these lessons!'

You have to balance risk and reward, however. If you eliminated

33

all companies which were less than perfect, the available stock universe would be too greatly reduced. 'One has to be prepared to play these games. As a Hong Kong fund manager visiting any company in the region, we are playing away from home. So I have to know the rule book, and this only comes with experience.' And part of the key is not to be too greedy. 'I played the game away from home, got a couple of goals, packed my bags . . . if you can do that a few times in each country you're doing well.

'You've got to overcome the fear of selling a stock and watching it go up. If you bought it at the right time, there is nothing wrong with selling it in the knowledge that it may go higher, because when things come down they can come down a long way. 1994 has been great for teaching us this! You have to accept that stocks can go from overvalued to ridiculously overvalued, but don't try to hang on for the last bit. You don't have to sell every share in the holding: you can say, well it's overvalued but I still like it, and sell 50 per cent.'

Small incremental purchases and small easing-back sales are a feature of the style. Cantwell often leaves limit orders on while he goes away for a trip, and will review their progress and the portfolio only on return. He refuses to worry about missed opportunities. At the end of the day, he says, it is not the decisions which might have been taken which matter, but those which he actually took. The record suggests he has made more than a fair number of good ones.

Chapter 3

Long cyclical plays

David Lui of Schroders Asia

David Lui has one of the best long-term institutional track records in Hong Kong, although slightly outpaced by the other featured managers – Peter Phillips (see p 16), Adrian Cantwell (see p 27), and Colin Armstrong (see p 44) – over the last few years. Lui's style is characterized by a very long approach to sector cycles, very broad diversification within his chosen sectors, and extraordinarily low turnover.

His analysis is in very broad strokes. He watches the US markets very closely, he says, because this gives him an advantage of time. 'People think South-East Asia is so strong now, because of growing regional trade, but the worldwide situation is still the key.' He believes that 1994's turbulence is no more than a correction in a long-term Asian bull market. He sees interest rates moving upwards until 1996–97, but reckons that by 1995 'the rise in interest rates will be much slower from there onwards, until the late stages of the cycle, and the impact on the market will be less, so the next phase of the market will be earnings driven. Hong Kong is probably an exception, because Hong Kong and China have been in a recovery phase since 1990 while the rest of the world was slowing down, so the cycle in Hong Kong and China is out of synch with the rest of the world.'

He pulls out tables of historical PEs and yield ratios to show that valuations in Hong Kong are at the time unusually high, and that the PE low for a calendar year has never in the last twelve years been more than nine. In marketing for institutional accounts, he is stressing the positive long-term picture; shorter-term, he is cautious, and is advising friends to wait for more opportune market conditions, perhaps the following year, before buying.

CYCLICAL SECTOR SELECTION AND LOW TURNOVER

Lui likes to be very early in identifying cyclical turns, and says that a year or eighteen months is fine. 'This gives you time for positioning; an institution is not an individual investor, and for an institution this takes time. It also allows you time to research individual companies.'

Now in his early forties, Lui studied at the London School of Economics, and then worked for other financial institutions in Hong Kong. He took over the Schroders Asian Fund from Edward Kong on joining the group in 1985, and also runs the Schroders Asia Hong Kong Fund and the Hong Kong Smaller Companies Fund, plus a number of institutional accounts. The Schroders Asian Fund has grown at a compound 30 per cent per annum over the ten years to September 1994, resulting in an increase during that period of over thirteen times. That rise, of course, was from a low base, when the Hong Kong market had been depressed by the Sino-British negotiations as to its political future, but subsequent performance has been consistently good.

Lui bought into Singapore shipyards in 1986, when nobody else was interested. (The sector had been all but written off by the government in the early eighties as a 'sunset industry', and earnings had been in decline since 1981. Moreover, the stock market had just completed a three year downward slide.) Schroders was very bearish again on the shipyards by late 1989, by which stage all possible good news was in the price. 'But we invested in the sector for three and a half years. In between, there was a lot of volatility. People often get confused, and mistake a correction for the end of the bull market. Or they try to be too smart, and trade too much. Short-term movements don't bother me.'

He also liked the overall markets in Singapore, Malaysia and Thailand in 1986. In 1989 he reduced that exposure, and by the end of that year had substantially overweighted Hong Kong, a stance which lasted through to late 1993. He always buys on a two to three year time horizon, and changes the portfolio only at major turning points of sectors. Portfolio turnover is a very low 20 per cent. He says he never worries about index weightings.

Since 1992, he has been very bullish of the hotel sector in Hong Kong – and I remember him thinking about the timing of the turn well before that. 1992 was the year in which the hotel fundamentals turned, after being battered in 1989–91 by new buildings, the Tiananmen massacre, and the Gulf War. The sector kept pace with the soaring stock market until late 1993, and then held up well as the rest of the market collapsed; consequently it has outperformed very strongly in 1994. Lui expects the fundamentals to be very favourable until 1996, which he expects to be the peak year for earnings, and would envisage starting to sell towards the end of the previous year.

The hotel sector accounts for less than 2 per cent of the Hang Seng index, but Lui has about 16 per cent of the Hong Kong fund in hotels, and almost as high a percentage of the Asian fund. Within the sector, Lui has bought virtually every Hong Kong hotel stock. He says that liquidity in the sector is too poor to buy just one or two, and that in any case the cyclical upswing will be enough to generate an earnings upturn for every company.

In 1993, he became cautious at an early stage on the Hong Kong property developers, and says he missed the boom in the second half. He remains wary. 'I think the property cycle has peaked. Interest rates have reversed. The growth in the Chinese economy has peaked out for the next one to two years. Even though China will recover, it won't show much growth in the next couple of years, because of infrastructural constraints. Another factor is the increased supply of land for development in Hong Kong. I think price rises will definitely slow. Whether prices fall dramatically, it is too early to say. Interest rates will probably move up only slowly; on the other hand affordability is already strained, so any change in interest rates has an effect. We still have the 1997 problem, and some people will continue to leave the country. It doesn't take much to change the market, with prices at such a high level.' Anyway, he adds, even if property prices were to stabilize, developers' profits might come under pressure, because of the extraordinary inventory profits they have been able to book in the past.

'Also, with interest rates rising, office yields will have to rise. In 1991, we argued that although rents were falling, capital values would not fall because of the declining interest rate. Now we have a rising interest rate, so capital values will not rise, and will probably tend to fall, despite rising rentals.'

CONSERVATIVE GEARING

The Hong Kong portfolio is at present conservatively invested, in hotels, conglomerates, high-yielders such as the *South China Morning Post*, and other stocks which he regards as low-beta. It is however 15 per cent geared. Despite the gearing, it has performed in line with the market during the first half of 1994, which vindicates Lui's sector and stock selection, and he was probably not geared going into the downturn. 'If clients are selling when the market is depressed, I often just gear up the fund. You need the patience and the guts to go against the market. You try not to sell along with others. After the market has begun to recover, if necessary I sell, but I find very often people then give you new money as the market rises.'

Generally, he is cautiously optimistic on Hong Kong. 'With the political reform package out of the way, China will have to accept it; they will change it in 1997. The economic way of life has to go on; why not come to an early agreement on the airport? The Chinese are taking a more practical approach to Hong Kong now. The most important things affecting the Hong Kong market are properties and confidence: confidence reflecting how the Chinese will handle Hong Kong over this period up to 1997. That is very important. There was a major outflow of funds and manpower in 1983–84, up to 1989. Then the confidence returned tremendously in the last two or three years. Now people in Hong Kong are generally very confident; everyone wants to invest in China. Up to the end of 1993 there was overwhelming confidence in Hong Kong, if you look at consumer spending, car registrations, property . . . Everyone who wants to buy a car now probably has one. Everyone wants to buy property in Hong Kong, even though prices have risen so much, beyond every wage-earner's affordability, and they don't realize the change in interest rates. China's economic slowdown in 1994 is probably only temporary, but even if China has strong growth in the long term, from time to time there will be setbacks and corrections. We cannot ignore the effect of all this on Hong Kong. Especially with only three years to go. This is a very delicate point. It has to be handled very carefully. It will be very volatile. Hopefully we can avoid any major downturn. The OECD (Organization for Economic Co-operation and Development) recovery will help Hong Kong and China quite a lot. Without the OECD recovery, Hong Kong would probably have been affected more, but the OECD has helped to offset the negative impact from China.'

Lui is also becoming a little concerned about residential property in Singapore and Malaysia, where he reckons the cycle is a year or so behind Hong Kong. Indonesia he regards as commodity based, and therefore likely to do well in the later stages of the economic cycle.

'In Korea and Taiwan we don't see that at all, and that's why I am so comfortable with those markets. When you talked to people last year they were not that bullish, still very cautious, no speculation in the stock market or the property market, so they can move quite a long way from here. The risks seem very low. Also, Korea and Taiwan are not just original equipment manufacturers; they are in a position to take advantage of rising demand for higher technology products. The same cannot be said of Hong Kong, Malaysia, or Thailand. I think these countries are much better managed than the South-East Asian economies. I find Korea exceptionally well managed. People are very learned, they pay a lot of attention to education, and the country will do very well; there is still much further to go. Taiwan is a wealthy country but it is chaotic. Whether it is as well run as Korea I am not sure.'

In practice however he says these markets are 'very difficult', because of the restrictions on foreign investment. 'We bought into some Korean stocks in 1992–93, but to get into the market at this stage is not possible. The stocks that are well liked are all full. Sometimes I buy foreign stock; in 1993 if you paid a five or ten per cent premium you could buy the stock. But now you can't, because everyone knows the market is going up, and premiums have been rising. Taiwan is OK, and we've applied for quota, but it depends on the specialist's ability to pick stocks, which is another difficult problem.'

There is a rather Confucian streak in Lui. He emphasizes public responsibility and service, and helps with educational seminars. He thinks remuneration in the financial sector absurd compared with other professions, and contrasts the rewards with those of hospital doctors. While generally disparaging of broker research, which he finds 'non-anticipatory', he has great respect for various 'well-informed, learned people', including the US strategist Elaine Garzarelli. He is very fortunate, he says, to have learnt from a number of talented, experienced people in Asia.

Despite the very long-term orientation of all Lui's public comments, his attention to execution detail is such that some brokers have been convinced for years that he is a dealer oriented only to the short term. Colleagues in London say that he 'likes to be part of the buzz in Hong Kong, in a way that no London fund manager could ever be'.

MANAGEMENT UNCERTAINTIES AND DIVERSIFICATION

There are almost three hundred stocks in the Asian fund; when he likes a sector, Lui will diversify his holdings broadly within it. In the Hong Kong fund he will buy sizable holdings in individual stocks which are liked. Swire Pacific for example accounts for 9 per cent of the fund, in the third quarter of 1994, and in keeping with the firm's value orientation the holding is in the cheaper non-voting B shares; HSBC accounts for 8 per cent. Around South-East Asia however he goes for much more diversified holdings, firstly because of liquidity, and secondly because the degree of confidence in management is much lower.

'If you are investing in Indonesia, whether in banks or conglomerates or smaller companies, you are not that certain about the management. The problem comes from disclosure and regulation. It is not like the United States or the UK! Often you cannot read too much in the annual report. What you can do sometimes is to anticipate the sectoral economics, the macro-economics. When it comes to pinpointing the micro factors, at company level – how management deals with different possibilities, how the company is positioned, management integrity, and the treatment of minority shareholders – this is far from satisfactory, and the risk of falling into major problems is quite high. Especially with some of the industrial companies, which in most of South-East Asia are original equipment manufacturers (OEM), not highly technical, or technology driven. They are not companies where the management is committed, and investing for the long term, in terms of research and technology and upgrading, and keeping in front of the market demand – companies like Johnson Electric, there are very few companies like this. It is a great disappointment that some of the companies in Hong Kong and South-East Asia are not of this level. They are very prone to changing the nature of the business. Unless you see them every six months, you are not in touch with the companies. Very often I find people are way behind the changing trend.'

Lui says that, in covering the nine countries for his portfolio: 'I

often have to rely on other people to visit all these places, so I need
to be extra careful. Those stocks I cover myself, I know very well
and have complete control and tend to be very aggressive. I tend to
be more aggressive in Hong Kong, Singapore and Malaysia because
I know these companies much better, and my feel for these types
of companies is much stronger, because of the years I have been
covering these markets. But in Indonesia, the Philippines or Korea,
the influence is more how I see the market in the next year or two,
and then at the stock level I let the other analysts or fund managers
decide. So in these markets each holding is smaller.'

When visiting countries, he visits both economists and companies,
to see how they feel about the local market and the local economy,
and to relate regional sectoral demand to his worldwide economic
scenario. Very often, he says, the locals focus too much on their
own economies, and tend to be very short term, thinking at most
six or twelve months ahead, whereas he is trying to assess the market
outlook for the next two or three years. 'I look at the rate of change.
The monetary indicators, the rate of change of earnings growth, the
rate of change of orders. Hong Kong used to be an export economy,
and the rate of change of exports indicated the rate of change of
economic growth, which indicated very early the rate of change
outlook for the stock market. Now it is probably the rate of change of
interest rates which is the key, depending on the stage of the cycle.'

COMPANY MEETINGS

'When you visit companies, it is important to see the major shareholders, and not the executives, if you can. If you talk to people for
half an hour or an hour, more or less I can detect something which
is not consistent in what they try to put across to me. I may have
formed some views about the sector because of the overseas operating environment, or because I know about the supply-demand side,
but not necessarily the company side. If during that hour I ask a
number of questions, and they try to avoid answering it, then I
really have reservations, I know something is not forthcoming. I'm
looking more for non-confirmations. People often don't ask the
right questions and are led by the company. The experience of
the fund manager or the analyst is very important, to be able to
foresee the pitfalls.

'I try to have one-on-one meetings, whether in office hours or

41

lunch time or drinks. I find office meetings are very formal, people are very guarded – especially if there are other people around, or if they are not in the mood to tell you anything. I prefer chatting over lunch or dinner; it is much more informal, people are more relaxed, and you probably end up knowing a bit more. The best thing is to have a good relationship with some of these people. If you don't know them, it is much more difficult. If you know them, then they are likely to let you know more than they are prepared to say to other people.'

There are some stocks with which Lui says he is 'totally not comfortable', and from time to time events tend to bear out his suspicions. 'I was in the States in the late eighties, the stores were full of Cabbage Patch dolls, and they weren't selling. When I came back to Hong Kong I went to all the four toy companies and asked them how they saw the market. Everyone except one told me all bullish things, and to me the facts did not substantiate that. Only one company, Universal, gave a direct answer. The rest were all highly misleading. Later, when one of these other stocks went up substantially in 1993, promoted by a broker, I was highly suspicious. It crashed.

'The new US managers – in terms of academic knowledge or investment techniques, they are very sophisticated. But I think they may be unfortunate not to know the people investing in South-East Asian markets: the liquidity, the sentiment, the qualities of management. Very often young analysts only look at the figures and ignore the management.'

Young analysts, he says, may even ignore rapid changes in the competitive environment. 'Like pagers. Last year some of the pager companies did very well. They have a head start over the other major competitors, like Motorola and NEC. But once these other players come in, how are they going to compete in terms of price? The margins will come down substantially. I saw last year that this was not sustainable.' When senior people deny such problems and say that their stock should be valued in line with established US telecommunication companies, Lui says, he doesn't want to get involved.

Local fund managers should be able to outperform, Lui believes, 'because they understand the culture and should be able to understand the thinking. If you were a Chinese in 1989, you could probably expect an outcome like Tiananmen Square. If you were not born in China or Hong Kong, you probably wouldn't anticipate that sort of outcome.'

BUYING WITH BLOOD ON THE STREETS

He was an aggressive buyer after Tiananmen. 'Not many people were bullish at that point; I only know two others who were bullish. But you don't get that sort of buying opportunity very often. It's important to take advantage of it, if you have the guts and the temperament. Political risk is a major opportunity. I illustrated this again in 1992 when Thailand had a coup. The stocks I bought then had doubled, tripled, or quadrupled by 1993. It is always the long-term economic outlook which prevails. The economic trend is very much embedded in a country, and most political changes do not have a major effect.

'It's the factors which are totally unanticipated, which ninety per cent of the market participants are not paying attention to, which may affect the market substantially. When people talk about their worries, ninety per cent of the time they will not have an impact on the market. Like most-favoured nation status. If China was going to lose MFN, then it would have lost it in 1990 already, because the American public was so disgusted with China. By 1991–92 you could see the drive to normalization with China everywhere. Every major country wanted to trade with China, to do business with China, knowing China's longer term prospects – especially by 1992, when Deng said speed up the reform. No one could afford not to trade with China.

'Again, in the airport row, when Lu Ping held a press conference, that was a major shock, a major Chinese official going against Chris Patten. That was the major impact on the market. After that there were still outspoken statements by Chinese officials from time to time, but the impact was gradually lower and lower and lower.

'But also, that kind of thing matters when the market is already overextended. If it is too high it is vulnerable to negative shocks. But in 1983–84 when the Hang Seng index was at 600–700, or in 1990 when it was at 2,000, how much further downside pressure can you have, when the market is at that low valuation? It is more prone to gradually more and more positive news which people did not anticipate. At a certain point you have to lead the market, to form an opinion, to reverse the trend.'

Lui's distinction is his proven willingness to do just that.

Chapter 4

Bold and intuitive

Colin Armstrong and Jardine Fleming

Colin Armstrong at Jardine Fleming is described by many of his competitors and colleagues as 'the best bull market fund manager in Asia'. Some intend this as a back-hander, and others, including some of his strongest competitors, as a genuine tribute.

Armstrong himself is wary of the description, evidently suspecting the former. Indeed, after a rough six months during which he was on the wrong side of the markets, he is wary of talking about his style at all. 'After a period like this you become less sure as to why a certain approach worked at that particular time, but doesn't appear to be working now; or maybe it really is still working, but the results will just take a little bit longer to come through. What consoles me in a bad period is that if you use it properly, and you're accumulating something which is out of favour, then you may get a much bigger move coming out, as the market moves in your direction.'

JAPANESE SUCCESSES

He considers the label unfair, since he did particularly well in the Japanese bear market. He also believes that Asia as a whole remains in a structural bull market, so that identifying someone as a good bull market manager is tantamount to saying he is a good fund manager, period. Japan was where he first made his reputation, and the account is illuminating.

He had moved to Japan from Hong Kong in 1984, to double the size of the Tokyo fund management team and broaden the coverage of small companies and technology stocks, then firm favourites with foreign investors. These sectors performed poorly, however, and by the end of Armstrong's first year, his funds were down, 'although

44

actually they weren't down as much as they should have been if I'd stuck strictly to my brief!' All of the stocks which foreigners wanted to buy, such as his target small companies and technology stocks, seemed to be doing badly; all of the stocks which foreigners hated, like banks and construction stocks, were doing well.

Poring over 25-year historical charts one evening, while waiting for a business dinner, he discovered that comparable shifts had taken place in the early 1970s. 'We'd had moves of around 50 per cent in the banks over twelve months, but before that they had been flat for about fifteen years; I discovered that in the early seventies banks had gone up by about eight times! The technology stocks, in which I was now supposed to be specializing, had gone down 50–70 per cent over the same period . . .' He explored what had happened to other sectors at that stage: construction, real estate, railways, and so on. 'Today there would be so many analysts looking at this, but then there weren't. I was able to fit the bits of the jigsaw together, and realize that what happened then was exactly in the process of repeating itself, and you could see why. It was all to do with the huge increases in the Japanese trade and current account surplus, the yen appreciating, interest rates plummeting, and a huge domestic boom; we were working up to the Plaza Accord, but it was also exactly what Japan had to do to placate the west.

'I began to write a few internal papers saying, "Look, you've got to realize this is going to happen, you've got to get me off technology and small companies, I'm actually a good fund manager . . . If you give me a chance with something like Japan Trust it'll work, because what I will do is this, I'll sell all this stuff which the fund holds, because it's the wrong stuff, and I'll buy all this stuff which the fund doesn't hold, because it doesn't want to hold, but it's gotta hold, because it's the right stuff." Anyway, I was backed to do that, and it worked out. The Japan Trust performed incredibly well, and was the best performing large fund . . . And then in 1987 I got the crash right, in that I'd managed to go quite liquid ahead of that, and I don't know quite why, I must have picked up a signal from somewhere, but I did. Just after that, I had a strong feeling that it wasn't the end of the Japanese bull market, and I managed to get everyone convinced that Japan was again going to double, from 20,000 to 40,000, and I managed to get everyone back into the market, and that worked out. That re-enhanced the performance of Japan Trust etc, and I suppose my reputation internally, if not externally just yet. I didn't get the top of the Japanese market, I don't think anyone ever does . . .

45

I knew it had gone too far, but I recognized that once it broke down through 36,000 it was all over, so at that stage we went quite bearish, took a lot of money out, launched JF Ninja Trust to give us a vehicle which could go short, and took advantage of that.'

A SWITCH TO OTHER ASIAN MARKETS

One of his colleagues says that Armstrong loses his edge in dull market conditions; he loses interest if the market is unexciting. His own comments bear this out. 'I left Japan in the summer of 1991, mainly out of boredom, because I'd seen the great bull market, and the most exciting phase of the bear market, and all that was now left was the grinding-out phase of the bear market, which isn't any fun for anyone.' Fortunately he then moved down to Hong Kong and assumed the leadership of the Pacific Regional Group. 1992 was a year of relative consolidation in the regional markets – Hong Kong rose 28 per cent over the year, and Thailand 26 per cent, but other markets were subdued and this paled in comparison with the surge which followed. The funds, in the meantime, were repositioned, with dramatic effects on performance.

'Jardine Fleming did quite well for a couple of years. If I had a role in that, it was emphasizing to people who are very well qualified and generally very good fund managers in their own right, that you should be positive about things. If you believe something's right to do, you should do it, because that's why clients have given you money in the first place. I don't see any point in giving money to managers who take a neutral view. To have no opinion is OK in the short term, but clearly not sufficient in the long term. The key to doing well as a fund manager is to try to have a positive view. I do emphasize try, because you have to weigh up a lot of considerations before you come to a specific opinion, and then be in a position to back that opinion.'

JARDINE FLEMING AND BULL MARKETS: A HOUSE STYLE

The strong bull market performance of the whole Jardine Fleming stable of unit trusts was enhanced by gearing. When the markets turned sour in early 1994, JF funds accordingly slumped in the performance rankings, to the unconcealed glee of many competitors. Jardine Fleming as a group is relatively sanguine: the aggressive positioning of the retail funds is a conscious business decision.

Firstly, Asia as a whole is believed to be in a secular bull market. In the future, as in the past, bull phases are expected to be longer and stronger than bear periods. Over the course of a cycle, therefore, an aggressively bullish view will outperform; and in the meantime the JF funds will feature at the top of league tables far more often than they are at the bottom.

Secondly, in JF's experience, the typical Asian unit trust investor is an aggressive punter. Conservative investors who trickle funds in with dollar cost averaging are far outnumbered by those who move large sums in and out of markets on a timescale of weeks or months. Hong Kong investors rarely buy the Hong Kong trust, preferring to play the local market themselves, but elsewhere they less frequently want to play individual stocks. If they want to take a bet on the Malaysian market, or believe that Australian resource stocks are on the move, or an uncle has tipped them off to buy Taiwan, then unit trusts are the vehicle of choice. These, therefore, are sophisticated investors – at least in their risk tolerance, if not in the quality of their analysis. When they are in the fund, according to this argument, they are taking an aggressive view of the market, and they want their fund manager to do likewise.

JAPAN V REST OF ASIA: THE SECULAR TRENDS CONTINUE

In any event, current market conditions are far from dull, in Armstrong's book. 'My fundamental structural view of Japan is that it's still in a bear market. I don't think that people will see a new high in the Japanese market for the next twenty to thirty years. It's a structural bear market because the economy is in structural decline, relative in particular to South-East Asia and the developing world, and that will be reflected in the stock market over the next few years as well. Four years ago, Japan would have been 85–90 per cent of the MSCI Pacific index, but I would argue that within the next ten years it will be 50 per cent. So if Japan is going to go from 90 per cent to 50 per cent over that period, it makes sense to have all your money in the rest of the region, the bit that's growing from 10 per cent to 50 per cent.

'I think the markets in the rest of the region have a lot further to go. Basically the economies are still at a developing stage, not a mature stage; and you've not yet seen the asset inflation and multiple expansion which will coincide with the all-time peak of the market when the markets are largely domestic driven – like Japan in its final surge in 1984–89, and Taiwan in 1987–89. You haven't seen that in any of the other markets because the domestic capital is not yet there, but it's growing all the time. It probably argues for the next cycle, not this one, being the final blow-off, or at least one of massive proportions. If you believe in hops, skips and jumps and all that stuff, in terms of charts, this is probably the skip, and this is probably the second leg of the longer term pattern. So you probably won't see these markets peak until they are roughly 3–400 per cent above where they are at the present time, and that will probably be sometime in the next five years.

'The amount of international money allocated to Asia is still small in percentage terms, and the Japanese in particular have almost no money in Asia. The key there is the yen. If they think the yen is beginning to turn, they will be much more aggressive in putting capital offshore. When that happens, and the Japanese see the Thai banks at ten times earnings and growing at 20 per cent a year, you won't see these things for dust. You've got to wait for it; it will happen right at the point when earnings momentum is about to turn negative. But you'll probably have a six to twelve month period, where just as earnings growth is tailing off, you have the liquidity flows coming in . . . It's not happened yet, but it will. As soon as the yen begins to turn, the Japanese *must* get huge amounts of money offshore. They won't do it while the yen is still strengthening, because they can't afford to take any more losses. So if the yen goes from 90, which it probably will, then if it starts to move the other way, it won't just go to 95, it will accelerate to 115 or 120. And Asia will be their preferred destination, which is why you haven't yet seen anything like the final blow-off in the other Asian markets.'

TRADING AROUND BUT NOT AGAINST THE TREND

Gearing aside, it was Armstrong's refusal to back what he sees as a short-term move into Japan by foreign investors in early 1994 which was the principal factor in a period of underperformance. He does not like to trade against his fundamental and structural view, he explains. 'I do think one can take advantage of short-term opportunities, but people do best trading around the trend that they believe in. So if I think that the trend is resolutely up, then you take profits occasionally, but you're always looking to get back in again around the rising trend.' Trading makes sense, he argues, to enhance the returns on a strategy which is firmly based on fundamentals, but he would not trade against the trend.

Moreover in late 1993, while Armstrong realized that the other markets had moved too far ahead of themselves in the short term, the team's collective view was that earnings growth in the other Asian markets would surprise dramatically on the upside over the next two years, and that the markets would therefore in the long run prove to be cheap rather than expensive. Some cash was raised, but reinvested after the markets had fallen 10–15 per cent; the magnitude of the subsequent decline caught him by surprise. A few quarters on, the strong positive view on South-East Asia and India remains broadly intact, with possibly a touch more caution on stock selection, and only Hong Kong downgraded because of the Chinese economic cycle.

MACRO AND MICRO

The decision-making process for Armstrong's fund management team 'starts off entirely macro, and then you try to fit the micro to the macro. If you then find a lot more interesting companies to invest in, in one particular market, where the macro picture determines that you should be underweight, then there is something wrong with your macro viewpoint. The best example of that was Malaysia, in late 1992 or early 1993, where the macro picture did not look particularly enticing, especially relative to the rest of the region, and seemed to determine fairly small weightings within a regional portfolio – but every time any of us went down to Malaysia we came back wanting to buy just about every company we'd been to see! At the same time other countries, Singapore for example, looked incredibly attractive from a macro standpoint but you couldn't get enough companies to fit the weighting, so we had to dismiss the macro allocation in favour of the micro. This turned out to be right, as the market began to move in the same direction. Part of the reason the JF funds did well in 1993 was places like Malaysia, where the micro picture got us there before the macro picture, because it was obvious that you had huge earnings turnarounds developing.'

The Indian experience has been similar. The overall market looked reasonable, but the cumulative message coming back from innumerable company visits had been much more exciting: earnings were growing not at 10–15 per cent per annum, but at more like 45–50 per cent. At the same time, the benefits of earlier structural changes could finally be seen more clearly to be coming through, so multiple expansion took effect as more money was attracted into the market by the reform story. 'The thirty stocks of the Bombay index appear to be on 50 times earnings and growing at 10 per cent a year, but if you look at the thousand companies below that, they're on about 30 times earnings and growing at 50 per cent a year. There's an anomaly there. You always hope to be in a position to exploit the anomaly before it's exposed by somebody else.'

TOMORROW'S BLUE CHIPS TODAY

I asked about JF's adventurous stock selection in Malaysia, which had stood it in good stead during the bull market of 1993 but had left it with what might to traditionalists look like some fairly racy names. 'If there is an element of bull market operator to me, or now to JF because of my influence on it, it tends to come from a view that the share price of most blue chips is adequately discounted by the market. The market already knows what it needs to know about most blue chips, and when it comes to adding value therefore I tend to look a little bit outside the mainstream to find the stock. I try to look for tomorrow's blue chips today, rather than buying yesterday's blue chips. UEM was a classic, a raging blue chip tomorrow, but priced at what at the time must have been two or three times earnings for two or three years out, because the market was viewing it from a position of ignorance, and a focus on yesterday's misdemeanours. Obviously UEM had disappointed when it was first listed and had been required to raise huge amounts of money to start building the North-South Highway. The market hadn't forgiven it for that, but here we were in a position where the highway was finally about to come on stream and start delivering revenue, and none of that at all was in the share price of the company. The price was only about $2.50 then – it's since gone up seven or eight times.

I was out of it after making four or five times, and have missed out on the bit since then, but the story is still getting better.

'Hopewell is probably Hong Kong's equivalent; I think it will do something very similar to UEM at some point over the next couple of years, and could go up 4–500 per cent from here. The market tends to view it with jaundiced eyes, as it has failed to deliver in the past, but any new money coming in will increasingly view it very favourably.

'All the stocks we bought in Malaysia at that time were stocks which on a two to three year view promised the fastest earnings growth, if you believed the story, and you had to work out whether you believed the story enough to go with it. Sometimes you could get around that just by buying a basket, and saying well, of these five stocks, two are going to be correct, which means they are going to go up 3–500 per cent, because that's the sort of earnings growth we're looking for; and three will fail to deliver. At worst you'll lose 10–30 per cent of your money in the ones that fail, so as a basket you'll come out well on top.

'We are growth fund managers in what are still growth markets, and that is the key. We are in a long-term bull market. People put their money into Asian markets because the economies are growth economies, and so by definition you are a growth fund manager. You're not going to buy conservatively-run blue chips, because you are destined to underperform perpetually if you do so. People often say you should buy blue chips for defensive reasons, but if we do hit a bear market then cash should be your alternative, not blue chips. So it's tomorrow's blue chips which are important, not today's.'

How does one put appropriate valuations on such stocks? 'When earnings momentum is slowing down and the PE is still expanding, that's a clear sign that you're beginning to get into overbought territory. But, more often than not, a sell is determined by an alternative making itself obvious. So you might sell YTL in Malaysia when you think it still has 20–30 per cent upside, but it has already quintupled, in order to buy another CEPA which is also in power stations and which you think could go up 3–400 per cent. It's more often a relative decision than an absolute decision.'

Derivatives are used 'if they give cheaper and more efficient exposure to a stock which we like. The equity consideration comes first. If there are warrants which require 20 per cent appreciation in the share price to double the warrant, and you think you've made the right decision on that particular stock, then it makes sense to buy

51

the warrant, and get the biggest bang for your buck. But I don't believe in buying Jardine Matheson warrants because they happen to be technically cheap when I don't like the underlying equity. Also, from time to time if you're taking a negative view of the Hong Kong market, then it may be easier to hedge through the futures than dumping the underlying stock, or ahead of doing so. But I'm not particularly interested in options for options' sake, or in straddles and complicated things.'

CHARTS TO GUIDE TIMING OF ENTRY AND EXIT

Charts are less important to Armstrong in the other Asian markets than they were in Japan, and are not always so readily available, but he thinks you still have to look at them. 'A chart is still the best immediate picture of what has happened, and what people's expectations are, and it gives you something to gauge your views against. I used charts a lot in Japan for trading decisions around the long-term trend, but I very, very seldom trade on the basis of charts in the other markets. The fundamentals, or our perceived fundamentals, dominate in the Asian markets, and I use charts more as a guide to the best entry or exit point.

'If there is a stock I like, for example Hopewell in Hong Kong, I can see in my mind's eye the chart pattern developing, and what it is going to look like twelve months from now. The moving averages are all over the place and still a bit negative, but you can tell that in the next couple of months it's going to break out there and be up about here in twelve months' time. You can recognize patterns which you've seen before; you can see charts which are building to do something; behaviour does repeat itself. Once you've become familiar with certain chart patterns, all you're trying to do is to spot the pattern repeating itself. If you can do that in a stock which you like, then you have a fair idea of what your target could be, and when you should begin accumulating.

'Hopewell is down, and I think it is a pretty good time to accumulate it. Sentiment is still negative, so there is no rush. I could wait for a dip to buy five million shares, but we probably want to buy a few hundred million, so we are looking to accumulate over say a four month period.' Size has reduced flexibility. In 1994, Armstrong's Pacific Regional Group has US$15 billion under management, about 60 per cent of the JF total, a sixfold increase in three years. He himself manages $1.5 billion. It's much easier to buy five million Hopewell than five hundred million, he comments. With larger transactions, you may drive the price up 10 per cent or more as you buy, and drive it back down if and when you try to sell. And *if* you realize you've made a mistake, it's much easier to extricate a small fund.

MANAGERIAL STRUCTURE

Armstrong himself does not spend a lot of time visiting companies. He likes to get out of the office about one week in four, but when visiting a country spends most of the time with brokers and analysts. He may visit a couple of the companies which JF already owns in size, but says that this is to get a feel for the management rather than anything more specific. The other members of his Pacific Regional Group, now around twelve strong, spend more time on company visits. The group, according to Armstrong, is increasingly self-reliant 'because obviously we have a clearer understanding of what we are looking for, which is fast growth where it has yet to be recognized by the market. I like to keep things simple, and you can't get more simple than that. You also need to maintain a feel for where the companies are, which enables you to take advantage of market sell-offs to accumulate the stocks which you prefer.'

Each of the fund managers in Armstrong's group has a country speciality. Like every other institutional manager, JF has had to adapt to the proliferation of markets and stocks in the region. 'This is the big change in the business over the last few years. It is impossible to really specialize in more than one market, but a fund manager can probably cope with four markets quite well, understanding the markets and knowing the stocks. Once you go beyond four, you're floundering. That's where you need really strong leads from the people around you.'

Armstrong is very selective about the marketing missions which he will allow his fund managers to undertake, and wryly admits that this causes occasional differences of opinion with the marketing department. Existing investors take priority, and at one stage he was reportedly prepared to see potential new clients only if they came in batches of five. He also refuses to get drawn into board meetings and wider management issues, in order to remain as focused as possible on investment.

He is regarded as an excellent team leader as well as an outstanding investor, and seems to have the knack of inspiring and motivating without intimidating.

DIFFICULTY IN THE 1994 CROSS-CURRENTS

He found 1993 much easier than 1994. 'Ideally, you sit down with your twelve experts, come out of the meeting, and say, OK, the ranking is 1, 2, 3, 4 . . . so we should have as much money as possible in markets one to four, and ignore the rest. That's fine when, firstly, the market allows you to have strong positive views on the ranking, and, secondly, you can get the money into your preferred markets. Ideally, you want to have as many of your eggs as possible in three or four baskets. That's what you're paid for; that's emphasizing the positive.'

It has been trickier in 1994 because it has been harder to choose between markets, and those which might be at the top of the list have been among the less accessible. 'Japan is the only market which is sufficiently different from the others. All the other markets are moving with roughly the same influences, all of the economies are growing quite healthily, and the flows of funds are into Asia as an entity, rather than into any one specific country. So stock selection rather than market selection is the key for the time being. Hong Kong is a bit different, as it is increasingly part of China, and China is such a big entity – so we effectively now have three blocks: Japan, Hong Kong/China, and South-East Asia.'

SEMI-OPEN MARKETS

'The unfortunate thing about Korea, Taiwan, and India is the limited ability to get money in and out. We would have more money in Korea if it was a free market, if we could have ease of access. We'll always tend to have more money in the markets where we can get money out. Getting money into India is no problem, but once you sell you can still wait twelve months to get your money out. If it wasn't for that, our weightings in India would be two or three times what they are, because we are particularly positive on the earnings

54

outlook, and we think the market could easily double or treble over the next two or three years, but you have to take account of your cash flow. If all proceeds appear as accounts receivable for twelve months, that obviously constrains what you can do elsewhere.'

OUTSIDER COMMENTS

Terry Thomas of Mees Pierson thinks outstanding Asian fund managers are characterized by 'balls of brass'. (Being a civil chap, he goes on to explain that such persons may be male or female.) The first person he thinks of in this category is Colin Armstrong.

Armstrong is also credited with 'innate good judgment', and with an ability to understand what really matters in economies and stock markets while soaring over the details. Stephen Hill of Jardine Fleming Securities in Tokyo – admittedly not an unbiased observer, being one of Armstrong's top brokers – believes that what distinguishes him is the ability to overlay an extremely fundamental long-term view with short-term trades; most people either rely on a succession of short-term views, or have a long-term view and are too inflexible to moderate or reverse it on a short-term basis.

He is both a fundamental and a momentum player, Hill explains. He will find an unidentified stock and buy it, and will keep buying it even though no one else is coming in. Then, when other people notice it and start to buy, he will gear up and buy more, because the story is yet to be fully appreciated. As soon as the volume of trading starts to flag, he will start to sell, even though the brokers by then have cottoned on and are saying that the stock has much further to go.

Stephen Hill thinks that Armstrong is 'as good as or better than Soros', with the caveats that he does not yet have the ability to move a market so far as to be self-fulfilling, and that he is subject to more institutional constraints and cannot afford to lose money for as long as Soros.

THE EXPERTS' NAP SELECTION

Will Armstrong's intuitive style stack up well in Asia in the long run? He himself is engagingly diffident about claiming any particular expertise or insights. 'I think it's impossible to analyse what you do as a fund manager. I may only be in a position to be interviewed for this book because I was in Asia early enough to specialize in what will be big markets when they were very, very small markets. I've been here for twelve years. A lot of people used to come out here for two or three years and then disappear . . . I always found it easier in Japan to explain what I was doing and why, because it's a single market, a single entity, so you're focused on one thing, and you can look at all the aspects of that one market, whereas as Asian managers we're covering every market from Pakistan through Japan down through New Zealand.'

If he is right on the magnitude of the market movements to be expected over the next few years, nevertheless, a lot of astute investors will put their money behind his judgment.

Chapter 5

Enigmatic consistency

The team at Aetna

The star of the Hong Kong pension fund scene in recent years has been relative minnow Aetna, which has shown by far the highest returns over seven years, close to the highest over three years, and easily the best risk-adjusted returns over both periods. In the Wyatt Company's annual comparative study of the territory's pension fund managers, Aetna's risk-return record has been coming out astonishingly close to the efficient frontier. Their two unit trusts have also been consistently strongly ranked.

The difficult thing is to figure out how they do it. Managing director Anna Tong says that stock selection is the key, and that they have mixed results on asset allocation. She thinks that size is an advantage, and that Aetna can buy small and medium growth companies, which larger groups have to pass by. Typically one third of the portfolio is in 'small cap stocks' capitalized at under US$1 billion, and another one third in 'medium-caps' at US$1–5 billion.

They have a fairly standard evaluation process, but one which has been developed by the present fund management team, to which there is therefore real commitment. Fund manager Winnie Lee explains that they first screen out all companies capitalized at less than US$100 million, and eliminate all stocks not in their 'growth sectors' – which rules out commodity and mining stocks. This reduces their universe to 900 – 1,000 companies, which are then evaluated on the basis of four factors: earnings growth, valuation, gearing, and management. Other people look at ten criteria, they say; they prefer to keep it simple. They don't take a trading view, she says: they look three to six months ahead, or even six months and beyond. They do not like to have a large number of small holdings: 1.5–2 per cent is the minimum unit size.

The Aetna difference seems to come down in large part to teamwork, on which there is great emphasis, and perhaps to good market instinct. Tong suggests that it is what you do when the performance is bad which is crucial to achieving good long-term results. The effort to maintain a constructive atmosphere appears very conscious. Mistakes are analysed without pointing fingers, and the attempt is made to identify strengths and weaknesses very rationally. According to Lee, 'we have our own companies we follow, and we really depend on our colleagues in terms of the companies they follow. We don't second guess each other, because we know that we too can pick bad stocks as well as good ones. We may joke about it, but we never make a personal attack. We give each other confidence, and we do our best. We always try to convince each other of our views. The others may not entirely agree, they may be cautious, but because we have worked together for so long we can still come to a consensus view. Because we put a lot of emphasis on the team, and the team has been working together for so long, and we have been adding members only gradually, a lot of things come naturally, and the working environment is fairly harmonious. This team is unique. Everyone feels pride in the company, because everyone helped to build it up. It feels like a family.'

The stability of the team is a major achievement in itself in Hong Kong. As Lee points out, many fund management houses pay lip service to teamwork but do not seem to achieve it in practice. Aetna does.

'In emerging markets, management is very important, and that is something a broker cannot tell you. It has to be someone you trust, maybe your analyst. At the beginning when we hire an analyst, we go out with him to do company visits, so that he becomes part of the team and we have a feel for how he approaches the companies – whether he may be too lenient, or too critical; how to interpret his assessments.'

Tong is low-key and efficient, and 'definitely knows what she's doing', according to competitors. Lee, much sought after by head-hunters as the manager of some of the top performing mutual funds in Hong Kong, says that her loyalty to the team is paramount – and anyway she couldn't do so well in a different environment. Teamwork is emphasized over and over again, and the adjective 'harmonious' comes up repeatedly. At the end of the day, the chemistry just seems to work.

Chapter 6

The incoming American

William Kaye of the Pacific Alliance Group

Bill Kaye epitomizes the brash American newcomer on the Hong Kong investment scene. Swinging into town in 1991, he thinks he is on the leading edge of Asian investment. Competitors respect his intellect, but say his ego is the size of a house, and his diatribes libellous. A gift to the caricaturist, he has repeatedly said at dinner parties that his hero is Gordon Gecko. Former employees say this is entirely in character, that he cultivates the tough guy image, and that he has no sense of humour so is unlikely to be joking.

He even looks a bit like Michael Douglas: a younger version, to be sure, with rugged good looks distinguished by balding temples and long hair curling just below the collar. He kept me waiting for fifty minutes on my first visit, and while perfectly lucid throughout the interview gave the initial impression that he had the other ninety-five per cent of his brain engaged in more interesting pursuits.

Sophisticated investors, in his definition, are those who give money to hedge fund managers like himself, with an incentive to achieve absolute returns. He is disparaging about money management in Asia, which he describes as 'plain vanilla', since the majority of fund managers have a more narrowly focused mandate, running regional equity funds, or single country funds. 'It's the customer who is taking the judgment that he wants to be long Asian stocks, or the specific market which is being offered. There is nothing wrong with that, but it is very rudimentary.'

AN EDGE WITH NEW INSTRUMENTS?

Kaye believes that he has an advantage in understanding derivatives, such as convertible bonds, because 'most of the products which are

59

only now becoming known in Asia were developed in the United States'.

This view would come as a surprise to the Singaporeans who have been trading warrants for decades, or to the investors of Bombay who cope with capital structures of amazing complexity, and a plethora of instruments such as zero-coupon fully convertible debentures. As international firms moved into Bombay in 1993 to work on Euroissues, talk of 'internationalizing the Indian markets' rapidly gave way to thoughts about 'Indianizing the international markets'.

What is true is that trading volumes in derivative instruments soared in 1991–93 with the arrival of major new American investors, and of the investment banks which trade these instruments as principals. Institutional investors who used to watch the Hang Seng index futures as a gauge of local Chinese sentiment now say that Americans have become the dominant futures players. But the increasing use of derivatives has been correlated in the past with the later stages of bull markets. In a downturn, liquidity in such instruments dries up even more quickly than in the underlying market, and the number of instruments typically declines over the subsequent cycle, as old paper expires or is retired and new issues dwindle to a trickle.

What is also true is that this illiquidity can be turned to advantage, and that many investors take simple share purchase decisions while failing to consider the alternative instruments. It is this opportunity which Kaye has identified. A lot of the Euro-convertibles in Asia, he says, were sold in 1993 to people who had no idea what they were doing; for example to private bankers in Europe who noted that the markets had already risen spectacularly and thought these provided a relatively safe way to play. 'A lot of them have been thrown out of the window, and there are actually some fairly attractive opportunities now.'

The examples he mentions, though – two Malaysian stocks described as 'blue chip' and having 'low credit risk' – would be regarded as notoriously speculative by local investors. I ask Kaye whether he regards his relatively limited experience in Asia as a disadvantage. He takes this one more thoughtfully. On balance he does not, he feels there are advantages in a fresh approach; and anyway, he says, one can always hire people who have local knowledge, and he has tried to do this. He initially had limited success in this respect, and the Pacific Group became notorious for its revolving door. A number of well-regarded locals had come and gone, with none yet lasting more than six months, and the consensus was that

Kaye was a difficult taskmaster. The problem seems to have been a particularly severe culture gap and the situation seems to have settled down in recent months. The information base also seems to have broadened, having initially been dangerously narrow.

PICKING THE BEST INVESTMENT ARENAS

Bill Kaye studied economics at Vanderbilt University, and joined the mergers and acquisitions department of Goldman Sachs in 1977 after completing an MBA course at Chicago. At Goldman he worked on a number of corporate takeovers, including the first large leveraged buyout (LBO) of a public company. Many leveraged buyouts had been done before, but never had sizable listed companies been the targets. Kaye says he recognized that this could be the beginning of a great business, and left Goldman after only a year.

He joined the risk arbitrage department of Paine Webber in 1978, and took over as departmental head in 1984, just in time for the headiest days of the LBO boom. Investing as much as $500m at a time of the firm's own capital, he says the department was profitable in every full year of his management, and in twenty of twenty-three calendar quarters. Unleveraged returns of around 25 per cent on the invested capital generally translated into returns on equity of 75–100 per cent.

These were rewarding years, as Kaye's small department received 20–25 per cent of the profits earned, and Kaye himself a large proportion of that pool. The game ended after the October 1989 failure of a proposed takeover of United Airlines' parent, UAL. The stock tumbled 59 per cent in the aftermath, inflicting heavy losses on the arbs, Paine Webber included. The high returns generated in earlier years had already fallen as the industry committed more and more new money to the business. Now, deal flow slumped as commercial banks came under pressure to reduce their involvement in LBOs, and financing dried up as the junk bond market collapsed. In August 1990 Paine Webber and its highly compensated arbitrage head parted company.

Kaye saw opportunities created by the panic selling of junk bonds and leveraged securities, and started investing in out-of-favour US securities, first for Paine Webber, and then as a private investor. In the twelve months from September 1990, he says that the value of the portfolio under his management increased from $13m to over $21m.

Meanwhile however he had been thinking about Asian markets, and decided that these were a yet more attractive investment arena. 'The greatest macro-economic story in the world today is the transformation of China into a multitude of regional market economies.' He and Jack Perkowski, who had run the investment banking division of Paine Webber before setting up an LBO partnership in 1988, established the Pacific Alliance Group with Tiger Management as an active shareholder. Asset management activities are concentrated in the Asian Hedge Fund, which started up in November 1992, and by mid-1994 stood at approximately $140m.

Kaye thinks that Asian market development is only just beginning, and that he has established a major competitive advantage by being here early. Evidently he sees his competitors as being in the US, not in Asia. 'As Asian markets develop, they will develop in a fashion somewhat similar to what you have now in the United States. They will become more efficient, liquidity will increase, derivative products will become more important, and managers who don't know how to use them will be at a definite disadvantage.'

At present, he notes, liquidity tends to dry up in bear markets. 'That is a serious mistake which newcomers to these markets frequently make. When they're in a buoyant period, they develop a misleading concept as to the underlying liquidity of the market.'

Trying to pick the market top, he points out, is frequently futile. 'As you get a little of your position out at the top and continue to sell, you now have no bids. So it appears to the casual observer that Jardine Matheson over a two month period goes from the high 80s to the high 40s. But in fact your ability to sell any sizable position on almost that entire path is extremely limited.' Kaye feels that the flexibility to protect his position through the futures market or through shorting other instruments is an advantage. 'If people think their money manager knows what he's doing, why not give him the maximum amount of flexibility to protect their assets, as well as make money?'

AN ENTHUSIAST FOR CHINA

Kaye remains very bullish on the potential for direct investment in China; much more so than for India, where he feels that local entrepreneurs have the edge. Although this does not translate directly across to the portfolio investment side, his logic is interesting. 'The advantage in China is, having been truly communist until very recently, it is much more of a level playing field. You have a country that wants to be a market-type economy, wants to be a member of GATT (general agreement on tariffs and trade), wants to have businesses that are globally competitive, and yet until recently it had a totally different agenda. What that means is that intermediaries like ourselves, who can be catalysts in getting some of the more important enterprises where they need to be, are operating without a disadvantage, to the extent that we can add value to the process. What China needs is technology, and a global partner who understands how the business is operated on a competitive basis outside China. And it needs management, particularly at a very senior level, because the degree of sophistication needed to transform a business or upgrade it probably doesn't exist locally.

'There are two aspects that I like. One is, you don't have to be cynical about why they're willing to do a deal with you, that might even be favourable to you, because you're bringing enormous value to the table. You're providing them with things that they currently don't have at their disposal, and that they need. The second thing is that you're not operating in an environment where a lot of other people, if this is such a good deal, would have done it already. If it's such a great deal, why is it that you can initiate it, or why is it being shown to you? That's one of the first questions I always used to ask myself on Wall Street. I can get over that hurdle much faster in China than in India.'

What about portfolio investment in these two giant economies? 'The public markets are too embryonic, offer too limited a menu of choices, and frequently do not represent either the best opportunities or anything close to the better quality companies that can be created within the country. I think that is broadly true for any emerging market. So the time to buy the public companies in China or the Indian subcontinent is when for some reason, usually investor sentiment or very negative capital flows, you have reason to believe they are artificially depressed. Where you really want to pounce on the public markets of these emerging situations is when they're just totally undiscovered, when it's: "World wake up!" You want to get there when they are dirt cheap, and nobody knows how to price anything, and the IPO can't be done unless you and maybe a couple of other guys support the issue. We're not in that environment now in almost any emerging country, and we haven't been for a while. The last emerging market I can remember that was like that was the re-emergence of the Philippines in 1991 when Meralco came out at 4.4 times earnings and we bought a pretty good chunk of the issue. Sentiment was so depressed, and people had made no money in the Philippines' public markets for so many years, that you couldn't interest people, even in the better quality issues. Now I wouldn't touch anything in the Philippines.

'We have a reasonably favourable view of Bangladesh, which is in a remarkable position in some respects. It's got a very strong currency and a good macro picture, an essentially balanced budget, stable pro-business government, extremely low wage costs, very cheap valuations. The tough thing is finding anything to buy. In those kind of markets, the game really is on the direct investment side. If there are technical and other reasons that we think an emerging market is unduly depressed, that's a reason to get at least somewhat excited and do a lot of work. Otherwise, the public markets frequently are not a very desirable way to access those markets, and direct investment frequently is about the only way to go.'

Although bullish on the long-term potential for the region, Kaye says he finds the trading environment very tricky at the time of our meeting, and that there are fewer themes on which he has any conviction than at any stage in his investment career. The yen had been soaring, and the yen-dollar rate was around 97, having just broken through 100 for the first time. 'This is fascinating, it's way overdone, but shows no sign of correcting. I think the yen will continue to appreciate against the dollar, it seems to have enormous strength. But I think if you came back in a year you could see the yen at 120, maybe 130. And that has enormous implications for all these other markets.'

A LONG-TERM BEAR ON JAPANESE EQUITIES

He is very bearish, for the long term, on the Japanese stock market, which has recently been attracting a lot of foreign buying. How do you support valuations, he asks, with the market on 85 times earnings. If earnings doubled, the market would still be expensive. And what would cause the doubling? Not exports, 'because the more they export, the worse the currency situation gets'. A real jump in profitability, he thinks, requires a pickup in final domestic demand, which in turn requires further deregulation.

'When they deregulate the retail sector, the way things are distributed, then obviously people in those sectors will get hurt, but the retail cost to the consumer will come down, and people will buy more. The reason they don't buy more now is it's a terrible deal, everything costs too much. When they deregulate, the aggregate effect for the population is quite positive. You get a pickup in domestic demand; you particularly get a pickup in imports. We're starting to see that by the way. Exports of US automobiles are at record levels, at a time when you're not seeing a big pickup in overall automobile sales in Japan, it's the mix . . . Now, with further deregulation, exports will just fly out the door from the low-cost places like the United States: semiconductors, automobiles, anything high value-added. On the margin, the winners are in the US at this stage of the cycle.

'Now the implications of that are: yes, you will have a pickup in aggregate profitability of Japanese companies. The current account surplus will probably be cut in half, in a two year period, from an unsustainably high level at the moment anyway. The current account deficit in the US, which is largely with Japan anyway, will also get cut in half. The US dollar will soar against the yen. Whoever owns Japanese equities will get killed.'

The two great sources of liquidity for the financial markets, Kaye argues, have been currency intervention by the Bank of Japan, trying to stem the yen's rise to protect its exporters, and the current account surplus. Both will dry up. The bond market will collapse. Equity valuations will follow. 'As soon as the real economy kicks in, the financial markets get wiped out. Some of the exporters may hold up. But overall, it's the death knell. How you can take that picture and say, wow, that's a great investment opportunity, let's go long Japan – I think you've got to have your head examined.'

I suggest that this sounds like conviction. Kaye agrees, but is very unsure of the timing; he is looking for a catalyst. Political paralysis and vested interests are delaying restructuring. 'They're in this weird transition phase. Their steps are just so glacial.' At the moment he is market-neutral. 'I'm assuming I'm not smart enough to know just when this thing is going to turn, but it will turn at some stage. It's easier for me to have a long-term view. The cross-currents are such that it's very difficult to have conviction in terms of what ought to work right now.'

For the moment, however, he is bullish on Korea. 'I think it idiotic that you can be bullish on both Japan and Korea. The logical beneficiary of what's happening at the moment is Korea, so surprises are likely to be on the positive side. Valuations are much more compelling, people debate the quality but that's improving, they are much lower-cost producers than the Japanese, and in the world today that's where you want to be. At some point it reverses. But that's in the future; I'm talking about right now.'

Kaye considers the best combination of macro picture in the region is New Zealand. He cites a projected growth rate of 4–5 per cent, low inflation, and high nominal and real interest rates. The bond market, he feels, is clearly oversold, and the monetary policies are just beginning to be recognized. 'The Kiwi dollar could end up being regarded as the Swiss franc of Asia.' He's just bought almost all of that day's auction of six month paper, he says, at a yield of 7.1 per cent.

He is wary of Hong Kong, and is slightly short. He feels the property market could fall 20–25 per cent. 'Why would you buy Hong Kong property shares? It's got to be one of the most expensive cities in the world in which to operate.' He is also concerned about the long-term future of the Hong Kong dollar, on the suspicion that Chinese-owned banks are lending to poor credit risks north of the border, and that a failure might cause jitters. Would there then be excess demand for Hong Kong dollars, as there has been in the past? Nevertheless, he finds some shares attractively priced. Jardine Matheson is the fund's largest long position, bought earlier in the year when 'battered for the unthinkable sin of de-listing from the local exchange. I will be happy to trade this stock in London in 1995.'

South-East Asia likewise generates little enthusiasm, despite recent stock-market declines. In Malaysia, for example, 'the real economy is doing well, the currency is cheap. The problem is the valuation of equities, which still fully discounts the very favourable growth picture. The opportunities in Malaysia are probably in the limited number of fixed income instruments, but it's hard to get leverage in those instruments. The currency is one of the safer bets, but you don't have a developed bond market.'

What makes a good fund manager? Kaye is not sure. Clearly he has no doubt that he is one, whereas some of his college contemporaries never really made it. But he says he certainly wouldn't put himself in the category of any of the masters. 'What makes a good fund manager, what makes a tennis star?' he muses. 'Why is Pete Sampras different from the pack?' Like other successful managers, he stresses the role of instinct. 'And judgment – almost a sixth sense.'

Travel, he says, is essential. 'And not because it's fun to travel. It's not always fun to travel. It's not a junket. You have to get out of the office. You can't develop conviction with respect to your investment ideas by reading research reports or talking on the telephone. Once you have an idea that seems sensible, you develop conviction by getting out there and testing your hypothesis.'

A client calls. Amongst other words of caution, Kaye identifies one of the main risks of the regional markets. 'These companies are family-run entities. They don't have a large free float. They can be manipulated by the controlling shareholders, and occasionally are. You have to be especially careful with the smaller companies.'

It is too early to judge Kaye's performance. In 1993, the fund rose 66 per cent before fees; respectable enough, but way below many straight equity funds. In the trickier environment of 1994, the fund is more or less even to date; in his worst down month he lost 5 per cent. Over-confidence is a principal danger for funds run in this style, and a lack of local experience and input could compound the dangers. Over-simplification is a risk. Yet Kaye has been learning fast. Confidence, investment-obsession, risk control and lucidity make him hard to ignore.

Chapter 7

Disproving modern portfolio theory

Edward Kong of E.K. Investments

Another recently started hedge fund is very different in character. Edward Kong, a Hong Kong-born Chinese, returned from the UK to start his own business in 1991. Its similarities are the timing, the size of the fund (slightly smaller than Bill Kaye's, at US$100m), and the fact that the fund's success is measured in absolute terms rather than with reference to an index. It differs in most other respects.

Where Kaye emphasizes the macro picture, Kong stresses value investing. Where Kaye is highly articulate, and writes chatty monthly faxes to his clients, Kong confesses readily that English is a second language, and writing in any case a weak point; he has as yet done little marketing. Where Kaye, despite his grumbles about Hong Kong office rentals, has established a lavishly spacious office, Kong's ten staff work in 1,200 square feet. Where Kaye thinks that local knowledge is a minor issue, Kong thinks his detailed understanding and long experience in the regional markets are critical: without these, he says, he would never have dared to establish his own company, competing ultimately with US giants such as Soros and Tiger.

Kong explains his strategy as two-faceted. His core portfolio is selected by value; he tries to look at companies with a corporate financier's eye, and consider the value of the enterprise as a whole. That valuation must then be adjusted for the fact that you only have part ownership, you don't have control. He particularly likes to look at companies which are not widely analysed, and which need expertise to understand. He then tries to control the risk of his portfolio, hedging individual markets when he thinks they are expensive, and taking advantage of arbitrage opportunities.

At the time of our meeting, he is very long of Japanese warrants, which he regards as irrationally cheap relative to the ordinary shares.

He is not gearing up, he says: he holds the equivalent number of warrants, and a large cash balance, and this limits his downside risk. If in three months' time the ordinary shares are cheaper than the warrants, he will sell the warrants and buy the shares.

US APPROACH NEEDS MODIFICATION

Kong says that US techniques cannot be used in Asia without adaptation, because there is so much less public information available. 'Warren Buffett can analyse a company in great detail and have great confidence in its future, because the information provided by the 10K' (the annual stock return filed by US companies) 'is extremely good, and the market environment in America doesn't change that much. Here, the market environment can change quickly, and the information is not as good. I cannot have the confidence to put 20 per cent of the portfolio into one single stock, and wait ten years for it to work out, because it may not work out. Not through any fault of my own; I may have made the best possible decision based on available information. But the visibility of the future in this part of the world is not as good as in America, even though the underlying growth rate is much higher.' I ask whether he is talking about fraudulent misrepresentation. This is sometimes a problem, he concurs, but 'even assuming the more straightforward managements, the disclosure requirements are much less here. And the markets are much smaller, more dynamic, so they change much more quickly.'

You consequently need to make more judgments, he argues. High-flying Malaysian shares provide a good example. 'It's easy to be wise after the fact, but before the fact there may not be enough information in the market. However, if you do know that there are close ties to the government, and you do know that the government wants such and such to happen, then you may be able to form a view. You need to take some risks, some judgments, in any market; more so in markets where politicians have greater influence. Politics has an influence in any market, even in the US, but it's a matter of degree.'

The mandate is global, but Kong says in practice he has a large concentration in Asia, because he believes that over the next decade this region will yield significantly superior returns. The mandate allows him considerable latitude, but equities are very clearly the focus. 'If we found a gold mining stock which was extremely cheap, but we didn't want to take a view on the price of gold, we might short some gold, to eliminate risk. We would not initiate a primary position in a commodity.'

Kong thinks he can call the markets to some extent, but says he is not that confident about timing, and takes only small positions. 'The core portfolio is not dependent on timing. I try to use timing on the margin, to improve the return, but I want to make sure that, if my timing is wrong, I still get the stock appreciation.' He emphasizes risk control, rather than timing for its own sake. He believes that this adds about 5 per cent per year to his annual return, although he has not tested the figure.

David Lui, who succeeded Kong as manager of the Schroders Hong Kong fund and is himself a very long-term, low-turnover investor, describes him as the best fund manager he has ever known. Nissim Tse of Arral, with whom Kong shared an office while establishing his firm, says that he is also a remarkable trader, and that his market timing is incredible.

Kong himself says that he is not a trader by nature, and it is only when he sees a framework and a pattern which he feels he understands that he is confident enough to trade short term. The most memorable occasion on which he did was during the Sino-British negotiations of 1982–84. He took the view that 'the negotiations would eventually be successful, because they were so important for both sides, but that with both sides jostling for position they would not finish quickly. So I would buy when the news was bad, and sell when the news was good. That worked very well. If you define a bear market as a 30 per cent decline in the index and a bull market as a 50 per cent rise, there were three bear markets and two bull markets over that period. We did very well by buying close to the bottoms, within say 10 per cent of the bottoms, and selling near the tops.' Kong was trading only a small proportion of the portfolio – he thinks perhaps 10 per cent but nevertheless the fund outperformed by about 30 per cent over the period. 'Part of that was stock selection, but part was buying low and selling high, twice.'

INEFFICIENT MARKET THEORY

Kong says he knew nothing about stock markets until he was at university, unusual as this may be for someone brought up in Hong Kong. He studied mathematics at Imperial College London. One of the subjects he studied there was time series analysis, although he had no idea at the time how relevant that would later become. He went on to do an MBA in Chicago, and it was there that he was introduced to stock markets. He started to study stock-market time series with the help of the university computer and databases, and gained first hand experience in the development of quantitative models.

While he was at Chicago, efficient market theory was very much in vogue. 'Like any theory developed in the academic world, if you accept the assumptions, the conclusion follows. You cannot fault it. But how closely do the assumptions match the real world? I was a non-believer in efficient market theory, so I worked backwards. If the market is not efficient, what is wrong with the assumptions? I wasn't a model student; I asked questions about what was considered sacred. I didn't get along very well with the professors. So I have mixed feelings about Chicago, although I benefited greatly there!

'When I entered the investment field, I looked for areas of inefficiency. I believed I knew where to look. I just worked back from efficient market theory, and the assumptions with which I disagreed.

'*First assumption: information is free and equally available.* So I focused on research. If you get better information, you get better investment results.

'*Second assumption: given the same information, you come to the same conclusions.* So I focused on better interpretation of the data.

'People thought I was crazy when I first went to Schroders in Hong Kong in 1982. I concentrated on research and analysis at a time when people thought this was a crazy speculative market. I had a great deal of difficulty convincing my colleagues. I have to thank Chicago for giving me that insight, and that was the single greatest influence in my early years.'

BAPTISMS OF FIRE

'After that, I was lucky, in that I have seen more bear markets than the average fund manager. When I joined GT, I was assigned to cover the Australian market, just in time for the resource boom and bust of 1980. I shifted to the South-East Asian desk just in time for the 1981 crash. I managed the Schroders Hong Kong Fund during 1982–84: very volatile markets.' (This was the period of maximum political uncertainty in Hong Kong, leading up to the Sino-British

Joint Declaration in December 1984.) 'I went to London in 1985 and was given the Australian market: again a long bear market in Australia. I went to Morgan Grenfell in 1989, and became head of the Japanese team: lo and behold, the crash of the Japanese stock market. This has been extremely good training! Even though I have only been in investment for fifteen years, I think I have seen as many bear markets as anyone.'

I asked Kong whether this makes him unduly cautious in bull markets. He thinks not, although he says he does not aim for top performance in a bull market. Experience 'gives me a more balanced perspective, which sometimes takes away from my performance in bull markets – but I don't see that negatively, I take lower risks. I make it back with a vengeance when markets have a downturn. For example, in 1987, my funds in South-East Asia returned 40 per cent for the year. That's a lead other fund managers need to do a lot of catching up with. They need to outperform me by a wide margin when the market goes up, to beat me in the long-term track record.'

The long-term track record is certainly impressive. The various funds under Kong's management have compounded over 30 per cent a year since 1983, allowing for an eighteen month period during which he can no longer obtain the figures. At this rate, the investor would multiply his money fourteen-fold every ten years. Given the bear markets Kong has experienced, this is not bad going. His funds have been consistently strongly ranked against their peer group.

THE REPUTATION-FORGERS

Kong says that when he returned to Hong Kong in the early eighties, there were a couple of things he found very strange, which prompted a lot of thinking about the investment process. 'One of the things I noticed was that Swire Pacific's shareholding in Swire Properties was worth more than the parent company itself, because Cathay was losing money. In those days all that analysts did was to look at the PE ratio. Obviously Swire Pacific's attributable earnings from Swire Properties were more than the parent company total. And because people knew that Cathay was losing money, the PE ratio of Swire Pacific was lower than the PE ratio of Swire Properties. That was a double-whammy. And I couldn't understand how this major regional airline could just be given to you, and you didn't have to pay for it;

especially when there were signs that Cathay was going to turn around, not that year, but maybe within a couple of years. I didn't realize the magnitude of the turnaround, but with that sort of pricing you don't need to! That was one of my major holdings, and I was a buyer of Swire for five years before selling a single share.'

Mostly he bought Swire B, the less liquid non-voting shares which trade at a significant discount; again, he says, this was contrary to conventional wisdom at the time. 'People told me that the discount would be maintained, but you get a higher dividend yield, so as long as the discount doesn't widen by more than the difference in dividend, you still win out.'

'I didn't buy as much as I should have initially, because I was relatively inexperienced, and I wasn't too sure whether there was something I was missing . . . did the old hands know something that I didn't? I didn't think so, but I didn't want to stick my neck out too much.'

Kong's most memorable stock call was a purchase of Hutchison Whampoa in 1984, 'when the market was crashing because of the Sino-British negotiation. Hutchison went from $24 to below $8. Part of the reason was that buildings had been presold to a corporate buyer who defaulted. At that time it fell to $12, and I did some analysis. The stock had $4 of cash per share, and earnings, as far as I remember, of about $2.50 per share. Conservatively, I could see 25 per cent earnings growth a year. The stock fell below $12, it fell to $11, it fell to $10, it fell to $9, it was 10 per cent of my portfolio. I was very nervous. I redid my calculations daily, and always got the same answer. Fortunately I had some credibility, because we had been the best performer in Hong Kong two years in a row by then, so my colleagues were prepared to bear with me! The last purchase I made was a very small amount at $8.00. The next day there was a large line at $7.80, which I didn't take, and that was the bottom. Within three months, Hutchison announced a capital payment of $4, and the stock went to about $40. At the time, it was very, very nerve-wracking. I remember that to this day!' (Kong was lucky he did not own the warrant. The exercise price was not adjusted for the issue, and the warrant price was decimated. Investors were wary of Cheung Kong group warrants for the rest of the decade.)

He is proud to have avoided both Carrian and Atlas, the two major Hong Kong bankruptcies of the 1980s. 'I think I was one of the very few fund managers, or possibly even the only fund manager, who didn't go into the restructuring meetings of either company.

As far as I can tell, most major firms were caught in either one or both.' Schroders stayed out of Carrian, although Kong recalls that this decision put him under enormous pressure as the stock outperformed. It was, after all, deemed to be virtually riskless, with a buyback guarantee from the company. 'There was an investment report which gave me the ammunition I needed to convince my colleagues. It's not always a case of whether you're right or not; you have to convince others, and that report made my job a lot easier. It was a recommendation to buy, but I think that the analyst probably had his arm twisted, because within that report there was enough information to form the conclusion that the net asset value was negative. Basically, the shipping interest was quoted at cost. I did a study on the world shipping market, I had access to some of the Lloyd's registers, and I knew roughly what a Panamax carrier and so on were worth.'

'Atlas was a similar case. It was the best performing stock in the Hong Kong market for two years in a row, at a time when the HK market was doing nothing. Atlas was just going up like a rocket. It outperformed the market by over 200 per cent. I didn't hold the stock, and everyone else was holding it. I was under tremendous pressure. The reason I didn't buy Atlas was that I bothered to look at the listing document, and that made me suspicious right from the beginning. Atlas bought a shell company, and wrote down all its inventory to zero. That's suspicious. What I suspected, although I didn't have proof, was that they would then write it back, in the form of inventory profits. Many people were sceptical of Atlas at first, but when the company achieved its first year profit target, half of them were convinced. The second year, they doubled earnings again, as predicted, and a lot more people believed. But having read the prospectus, and become suspicious of what they were doing, I remained unconvinced.

'I also bothered to do the work on the market for electronics, which a lot of analysts didn't; it was just one company in Hong Kong. But I looked at the fortunes of similar companies in the United States and Japan, and concluded there was no way they could be making that much money. It was possible, but the odds against were so high, I felt it was highly unlikely. And what really convinced me was the plant in Penang. I had a friend who was going to Penang at the time, and asked him to check the plant for me. He said it was non-operational; and this was completely contrary to what the company was saying. That convinced me that my suspicions were right. I think within six months of that it went bankrupt. But it was a tough two years!'

In the difficult conditions of 1982–84, Kong's second largest holding was Winsor. 'Not because I found it a particularly exciting company, but in the middle of a bear market you want safety. Winsor was trading at three times earnings, and something like two times cash flow, and yielding about 17–18 per cent. They also held a lot of textile quotas. And again, the market value of those textile quotas, which we checked independently, accounted for a large part of the asset value, and there were also a lot of properties. Added together, it was just ridiculously cheap, in terms of earnings, and in terms of assets. I felt extremely comfortable to buy, even though the price was dropping every day, because I knew that within six months I had to make money. As it turned out, because the market turned, I made more money than I had bargained for. One reason that the Schroders Asia Hong Kong fund was the best performer even though we didn't hold Atlas, was a major position in Winsor which was the second best performing stock. The performance gap was wide – but then I had 10 per cent in Winsor. No one in his right mind would have 10 per cent in Atlas. That saved my skin, and allowed me to withstand the pressure.'

After the Tiananmen crash in 1989, Kong sold Swire and switched heavily into property stocks. 'I didn't have any more foresight than others as to whether there would be civil war. I wasn't bullish or bearish; I had no idea what would happen. But I was sure that property stocks would outperform. It didn't make sense for property stocks to have fallen that much more than the rest of the market. If things were going to go wrong, they would all go wrong. Anyway, there were a lot of other stocks with a big property component.'

THE SAME APPROACH IN ALL MARKETS

Kong has applied the same techniques successfully in all of the markets in which he has been active. 'My thinking has been refined and reinforced year after year. The approach applies conceptually to all markets: I think it is universal. It's the implementation that's difficult!'

He cites a Japanese example from the past which parallels some of the fund's recent moves. 'Several years back, I found Hitachi to be very cheap. The whole sector was cheap, but Hitachi was extremely cheap. There were three risks: the mainframe market, the consumer electronics market, and the yen. But Hitachi was so cheap that the risks on the mainframe and the consumer market were minute – well, adequately discounted. One risk that you could not discount adequately was the yen. Profit margins were 4 per cent. So a 4 per cent movement in the yen, everything else being equal, would wipe out all your profit. At the time, this didn't seem to be an issue, since the consensus at Morgan Grenfell and elsewhere was that the yen would weaken and go to 140. I was very suspicious of that view; I actually felt the yen would strengthen. But what made me feel it was such an anomaly was that, despite the fact that people saw the yen going to 140, they were bearish on Hitachi. That made no sense whatsoever. If you were bullish on the yen, you might have been able to make a negative case; but if you were bearish on the yen, it was a screaming buy.

Obviously a traditional fund cannot hedge the yen, but when I started my own company we bought heavily into Hitachi, and we were also long of yen futures contracts. We hedged Hitachi's expected five-year sales in yen. Now what actually happened was that the yen strengthened from 130 to 110 over a period. Hitachi underperformed and then it outperformed; over the period of the trade it was probably in line with the market or slightly underperforming – but we made a bundle on the yen. And to me that is really not taking any risk, because one or the other has to happen. Also, to me, this was a confirmation of my analysis, that despite the run in the yen, Hitachi did not underperform by a wide margin.'

Another buying opportunity was presented by Japanese convertible bonds in 1990. 'It was obvious that there was going to be a supply-demand imbalance in the market, because of the unwinding of the tokkin funds. But there was again a glaring anomaly in the market; you had Yamaichi or Daiwa convertible bonds selling at a yield of 10 per cent. This was unbelievable; they weren't going to go bankrupt! Or at least, they might go technically bankrupt, but the government would support them. The convertibles were selling at a premium to exercise price of about 35–40 per cent; people were looking at them as straight bonds, as junk bonds. But those bonds had ten years to run. It doesn't take much to get that degree of appreciation in ten years. So, you were getting 10 per cent yield to maturity, and as long as Japan had a bull market somewhere within the ten years, you would make money on the stock too. So I tried to persuade my colleagues to go into convertibles very heavily.

Because it was an unusual investment for a fund manager I had very little success. We ended up with 1–2 per cent of the Japanese portfolio. But again it was an anomaly that turned out much better than I expected. I tend to look at the downside. Because interest rates in Japan came down so sharply, these stocks would have made huge money.'

THE CURRENT PORTFOLIO

Buying opportunities in convertibles recurred in the first half of 1994. Kong bought the Pacific Concord convertible. 'If it was a straight bond, yielding 10 per cent, I might say that it was not that exciting. But for a convertible, with only 18 per cent premium, yielding over 10 per cent, I think it is very exciting. That's an anomaly in the market – certainly compared with all the warrants, because basically a convertible is a straight bond and a warrant. Here you get a free warrant, whereas other instruments are trading at a huge premium. Regardless of the merits of Pacific Concord, which people debate, I think the credit risk is low.' The stock had risen over the couple of months since purchase, and at the time of our meeting was yielding 7–8 per cent. 'Even now it's probably still cheap, but you need to take a view on the stock more than I had to.'

In contrast to the prevailing consensus, he does not have much of the portfolio invested in the emerging markets. Indonesia, for example, he regards as abnormally risky because of the poor liquidity; Taiwan and Korea because of the barriers to foreign investors and possible premiums. 'If I didn't look at the risk factor, they would be a lot more attractive. In terms of risk-adjusted return, they are a lot less attractive, based on my analysis, than they would otherwise be.'

At the beginning of 1994, when most of the South-East Asian markets were looking very stretched, 'we took the view that the two ASEAN markets which would hold up best would be Singapore and Thailand. In the case of Thailand, we felt there were huge anomalies in the valuation of companies, and we found some companies which were very cheap. The market itself has actually done very well, but that was not my premise. My premise was that I found these stocks I liked so much, I didn't care what the market was doing.

'Even in Malaysia, where I don't like the market, rightly or wrongly, we hold one stock – Oriental Holdings – because I find that stock to be very cheap. It didn't go up during the entire bull market. So late last year I switched my Malaysian holdings into Oriental Holdings. Sooner or later, either the market had to collapse, or Oriental Holdings had to take off. As it happens, the market has collapsed, and Oriental has gone up, although not by much. We are driven by stocks and not by markets. I will buy a stock in a market that I hate, if that stock is attractive enough.'

Risk management is based on the overall portfolio. 'I do sometimes take huge risks on individual holdings, providing the holding is small. Two weeks ago we took a position in the Venezuelan Brady bond, but it is only one per cent of the portfolio. That is a risk I can take. The bond is yielding 28 per cent to maturity. The risk of course is that you lose it all. But my judgment is that you would not be able to tell whether you will lose it all for some time. So over the period, my risk is not my entire holding. They may go down more; my risk is maybe ten to twenty per cent. Twenty per cent of one per cent is 0.2 per cent, and I can afford to lose that. It doesn't make sense that the yield on a Venezuelan bond is higher than the yield on a Russian bond or some of the other less developed countries, given that the Venezuelan currency is based on oil, an easily saleable commodity, much simpler than the others. It doesn't make sense to me when Chilean bonds and Brazilian bonds yield in the teens, so there is a big gap.'

BABY STEPS IN THE DOWNSWING

Kong tends to buy stocks gradually, a little at a time. 'I never try to buy at the bottom; I never try to sell at the top. If you look at a stylized cycle, I tend to buy on the way down, near the bottom of the cycle, even if I think I will probably lose money. If the market goes down, I can buy more. But I cannot be sure of the market, so if I think the stock is cheap I want to lock in some of it. Most people buy after the bottom, on the way up, and that's my difference. I have a theory on that. If you buy on the way down, the pain threshold is high, and the amount of time you are wrong is longer, but your average cost is actually lower. If you buy on the way up, you look much better, and you're under much less pressure, but you actually get worse execution.

'This gives a performance edge. The trade-off is that you need to spend more time managing your colleagues. It's human nature: if a stock is bought and goes down and it's not your decision, you get worried. That's why I'm so pleased I started my own company!'

He learnt not to be too greedy, he says, in Hong Kong's small electronics stocks in the mid-80s. He didn't lose money, like many other investors, but it was an educational experience. 'It was a new sector in Hong Kong, and a lot of funds were caught because they had to believe what the companies told them, there was no other way to judge them. I took the time and trouble to look at the market for printed circuit boards and consumer electronics in America and elsewhere, and that gave me warning signs. I took some profit, but I tried to wait for the market to turn to maximize my profit, and then I couldn't sell – I underestimated how much the trading volume would shrink. Had I just sold and forgotten about it, I would have made a lot more. Now I always tell people not to be too greedy; leave the last 20 per cent or even 40 per cent to other people.'

In 1987, he started selling in May – with hindsight, much too early. 'I didn't sell a lot at that top – but I sold a lot in June, July, and August.'

Broker research, he says, cannot make you outperform, because it is available to too many people simultaneously. Where it may be useful is to level the playing field in areas where you do not have specialist knowledge, to get you speedily up to par, and to save you from mistakes. 'If I receive good quality broker research, it means that I start at a very high level to do my additional research; but our emphasis is always on that additional research.'

Kong reckons that his biggest mistake ever related not to investment but to administration. When he set up his company, he thought he could contract out all the administration to custodians and accountants, admittedly paying a premium but freeing him to concentrate entirely on the markets. This was a disaster, and he spent eighty or ninety per cent of his first year chasing up these companies, caught in a trap where he had little time to interview prospective employees who might be able to alleviate his workload. Performance suffered, and the fund was down 6 per cent in 1992. His brother-in-law Edmond Kung came to the rescue in 1993, and he got on track with a gain of 67 per cent for that year. Now, he says, a good team is falling into place, and he can begin to relax. He no longer has to spend all Saturdays and Sundays in the office, and at last has time to spend taking his two small children swimming, and doing other things that children like to do.

STRAYING OUTSIDE THE CORE EXPERTISE?

1994 has been treacherous. A creditable 7 per cent rise in the tricky first half was given back in the third quarter, leaving Kong level for the first nine months of the year. The third quarter fall was due to Kong being long of Japan and short the US. Kong's argument is that he expects a global interest rate rise to dominate international markets, leaving the US market extremely vulnerable. The move might seem to diverge from his declared analytical strengths, but Kong maintains that his degree of certainty on this score is as great as that on his stock selections.

Where risk control veers into risky speculation is sometimes hard to judge. With individual stocks, it clearly is possible at times to have insights superior to the market consensus and a reasonable degree of certainty on that analysis. With international economies and markets, the number of variables is so huge that one can far more easily be proven wrong.

Michael Sofaer says that obstinacy is disastrous for a hedge fund manager: that it is necessary to reassess your hypotheses continually, and to cut a position very quickly if the market says you are wrong. Clearly, stubbornness has stood Kong in good stead on individual stocks. Buying a stock as it is falling, continuing to buy, and sticking to your guns, can be extremely effective, and the likelihood of a serious mistake can be minimized by thorough study. It may not be appropriate for calling whole markets, where you can be correct in your own assumptions but overwhelmed by other factors or by the elapse of time.

FOCUSING THE EFFORT

Kong says that he has no problem keeping track of all the regional markets, because 'we don't look at very short-term trends. We look at the prospects for the market for the next three to five years. They don't change that much. If there are underlying themes which will drive several markets over the next three to five years, then you can look at those like a single market. We're not geared up to capture the divergences between markets over a six to twelve month period.'

He does focus his efforts, however, and leave deliberate gaps in his coverage to save time. When he was running a regional portfolio in London, he says he didn't look at Singapore or Malaysia for a year, because he thought Hong Kong was more attractive.

'When I was running an Australian fund, in 1985, I focused entirely on the mining shares, because I felt that there was a discrepancy in valuations. People didn't look at the balance sheet, and they didn't distinguish between operating earnings and currency losses. Those companies turned round for a year, and people didn't realize. The supply-demand situation had turned around for three years. I went to Australia and nobody showed me a balance sheet. People said they didn't think fund managers were interested in those. 90 per cent of my portfolio was in mining stocks, and eight or nine of my top ten holdings; the only non-mining stock I remember holding was Lendlease. And so there were huge gaps in my Australian knowledge, even though I was the person responsible for the Australian portfolio. When I say gaps, I knew something about these areas, obviously, but I didn't have any insights over and above what I read. I would still read the broker reports so that I knew what people were saying, but I didn't do a lot of homework myself.'

Kong says there has been one change in his approach over the years. In the early days he paid more attention to the flow of funds than he does now, when more people are trying to anticipate such flows and fewer are analysing the fundamentals of stocks. Now, 'we don't buy on the basis of greater-fool theory, or on specific categories of investor coming in; we buy the stocks we think are most attractive, and hope they come to the same conclusion. If they don't, we underperform in the short term, but eventually we are right, we catch up.'

He also says his portfolio is less concentrated than in the past – when you are running a hedge fund, there are more themes to play. When you are running a single country or traditional fund, it is easy to find some ideas which are much more attractive than others. When you are running a hedge fund, there are so many opportunities, and the risks they face are very different. We spend a lot of time structuring the risks so that we are not that exposed to a single risk. Whether you will make more money buying a very cheap stock or shorting a very expensive market, that is a very difficult judgment. When you have two stocks, and one is more attractive

81

than the other, that is a much easier decision. So it's much easier to have a very concentrated portfolio when your degrees of freedom are limited; when you see anomalies you are quite confident. But how do you judge the risk of a Brazilian bond versus a speculative share? We do try to do that, but my confidence in that judgment is less than if I were to judge the risk of Hongkong Land versus Great Eagle.

'I do believe in concentrated holdings, if you've done your home-work. If you know something is good, you shouldn't diversify. And that is borne out in my experience. I did a study of the Australian fund I ran in London, which was the best performing fund over a two year period. The reason was that I kept running up against the guideline constraints which said that the top ten holdings should not account for more than 55 per cent of the fund, and I kept having problems with that. I would ask: 'You mean market value or cost?' and they said market value. I said I shouldn't be forced to sell something just because it doubled. So I did a study. If you took away my top ten holdings, which accounted for 55 per cent of the fund, the rest of my holdings actually underperformed the Australian index. So all of my outperformance and more came from my top ten stocks. With the others, I relied on news, and other people's research – they were small holdings, I didn't bother. But nine out of those top ten stocks I had researched myself. The difference was huge.'

Kong has an outstanding track record with institutional funds, where he fretted about the diversification constraints. Running a successful hedge fund is a matter of risk and reward; the manager's judgment of the risks is critical. Edward Kong is one of the most interesting new names in the field.

Chapter 8

Thai salad days

David Crichton-Watt of Asian Investment Management Services

David Watt may be one of the most unassuming of all hedge fund managers. He is also highly successful – and tells some of the best stories in Asia. He has trekked extensively in the mountains of Pakistan, on which he is something of an expert, and once lost a horse over a cliff on an expedition near the Afghan border. The horse, unfortunately, carried all his spare clothes, his sleeping bag, and all the cooking equipment. They did still have food: a bag of flour remained. It was eight days' walk to civilization, during which the expedition occasionally managed to cook flour and water on a big slate, and thus survived on chapatis. The team emerged looking like victims of Belsen. Somewhere out there, Watt grumbles, is an Afghani wearing his clothes and using his sleeping bag.

He has done the gruelling hundred kilometre Trailwalker hike, over the rugged terrain of Hong Kong's New Territories, about six times – usually every other year, he says, because by then he has forgotten the tedium of walking for twenty hours. (This time is definitely at the fast end of the scale.) He is also no mean squash player. At the time of our last conversation, however, he was about to depart for an unusually hedonistic break in Italy.

He is a famously astute, if controversial, investor. Three of his calls are particularly well known. He was very early into Thailand, where he started buying personally in 1982; he was short the Japanese market at 38,000 when the bubble finally burst in 1989, and covered the position at 19,000; and he was an early buyer of Sri Lanka, from 1991 onwards.

Now he has some US$200 million under management, of which about half is sub-contracted from George Soros' Quantum Emerging

Growth Fund. The rest is in the Crescat fund and the Floreat fund – all the old Latin names coming out, he says, obviously remembering more of the language than most of us who studied it throughout our schooldays. ('Crescat' means 'let it grow'; and 'floreat', 'let it flourish'.)

In mid-94 he can find few stocks offering reasonable value, and feels that direct investment in the emerging markets now seems more attractive – especially mezzanine deals, a year or so ahead of listing, 'where you don't have to watch it frittering away every day!' He has been at least fully hedged for several months, and the shorts for the time being are costing him money. Up to 10 per cent of the funds may go into direct investments. 'There is a lot to be said for investing in basket-case countries, where the downside is only political.'

He will be off to Mongolia soon to inspect a new investment which is being negotiated by an American company, to reactivate some oil wells which were discovered in the 1960s. Mongolia's only refinery met with a mishap shortly thereafter and the country has since been dependent on Russian oil. In return for building a small refinery, the new venture will be entitled to 50 per cent of the oil output from existing wells and future exploration. As a bonus, the venture has the right to rework old dumps of copper tailings with new leaching technology. Toronto and NASDAQ listings are planned.

He is also an investor in a company called Odin, recently acquired as an Australian shell by the Malaysian property-based conglomerate Land & General. Odin will undertake construction and construction-material projects in countries such as Bangladesh, Burma, Uzbekistan, and Vietnam. Tan Sri Azmi wan Hamzah, the well-connected chief executive of Land & General, has been a friend of Watt's since the early 1980s, and a few years ago was persuaded to forsake more sedate Malaysian pursuits to join one of the strenuous Pakistan hikes. Azmi is now president of the Malaysian Chamber of Commerce, and while accompanying Malaysia's very business-oriented prime minister in his trips around the region is sometimes offered interesting privatization deals – a PVC plant in Bangladesh, for example. A steel mill in Vietnam is another possibility, an import-substitution project. A construction boom is already under way there, but there is a danger of overbuilding of hotels and office space; the property game, Watt feels, is overplayed. This is the ideal emerging market investment, he suggests: Azmi will take care of all the management headaches, and liquidity will be available through the stock market.

Watt first moved to Asia in 1972, when he worked for a while with the stockbroking firm of J. Ballas in Singapore. He moved to Hong Kong in 1975, and worked for a few years as a half-commission man in a local broking firm, setting up his own fund management company in the early 1980s. He spent a few years representing the stockbroking firm of T.C. Coombs, before reverting to a quieter life with the company in its present form.

In Singapore, he recalls, he used to make a habit of registering all stock. Dividends would sometimes flow for years afterwards, as the local Chinese invested for capital gains and rarely bothered either to register or to chase the dividends through the system.

EARLY ADVENTURES IN THAILAND

Watt started investing in Thailand in 1982, when good quality companies could be picked up for one to one-and-a-half times cash flow.

'The market was very illiquid. I was almost the only buyer, and volume then was 10 million baht a day – about US$400,000. The only other groups who traded in any size or had any interest in equities were the Mutual Fund Company, which was very small – only a few funds – and Siam Commercial Bank, which traded Siam Cement and some of the property companies within the group.' Custody was the next problem. 'Hongkong Bank didn't want to do it, because there was no business and they therefore didn't want to set up a department. Standard Chartered didn't want to do it for the same reason. So I persuaded Siam Commercial Bank to set up a custodian department, and became quite good friends with some of their people. I used to get offers of stock which were good for two weeks. Fifty thousand Siam Cement say, which was a big trade. It's changed a bit now!'

Financial statements were usually available, although not always in English; they were not however printed into glossy annual reports, and were usually presented in a folder from the auditors. The companies were very friendly, he recalls, although they really could not understand why this peculiar foreigner wanted to visit. Siam Cement used to invite him to lunch . . . this gesture of hospitality is almost inconceivable to present-day analysts, who find this ultimate Thai blue chip notoriously uncommunicative.

After a disastrous crash in the late 1970s, equities were regarded as extremely risky: dividend yields were therefore required to be higher than the bank deposit rate, and the bank deposit rate was of the order of 18 per cent. When Singer was obliged to divest 51 per cent of its local company to Thai investors, the American parent company had to guarantee dividends of 15 per cent for the next three years; the underwriting fee was 7.5 per cent, and the under-writers were sweating. Watt remembers borrowing money to buy Siam Cement, with a cost of funds lower than the dividend yield. 'It was great!'

He goes on, 'But the prices didn't really move much. They crept up slowly. And then in 1984 we had a coup, and a threat of a devaluation, and then the threat of another coup because the army hadn't been told about the devaluation, and hadn't got their money out . . . So it was really only after the oil price came down sharply in 1986, and the dollar slumped, and the yen rose to the point where many Japanese labour-intensive industries were forced down to Thailand, that the boom started. Thailand for the first time had a current account surplus, so there was a big build-up in liquidity in the stock market, which finally soared. Then Soros came in as well, adding fuel to the fire. He bought the Krung Thai fund, set up in 1979 to rescue the stock market from an earlier lunatic bull market. The market had a spectacular rise from 1986 up to 1990. Then it fell 50 per cent without a trade, essentially, in seven or ten days' trading. But it was a great party while it lasted. Siam Cement went from 180 baht to 11,000; and many stocks did just as well.'

I asked about Mahboonkrong, a high-flyer of the early 1980s which came to grief in 1985 and has never been relisted: a fascinating story.

I never lost money on Mahboonkrong. We bought it so cheaply. The stock had collapsed from 1,600 baht in 1983, or thereabouts, to 60, where I started buying, and I bought down to about 30. It collapsed after the devaluation, because high interest rates had made property development a pretty unattractive business, and the com-pany had borrowed US$ out of Singapore, so the devaluation put a nasty hole in the balance sheet. This was the *coup de grâce*, because the company had been limping along in a difficult property market. But it had tremendous assets, and it was just a problem of liquidity. At 40 baht, or even at 50 baht, the total market capitalization was about US$12 million. They had 2.5 million square feet of commercial space, 750 acres of industrial estate in Bangkok, the biggest rice mill in Asia, the biggest tapioca silo, a 5 km long conveyor belt and loading facility; they had 25 per cent of Toshiba in Thailand, and a lot of other good assets. So they really just needed a rights issue.

'My clients and I had acquired about 50 per cent of this company. At that point, Siam Commercial Bank, the main creditors of the company and of the former controlling shareholder, rang up and suggested that I should perhaps take a closer interest, because it was probable that the interests of Mr Sirichai and those of the company no longer coincided, as they had sold all his shares, which was why the shares had collapsed . . . he ended up with 2–3 per cent of the company. I wrote to him suggesting a rights issue, and didn't receive a reply. Later I was told that he was doing all kinds of strange things, and the Thais advised me to throw him out. We tried to do this ourselves, but quickly realized that going through the Thai courts, foreigner against Thai, was going to be impossible. So we looked around for someone to get us out of the mess. Khunying Chanut Piyaoui of Dusit Thani was one of the two ladies who were the only people willing to take Sirichai on, because he was quite a tough character . . . so we sold all our shares to her for ten baht a share, with the right to buy back 90 per cent for eleven baht a share, and she threw him out. As the thing dragged on, some of the foreign investors decided just to sell to her outright, but others bought their shares back. I still have some. The company's doing well.' The shares have still not been relisted, because of outstanding counter-suits, but after a rights issue the net asset value is estimated to be about 500 baht per share, and they have traded reasonably frequently over-the-counter at 400.

HOTELS IN SRI LANKA

Watt first visited Sri Lanka in the early eighties, at roughly the same time as he first became involved in Thailand, but was deterred by political violence until 1990–91. It was quite difficult even then, he found, to invest serious money. 'We decided we had to buy on the privatizations, because the volume was pathetic in the stock market. We tried to bid for the distillery company, and a television company, and then eventually bought the Asian Hotels Corporation. We being Azmi and myself. I needed Azmi's hands-on property experience.

87

When we went there he rather liked it; he could see the old Malaysia of the sixties. And there is no question the country has tremendous potential.' If the politicians get it together, he adds – but he is encouraged by the new government, and its choice of senior administrators. This allows the possibility of a major privatization programme, and a serious reduction in the budget deficit. 'Even though they are coming in on a socialist ticket, they are the only people who may be able to teach their union followers the harsh realities of life.'

The hotel investment, Watt feels, is the best possible warrant on the market. He and Azmi have a controlling interest in the company, which owns the Oberoi, the Renaissance, and the Intercontinental: two thousand rooms, or 60 per cent of the Colombo total. At present, occupancies are only 60 per cent, and room rates are US$40 per night. If there is a surge in the market, and in business, and international contacts, then the vacancy rate could easily fall below 5 per cent, and room rates could quadruple without international businessmen thinking them unreasonable.

Now, however, markets do not excite him. The job has become quite horrible, he grumbles: how can you possibly cover so many markets? In the eighties, for example, only Hong Kong, Singapore, Malaysia and Thailand were worth thinking about. Korea and Taiwan were shut, and Japan too expensive to bother with. 'Now everything's picked over, down to darkest Africa, and we have these floods of mindless research. I don't want to pay four times book value and twenty times cash flow.' I ask about Russia. There may be value there, he agrees, but when he visited in 1991 he was very unconvinced about the settlement procedures. 'I don't like handing over all the money up front. You have 100 per cent downside risk in the first two weeks.'

Whatever the temporary lack of enthusiasm, he does not appear to be losing his grip. The hedge fund was up 120 per cent in 1993 – 'and we were very cautious, buying puts all the way up' – and 8 per cent in the first half of 1994. He has not participated in the flow of foreign money back into Japan, because he could not see value, and notes that there has been no follow-through of domestic buying. In 1994 he has made money in selected Thai stocks and in Australian resources. The Sri Lankan investment bank, Asia Capital, in which he invested a year ago, is about to be listed. He is unlikely to be short of ideas for long.

Chapter 9

Asian manager learns new tricks

Peter Everington of Regent Pacific

Peter Everington admits that he didn't know much about deltas and volatilities until 1992. He did however have an excellent eight-year track record in Asia.

There are two ways to run a hedge fund in Asia, he comments. 'You can come out here and learn about Asia, or you can be someone who has reasonable experience in Asia and learn how to run hedge money. I don't know which of the two is going to be the better; I suspect the latter, because I think it's easier to learn to run hedge money than to learn Asia. I've been here for many years and I'm still learning. Even the basic elements of Asia take a long time, because it's so different. If you're too set in your ways in a western market, I don't think you can adapt to Asia that easily. On the other hand, learning risk management techniques has proven to be relatively simple. Even for someone in the dark ages like me, I'm really getting into these computers!'

The key partnership at Regent Pacific, a relative newcomer on the Hong Kong investment scene, is between Jim Mellon and Peter Everington, who are respectively chairman and managing director of the fund management operation. Both joined GT Management after leaving university, and they worked together in San Francisco in 1982–84; both left together to set up the Asian side of Thornton Management on start-up; and after a short interlude they ended up together again at Regent.

Richard Thornton, the 'T' of GT and founder of Thornton Management, had an extraordinary track record of attracting bright young men fresh out of university (almost invariably Oxford or Cambridge), and giving them their head. On occasion he caught them even younger: he recalls recruiting Jeremy Hosking, who went on to become one of the founders of Marathon Asset Management,

89

at the age of about sixteen when he came round to tea with Thornton's daughter. Thornton offered him a holiday job, and then more, sending him during the vacations first to San Francisco to work with Jack Mussey, and then at the age of seventeen to Hong Kong. The holiday jobs continued through university. Thornton remembers Hosking graduating fully trained at the age of twenty, and immediately taking over the GT Asia Fund. Thornton grumbles that he has only one major black against Hosking: the introduction to Peter Everington, whom he remembers as his most difficult trainee ever – 'absolutely impossible, he *would* not listen!'

JIM MELLON

Jim Mellon joined GT in 1978, and covered Japan for a year before moving to San Francisco. Peter Everington joined in 1980, and initially covered UK equities. In mid-1982, Everington was transferred to the US to help Mellon build up the US portfolios, with GT adding resources to back up Mellon's April 1982 prediction of the imminent start of the most powerful US bull market in thirty years. The market took off in August, and for the year as a whole the fund was the top performer in its class. In early 1984, ructions at GT resulted in Mellon, Everington and David Harding leaving to set up their own company; they were looking for backers when Thornton announced that he was setting up Thornton Management, and invited Mellon to join him. Mellon insisted on bringing Everington and Harding, and they moved to Hong Kong in 1984. By 1985, at the age of about twenty-eight, Mellon was managing director of the Asian operations.

Thornton describes Mellon as 'a terrific, a peerless investor'. He remembers sending him to see San Miguel in the early eighties. Mellon offended one of the leading brokers in the Philippines, a lifelong bull of San Miguel, by demolishing his case for the stock. The price would halve, Mellon said, if not quarter. The broker rang Thornton to complain about the behaviour of this arrogant young man; Thornton says he advised the broker to take note of Mellon's views. The stock market was decimated in the final years of the Marcos regime. 'Then, just before Cory (Aquino) succeeded, Jim nipped down to the Philippines, and made a huge purchase' – through the same broker, who became a firm friend. Mellon's Philippines Redevelopment Fund was the world's best performing mutual fund in 1986.

Mellon left Thornton in 1988, after a row over delays to the UK listing of the company, which had then to be aborted after the October 1987 stock-market crash. He joined Tyndall, temporarily abandoning fund management in favour of structuring and marketing funds, but in 1991 moved to join Regent Pacific, where he became group managing director and has been the prime mover in building the firm in its present form. The expansion has been rapid, aggressive, and effective. Mellon is a controversial character in Hong Kong, but few would dispute his entrepreneurial and marketing flair.

Although business development and marketing are now Mellon's main priorities, he remains good at spotting under-appreciated investment opportunities. This is 'one of the great tragedies', in Thornton's view – 'if only he would sit still and invest, he'd be an even better fund manager.' In 1991 Mellon established an Under-valued Assets Fund, investing in closed end funds trading at substantial discounts, and where possible encouraging or forcing restructuring to narrow the discounts. The concentration of this fund, which could at times have 25 per cent of the fund in one target, was the initial spur to investigate risk management systems, vitally important to the subsequent hedge fund.

TIGERS AND DRAGONS

Everington meanwhile has remained firmly focused on investment management. In late 1985 he predicted a major bull market in South-East Asia, on the assumption that the doubling of the Japanese yen and the halving of the oil price would lead to the most powerful economic boom for the region in over twenty years. Others may have held the same view, but I remember Everington as by far its most articulate exponent. Certainly he capitalized on it most effectively, initiating the 'Tiger' description of the newly-industrializing Asian economies – a term which has passed into daily usage – and launching a series of funds under the Tiger name. Later the concept was extended with 'Little Dragons', and Thornton's lucid marketing materials and topic papers frequently invented metaphors which explained regional economic developments so succinctly that they were widely adopted in financial circles. More importantly, the funds featured regularly at the top of the performance tables.

In 1992, Everington joined Mellon at Regent to take charge of the fund management operation, and initially launched a similar range of 'plain vanilla products': standard equity vehicles including a Pacific Basin Growth Fund and a Tiger Fund, under the Regent Global Fund umbrella. (These were no-load funds, an innovation in Hong Kong. This inspired marketing move, like the 'raiding fund', won Regent no friends in the rest of the fund management community. The company is regarded as aggressive in its fee and cost structures, and although in this case it scrapped the front-end load, the funds came with redemption and performance fees.) Regent then combined Everington's expertise in traditional equity investment with Mellon's new appreciation of risk management and imported US systems expertise, and established its hedge fund in 1993.

'These days you cannot say that the Asian markets are cheap; they're not cheap at all,' Everington says. 'That's why I'm moving away from plain vanilla towards risk-managed products.' (Hefty hedge fund performance fees do nothing to deter this shift of emphasis.) In years gone by, he focused solely on return and paid very little attention to risk. Now, with the price of entry into stock markets much higher, he is focusing much more on risk control. 'Fortunately, the tools to achieve that are developing at a prodigious rate. The flip side of all that money flooding out of America has been the arrival of the investment banks and all their capital, and with that comes their derivative capability. The Americans lead the world by a country-mile in derivative capability; they exported it to Japan first and Asianized it, and now they are learning the lessons from Japan and bringing the capability down to South-East Asia.'

Everington says that, when he first came to Hong Kong and set up the Thornton Tiger Fund, investment was relatively easy. 'The price of entry was incredibly cheap, Thailand for example on four to five times earnings. We bought the Philippine Long Distance Telephone Company on what we thought was 1.5 times earnings, but it turned out to be 0.6 times earnings.'

HEDGE FUNDS IN ASIA

Even now, 'you don't have to be that smart when the economies are growing at 8 per cent a year – or have been in the past, let's say 6 per cent going forward. The wind is so powerfully in your favour, you don't have to be a genius. When I go to the United States to talk about my hedge fund, I almost apologize and say, look, we're not doing anything greatly scientific, it's nothing like you guys are doing, it's just that we happen to be playing in a pool where there's that much less competition and the pool is that much more inefficient. In the States there are three thousand hedge fund managers; in Asia there are less than a dozen.

'The Asian markets are still hugely inefficient, with tremendous market anomalies. Ninety-nine per cent of investors are still long only, and while that prevails you can't have an efficient market. That's why if you have the technical and functional ability, and the inclination, to go short in this part of the world, you can make huge amounts of money, because you are just playing in a different territory to other people. The history of hedge funds is very short in Asia because, going back more than eighteen months or two years, you didn't have the tools. That's changed dramatically – you now have a form of hedge structure available on just about every market in the region, except the subcontinental markets. But even there, you are starting to be able to do various things. As the number of players increases, the instruments will improve but the markets will become more efficient and the opportunities for profit will diminish. For now, the ignorance margin that allows you to make money for virtually no risk is just huge.

'In January 1994, the Merrill Lynch India Fund on the London market went to a 20 per cent premium to asset value. True, a lot of country funds go to huge premiums – it's just that the India Fund's is open-ended! So I was able to short it on the Thursday night, on the lovely old three-week settlement system which unfortunately has now gone, and on the Monday I was able to subscribe to the fund at asset value, plus the three per cent rapist front-end charge. So I was able to make 17 per cent in four days. That's a pure function of ignorance. I don't know who the people were on the other side who were stupid enough to pay that kind of premium.

'In mid-1994 – you know the situation in Korea, where the quotas for many stocks are full, and Korean Airlines has been full for a long time – some wally sold Korean Airlines foreign straight into the market without realizing that he could have sold it for a 10 per cent premium in the OTC market. So I snapped up the stock and sold it an hour later in the OTC market, for a round-trip gain of 6.5 per cent and one hour's risk.

'That kind of thing would not happen in the US. It happens

continuously here. In the Hong Kong market, you have tremendous speculative activity by the locals, who are generally long only; there are very few Hong Kong Chinese who will play the short side to any great extent. As a result, when the market goes wild, the premiums on options go to unbelievable levels, just because people want to speculate. You look at all these covered warrants that have been issued, and at the number which are now expiring with no value. Inevitably a few people made a great deal of money early on, but the mass were sucked in and lost money.

'Most people who buy options lose money. If you look at the implied volatility, for example, Hong Kong has been trading at 45–55 per cent at various stages over the last nine months, whereas New York is on about 8 or 9 per cent, and Tokyo is on about 16 per cent. In the last week, implied volatility in Hong Kong has crashed, down to about 26 per cent. So you get very wild swings on the volatility of options, or the pricing of options, and you can take advantage of that. For us, either on a naked basis or on a covered basis, shorting options is usually a relatively easy way to make money. Right now, with the volatility so low, we are buying options, just as part of the ongoing process of risk control. The use of these tools is so common in the States, and yet so new in this part of the world.'

UNASHAMEDLY TOP-DOWN

Everington says he is 'unashamedly top-down', and thinks that is definitely the way to go in Asian markets, in these first decades of market opening. At the moment, he estimates, 65 per cent of his decisions are geographical and 35 per cent stock-specific. He says he is too cynical to be happy analysing companies, as there are few which meet his demanding criteria, and the few really great companies which he can think of are all in the west. 'In Asia, I have found some very good companies, and I have found some very good investments, but I have never found both characteristics wrapped up together in the same way. Probably because you don't get the same disclosure, or attention to shareholders, as you do in the west.'

'We have a strategic side and a tactical side. We trade market inefficiencies. There are a lot of messages in the market, if you listen to what the volatility is saying, and to the trading relationship between the spot market and the futures market. There are tremendous swings in the futures market here; much more than you would get in New York. And there are all those new indicators that not many people are watching.'

As an example, the Hang Seng index is calculated once a minute. Regent calculates it real time, on a bid, offer, and last price basis. So they have on average thirty seconds advantage – 'a small advantage, but it's nice', and can see how the bid-offer spread is moving relative to the last traded prices.

'First, there are arbitrage opportunities for making money, but second, we can listen to a whole range of indicators which weren't there before. In our business, half the time you spend forecasting what the markets are going to do. The other half you should spend listening to what the markets are saying, and trying to work out where you are, and what's in the market already.'

The trading opportunities are generally in the larger markets. In the smaller markets, transaction costs are high, and liquidity is a constraint. In the Indian subcontinent, for example, only strategic positions are taken.

Strategic selections are described as 'top-down/bottom-up. Make the country selection first, forget the industries, and go straight to the stock selection. In the Philippines for example you only have about fifteen decent stocks to buy.'

All company analysis focuses on cash flow. When analysing a market, Everington uses simple cash flow, net profits plus depreciation. When he gets down to individual companies, he goes into detailed source and application statements. Return on equity and the sustainable rate of growth are factors on which he focuses.

He tries to teach junior analysts to think of economies in the same way as companies, as single economic entities. 'The ploughback rate for a country is of course its savings rate. The growth rate of a country is directly proportional to its savings rate. The reason these countries are able to grow much faster than the western countries, without significant inflation, is the savings rate. Low savings equals low investment equals low growth equals United States. High savings equals high investment equals high growth equals Asia.'

In the second half of 1994 however, Everington is a strategic bear on Hong Kong, and sees the Hang Seng index going to 4,000 sometime in 1995.

THE HONG KONG DOUBLE-WHAMMY

'The excess in Hong Kong was caused by a combination of two virtuous stimuli, combined with a system that had a curious inability to sterilize that over-stimulation. The stimuli came from monetary expansion from the States, consequent on recapitalizing the US banking system but also on a poorly performing US economy; a poor US economy equals loose monetary policy in the US. On the other hand, in China we had massive economic expansion, and therefore a fiscal pull on Hong Kong. And so Hong Kong has had this great economic stimulus from China and great monetary stimulus from America, a great virtuous double-equation. As we go forward from here, China goes into a downturn, America goes into an upturn, that's a double-whammy the opposite way.

'More to the point, as all of this was happening on the upside in Hong Kong, when the money came pouring into Hong Kong, Hong Kong's exchange rate mechanism gave it no ability whatsoever to adapt to that huge level of monetary inflow. Part of the monetary inflow was manifested by huge portfolio flows from pension funds and the like in the States, and the other part was capital flight money from China. The Hong Kong fixed exchange rate system is a very simple, self-balancing, perfect system, in theory. But theory is one thing and the practice another. In any capital system you have essentially three variables to look at, the exchange rate, the interest rate, and the money supply. You can choose to fix any one of those three, so long as you let the other two float. Hong Kong chose to fix its exchange rate. The control variable in the Hong Kong link-rate system is the interest rate, which is set by arbitrage. That simple system requires that interest rates can go to whatever level is necessary to achieve balance, so conceivably they can be a hundred per cent, or zero, or minus ten per cent. But in practice Hong Kong cannot have negative interest rates: both because of the lack of legal mandate, which could be changed, but also more simply because the banking system cannot handle negative interest rates, the computers can't cope. So we had this massive inflow in 1992–93 and an inability to sterilize it. As interest rates approach zero they just level out and go fixed. So for all of 1993 you had the interest rate at 1 per cent, and capital still kept pouring in, so the money supply had to expand. The monetary base in Hong Kong in the last three years has exploded six-fold, but from August to October 1993 alone it rose 50 per cent, and that's what the bubble was all about.

'Since the end of the year the monetary base has contracted by 33 per cent. The money supply figures are very crude, there is no point doing any analysis on those; but we look at what one might call the monetary base, the free balances of the banks at the Exchange Fund, a figure that is on Reuters every day. It is illegal for a bank in Hong Kong to go net short of funds; it has to balance its books every day. That free clearing balance at the Exchange Fund represents the amount that the banks can borrow every day without penalty, but they can't borrow beyond that. The Exchange Fund has been contracting its window, because of what's been happening on the capital account, so the banks have been squeezing credit, and so the bubble is going into reverse.

'Singapore was washed with the same excess money, but they responded by raising their exchange rate, and therefore the elevation of the stock and property market was nothing like the elevation you had here. Hong Kong had no ability to sterilize; the bubble was that much more spectacular, and therefore the bust has to be that much more spectacular.

'If you want to take it to the micro-level, the market is superficially incredibly cheap, on say twelve times earnings, and yet that is struck on a market that is effectively entirely property based. Development companies like Henderson Land have net after tax margins of 73 per cent. You just don't make margins of 73 per cent on property development in the long run. Maybe 20 per cent is a good margin, but 73 per cent is a temporary aberration. The downturn is all set up.

'Right now there has been a 15 per cent decline in the property market, and most people see that as being good news. It would be, if it stopped at that. I don't see how it can stop at that level. There is hidden leverage in Hong Kong: leverage has moved away from the corporate sector to the private sector. I don't think you can have a twelve year bull market in property without a buildup of leverage.'

While property companies, badly burnt in 1981–84, now maintain relatively conservative balance sheets, many individuals have acquired multiple apartments at a relatively late stage of the boom. They will be hurt by rising interest rates; because of Hong Kong's astronomical prices, the service costs can be very high, even if they are ostensibly only lightly geared. A three bedroom flat in mid-levels, for example – where most expatriates live – can easily cost US$3 million. Even if the mortgage is only US$1 million, the service cost at a 10 per cent interest rate is US$100,000 a year. While brokers are assuming that, because there has been much talk of rising interest rates, the change has been discounted, Everington thinks not. 'That may be true in financial circles, but Mr Chan in the New Territories does not follow the US long bond rate. He does not anticipate rate rises; he dreads them – and when they come, he will finally have to deal with them.' A fairly high proportion of apartments are now empty awaiting resale. Many owners have been thinking of selling, but holding off a little because the market has been soft, waiting for a New Year rally or other improvement. Meanwhile, property accounts for 40 per cent of bank assets, against 30 per cent at the 1981 top. A soft landing looks unlikely.

POLITICS AND ECONOMICS INTERTWINED

'The question is whether this particular contraction will follow through to a bear market. I think given the approach of 1997, you have all the ingredients necessary for a panic. You have a contracting China, Chinese stock markets down 70–80 per cent, a reversal of US monetary policy against Hong Kong, and all the political confusion. People can confuse a downturn in the equity market with political factors. That won't have anything to do with it, but they can be easily confused. You have the same environment fundamentally as we had going into Tiananmen Square in 1989: plenty of scope for at least a correction, if not a bear market.

'The nice thing is, if I'm wrong, I'll be wrong on my own, I don't think there are many people around town saying this! But I'm not saying it deliberately to be controversial.'

The 4,000 figure for the index is based only on the extent of past declines, in particular the last bear market of 1981–82. (Bear markets, in Everington's definition, are falls of more than 50 per cent which are protracted. Corrections are short sharp falls, such as 1987 and 1989, which can still be of the order of 50 per cent.) So the view is at present essentially directional, with an idea of possible magnitude, rather than tied to a firm target level.

He is also predicting a surge in reported inflation. 'Consumer price inflation in Hong Kong repeatedly comes out at 8–10 per cent per year; if you try to work that out in relation to your own grocery bills, let alone your own rent, you know that's a load of hogwash. Inflation in Hong Kong has been running at probably 20 per cent, and I would think the consumer price index will start to reveal that towards the end of this year. It's just a lag effect; you've had massive property inflation, massive stock-market inflation, and that has to feed through to consumer price inflation, if only through the mechanism of rent on stores.

'There is a lot of significance in volatility in Hong Kong coming down to 26 per cent at the moment. In the last three or four years, Hong Kong volatility has never, except very briefly, gone below 25 per cent. This is telling you that people don't think Hong Kong's in a bear market. If you look at a chart, Hong Kong has bounced off its uptrend, so it's comfortable to take the last quarter of 1993 as an excess, ignore that, and continue the trend. I don't think that will hold; I think Hong Kong's decisively in a bear market. It's interesting that, given such powerful conflicting forces, the market has clearly concluded we're in an uptrend again. I think that's wrong.' Accordingly, he is buying options: effectively, buying volatility.

MONETARY EXPANSION AND BARGAINS IN KOREA

By contrast, he maintains that Korea is in a bull market which has only been going for two years, and has a long way further to go. ('Although if the yen did start to depreciate, we'd fairly quickly have to get worried about Korea.') The Korean market, he points out, is still below its high of five years ago, while Hong Kong even after a setback is still more than four times higher over the same period – and Korea should be capable of sustaining the faster rate of economic growth. On a price-cash flow multiple, the market is half the price of any other Asian market.

Moreover, money supply is growing fast. Trust accounts, which largely represent surplus corporate funds only one step away from the stock market, amount to 80 per cent of M2, but are only included in M3. The Bank of Korea is focused on controlling M2, and devotes inadequate attention to broader aggregates. In an upturn, therefore, the constraints tend to be readily bypassed. Everington thinks the resultant surge in liquidity may lead to an acceleration of the stock-market rise. However, he expects interest to rotate away from the large-capitalization blue chips towards domestic shares, banks, and insurance companies. Regent reckons that the value in the market now lies selectively in the small and mid-sized companies which have been uneconomic for brokers to research; they still regularly visit companies which have never met a foreign analyst.

TAIWAN CLOSED-END FUNDS

Another market Everington likes is Taiwan, where Regent has been buying large stakes in the domestically listed closed-end funds. These have been trading at a 25–26 per cent discount, a historic high, with a government instruction to the funds to narrow the discount. They normally pay out the majority of their capital gains as dividends, and therefore tend to run up in the second half in anticipation of the payout, which should be particularly good in 1994 after the strong gains of the first half. Other foreigners have spotted the opportunity, but 'you need quota in order to buy'.

THREE SOURCES OF MARKET INEFFICIENCY

This is another of the recurring reasons for market inefficiency in Asia, Everington believes. 'One is the cultural arbitrage. Another is the tax and administrative and legal aspects. The third is that, as you globalize these markets, people who were perfectly sane and rational in their home markets, as they go overseas become totally insane and irrational. Very sensible people do very stupid things in this part of the world because they have fallen in love with the long-term growth story.'

Telecommunications, for example, is clearly a growth industry in Asia. 'But VSNL, Very Sorry No Lines, was it really worth sixty times earnings? At that sort of price you should be getting down there and setting up your own company. There are, what, sixteen new pager companies just licensed for Indian cities? You should be down there bidding for a franchise. Portfolio managers don't think like that, but they could theoretically do so by getting down into the venture capital field.'

THE SECULAR AND THE CYCLICAL

Another common mistake is to confuse the secular with the cyclical. 'There are a lot of players in the American market who work very

100

efficiently there, and then come out here with total naïvety. They take one trip into China, see the great building site, and conclude that it's a huge growth story. There is no doubt that the secular trend in China is fantastic. But there is insufficient analysis on the cyclical front. China has clearly had a number of cyclical downturns in the last fifteen years, the last of which was 1989, and with it as a symptom of that downturn came Tiananmen Square. We're heading into the same situation now.'

Once again, Regent's tactical position is distinct from its strategic one. It had been buying China 'B' shares for the previous couple of months, with many of these shares believed to be on single-digit multiples. The domestic stock market at the time we spoke was down 80 per cent from its high. (It doubled the following week, with the announcement of support measures.) These purchases were on a short-term view. 'I think there is a 25 per cent fall in the currency to come. In the short term the currency is quite strong, because money is being sucked back into China at a hell of a rate, because of the credit squeeze there, to shore up working capital requirements. Despite all the capital inflows, China was running a capital deficit for the last two years. All the foreign suckers put their money in, and the Chinese were salting it all away offshore. That repatriation of capital has been a major element in the Hong Kong stock market weakness of the last six months.'

Overall, successful investing in Asia 'is nothing like as sophisticated as overseas, you just have to be a little bit ahead of the market. It's wrong to be too far ahead; otherwise you're probably like Marc Faber, indefinite timing. If I can manage risk just a little bit better than most, I think I can still capture the spectacular returns in this region, but lower the risk dramatically without giving up too much.'

He has been thinking about local versus foreign systems of invest-ment. 'It is easy to laugh at the Korean system which says a cheap stock is W10,000 and an expensive stock is W30,000. Previously the market was 100 per cent Korean, and now it is only 93 per cent Korean. Foreigners at present are dominating the market, and Kore-ans are apeing the foreigners. This won't last forever. As we've seen in Japan. But what happens when the Japanese dominate in our own markets? As has already happened with US bonds.'

The day after we spoke, Everington was off on holiday, with his wife and children – and a portable Bloomberg terminal, with the hedge fund portfolio on a spreadsheet. The full-time nature of the job is something which bothers him, although it is difficult to

101

imagine him doing anything else. He was late into the office that morning, he confesses, having been playing with his children; he is determined not to reach retirement age and discover that his priorities were all wrong. He seems to others to have them pretty well balanced, and there is as yet no dent in the performance record. Everington and Mellon have each achieved composite twelve year track records showing compound growth of 25 per cent per annum, a rate which multiplies the investor's money tenfold every ten years. If the relative performance can be sustained, Regent will be a major new force on the Asian investment scene.

Chapter 10

Continually reassessing

Michael Sofaer of Sofaer Capital

Michael Sofaer probably has the most pleasant working environment of any of these top fund managers: he works from his huge and elegant home, just off London's Belgrave Square. He is the longest-established hedge fund manager in Asia, and the largest, with around US$600 million under management, mainly in the Arral Asian Fund. Former colleagues ask enviously why he is still working – financially, there is clearly no need to do so, as he is the group's second largest investor. But to Sofaer there is no question: investment is fun, and he is still learning all the time.

Now clearly very much at home in London, and described by one Hong Kong fund manager as 'the perfect English gentleman', Sofaer actually has English as his third language – Arabic being his first, and French his second – since he is originally from Iraq, but left Baghdad as a boy in 1963. He attended university in Montreal, and then in 1977 joined Schroders as an analyst, first in London and then in Hong Kong. In Hong Kong, he was mainly a US specialist, but ran the Schroders Asian Fund as well as the Schroders International Fund. He is remembered as a maverick, and himself says he was a 'fish out of water' in that disciplined environment, and 'never really in the Schroder mould'.

By the age of twenty-six, which he now claims to consider far too young, he had left Schroders and wanted to set up his own business. He recalls that his ideas were very vague, but he visited New York to learn more about the sector, and was lucky enough to meet George Soros and Michael Steinhardt. He decided that hedge funds would become increasingly important worldwide, that the smart money was invested in vehicles of this type, and that it would be a good way to differentiate himself from other managers operating in Asia.

On returning to Hong Kong, he struck a deal with the First Pacific group and, as managing director, set up First Pacific Fund Management. His first client was Soros, who invested US$3 million; others followed.

In 1986, he concluded that the relationship with First Pacific had limitations, and set up an investment company in partnership with Arral, previously a pure direct investment house. The group appeared to flourish, but after an acrimonious breakdown in the partnership in 1992, Sofaer bought out the fund management company. The existing team remained in place, and the company was renamed Sofaer Capital.

PAINFUL LESSONS

During that early US trip, he had told Soros that he would double his money in Hong Kong blue chips. Sofaer made 40 per cent in the first three months, and appeared to be on a roll when Margaret Thatcher visited Beijing and fell down the steps of the Great Hall of the People. The Hong Kong market collapsed, and Soros pulled out. Fortunately, Sofaer had enough other clients to pull through, and the subsequent vindication of his original forecast led Soros to reinvest.

Meanwhile, performance was not what Sofaer had hoped; he says he was quite unprepared for the weight of running a business in addition to managing funds, and at times it felt pure agony. He reckons his two redeeming qualities were courage and perseverance, and these pulled him through. The first lesson, therefore, was: *have patience.*

A year or so later Soros reinvested. Sofaer put him into industrials, which appeared to offer unusually good value. The subsequent collapse of some high-flying electronic companies, and of the sector as a whole, was his second painful lesson: *bargains are rare; stocks which seem cheap – especially if unseasoned – should be closely examined.*

The 1987 crash was another memorable learning experience, and Sofaer's fund was down 45 per cent in the final quarter of that year, having previously been up 60 per cent. This taught him the importance of *disciplined adherence to a fundamental investment approach,* which would have prevented him from being seduced by the mirage of apparent profits in a rising market which, with hindsight, was hopelessly overvalued and vulnerable. The next lesson was to be *wary of leverage*; it can generate excess returns, or destroy your business. After October 1987 he feared he was in danger of the latter, and successfully pre-empted the possibility by returning to clients all fees charged earlier in the year.

Other important lessons he learnt at different times included: *listen to what the market is telling you; never buy a stock without looking at the chart; and remain in step with the technical condition of the markets – who owns stock, and who is left to buy?*

Despite all these tribulations, which caught out many managers less candid than Sofaer, he achieved a composite annual return with international funds of 17.0 per cent per annum from 1980 through mid-1994, against 10.5 per cent for the MSCI World Index, with notably lower volatility. The only full-year downturn was in 1984, although at the time of writing 1994 was also proving to be a difficult year. The Arral Asian Fund achieved annual growth of 29 per cent over the five years to September 1994, again amongst the best performances, and again with notably low volatility.

TOP-DOWN, LIQUIDITY DRIVEN

Sofaer starts with an attempt to identify economic trends and focuses particularly on liquidity. He is acutely sensitive to liquidity changes, and monitors a wide range of economic, monetary and stock-market indicators. He may watch a potentially attractive market for long periods of time and do very little while it remains quiescent, then jump in heavily as the market begins to move. On the other hand he may stick with a maturing market until it begins to crack; but his fundamental analysis will ensure that he is watching closely for the first signs of such danger. This does not always work; occasionally markets reverse too fast. The first quarter of 1994 was a classic example, in which the Asian fund dropped 14 per cent.

His analysis starts with the world's major markets – the US, Japan, world bond markets – and moves downwards. While the same can be said of many of the fund managers featured here, Sofaer is the only one who runs an international hedge fund as well as an Asian fund, and indeed the global fund preceded the Asian fund by several years. To some extent he bridges two worlds: the mentality is more clearly akin to that of certain classic US hedge funds than to some of his competitors in Asia, but by US standards Sofaer Capital would have a very strong Asian orientation.

Being in London may even help; it certainly shows no sign of hindering performance, and Sofaer has been there since his funds were established. He reckons that the time zone and its status as a time centre makes London the ideal location for global funds, with New York the main alternative contender. Being in London, he believes he talks to fewer people than he would in Asia, and that this helps to maintain the strategic focus and reduce unnecessary 'noise'.

The three Arral analysts in Hong Kong are crucial. They do all the stockpicking, while Sofaer sees his role as asset allocation; but the analysts have to state their case for every selection. A number of criteria are used in stock selection, and the approach is flexible. Stocks may be purchased because they fit into the thematic macro strategy, or on grounds of valuation, accelerating earnings growth or an undiscounted 'kicker', or a favourable chart pattern. Shorts tend to be chosen for the reverse characteristics, but Sofaer also does 'pair' trades where they play on the relative movement of two shares. He says he has to back the analysts' judgment in order to keep them motivated, and analysts' bonuses depend on their selections, but if unconvinced on a particular story he will either buy very little or may hedge by shorting something against it. The portfolios are well diversified in terms of stock selection, in contrast to the more aggressive asset allocation. Individual positions are typically 1 per cent of assets, although some core long-term holdings and trading positions account for 3–4 per cent.

Bob Rosner in Sofaer's San Francisco office liaises with the Asian analysts; Michael's brother Philip Sofaer works from New York on Europe and Latin America. Other key input comes from Sofaer's excellent personal network of contacts, which includes some of the leading US hedge fund managers. A competitor says that he is 'very good with people'.

Sofaer also stresses the importance of the administrative support team in Hong Kong. It is essential for a hedge fund to have all its systems in-house, he maintains (and not all do), because of the necessity to monitor a large number of detailed portfolio ratios.

Sofaer is convinced of the importance of discipline, not only in being sure to listen to what the market is telling you, but also in terms of sheer hard work. He finds that he cannot afford to be away from markets for long, and that it is therefore impossible to take long holidays; he is never far from a phone and fax. The daily routine starts with the first calls from Hong Kong at 6.30 in the morning, GMT. The global network is organized to ensure that the portfolio is monitored at all times. Sofaer believes that his was the first hedge fund to be not only international in the disposition of assets but also in the spread of managers across time zones.

A HONG KONG CHRONICLE

It is enlightening to track his exposure and thoughts over several years on Hong Kong, the most important of the Asia-ex-Japan markets. (The universe for the Arral Asian Fund includes Australia but excludes Japan.) Sofaer's quarterly letters, usually about three pages each on the international and the Asian markets, provide a remarkably cogent chronicle of market developments and of his analysis at the time. Even for local investors who may have had similar views as they went along, it is interesting to go back and review events as they unfolded; it may also be enlightening for investors who moved into the market at a later stage. Others will be intrigued, not only by the aggression with which Sofaer played the short-term market movements, within the context of a firmly based longer-term view; but also by the way in which he stayed on the market bandwagon long enough to capture a fair portion of its final explosive blow-off, while having identified critical risk factors very early and attempting to minimize portfolio exposure to such risks.

From 1989 onwards, he was consistently bullish on the long-term outlook for Hong Kong. By the end of March 1991, with the Hang Seng index up 24 per cent in the previous three months to just under 3,800, the market had achieved all the performance he expected for that particular year. It stood on a multiple of 12.6 times historic and 11 times prospective earnings, and he felt there was potential for a 'meaningful correction or at least a consolidation period'. Net exposure was zero, with some long positions offset by shorts on the stocks considered most overvalued, a strategy which had worked well in the first quarter.

By the end of the second quarter, the market was indeed slightly down, after a rise in interest rates and some political turbulence. With an apparent resolution to the airport dispute, Sofaer felt all was looking better and had increased exposure to 45 per cent. By the end of the third quarter, the stock market had rebounded, led by sharply rising residential property prices. 'Rising inflation and falling interest rates do not result in a stable or sustainable economic environment,' Sofaer noted. 'Ultimately the problem must be addressed, but under the circumstances we can expect the inflationary environment to prevail for some time. This is not necessarily bad for the stock market – negative real interest rates should keep demand for property buoyant while the banks, now charging premium spreads on mortgages, should also do well.' Net exposure had now been increased to 55 per cent. By the year end, with the market now 17 per cent above its mid-year low, the weighting had been slightly reduced to 50 per cent, with Sofaer thinking about scaling back in favour of Thailand and Malaysia in the event of monetary loosening in those countries.

By April 1992, the Hang Seng index was over 5,000, up more than 35 per cent in the nine months since he had rebuilt exposure to the market. 'The fundamental economic factors underpinning the market's strength are principally the huge rise in the value of trade with China and secondly, the Hong Kong dollar's peg to the US dollar which has translated easy monetary conditions in the US into high levels of liquidity in Hong Kong. More recently, promising political developments in China, which commit the country to further capitalist reforms, have begun to dilute the risk associated with the 1997 handover by Britain to China. This has captured the imagination of foreign investors who have rushed to invest in Hong Kong and anything "China-related" . . . There appear to be no serious drawbacks to a continued market advance, but we would sound a note of caution against unqualified bullishness. Firstly, and perhaps simplistically, the Hong Kong market has *always* been at its most vulnerable during periods of universal optimism. There is no logical explanation as to why an event happens along to knock confidence just when it is least expected but that has been the experience and, having been at the receiving end more than once, we feel we have learned enough to exercise restraint when it most seems wrong to do so . . . However, the market is still cheap, and should go higher over the year.'

The market surged onwards and upwards to over 6,000 by the middle of the year, at which point Sofaer wrote that, 'having risen so sharply this year, the Hong Kong market is fairly valued given the propensity for China and Hong Kong to clash over ongoing airport negotiations and Hong Kong's faltering steps towards greater democracy. Although we are certainly more cautious than we have been for some time and have begun to hedge our exposure, we remain bullish longer term with the expectation that if all goes well with China the Hong Kong market could easily trade at 18 times earnings. For the time being we intend to maintain our 38 per cent net exposure to the market, but further short-term strength or signs of overheating in the south China economy will encourage us to increase our hedge.'

By October 1992 the index had fallen back to 5,500 and rebounded; Sofaer remained happy with the fundamentals but cautious about the market, at least above the 6,000 level. He was concerned firstly about political succession in China, 'although others remain confident of a relatively smooth transition . . . evolution is not a word that describes political change in China.' A second concern was that the implications of a Clinton administration in the United States might not have been fully appreciated by the market, in terms of likely reflation and higher interest rates. 'Finally, the residential property market has peaked in our view and prices may well correct over the next year. Historically, the market has generally moved in the same direction as residential property prices. However, until the market decides to focus on these real issues, it will pay to be long the market because Hong Kong remains one of the few places where growth (earnings should increase 20 per cent in 1993) and valuation (just over 10 times 1993 earnings) are compelling.'

The final quarter, in the event, saw the market end the year flat at just over 5,500, with the strained Sino-British relationship to the fore. Overall, 'our long held belief that South-East Asia is no longer hostage to the fortunes of the industrialized economies was vindicated in 1992 when the OECD economies, without exception, suffered their worst collective recession for fifty years while Asia barely missed a beat.' However, Sofaer remained cautious on Hong Kong, given the continuing dangers of an overheating mainland economy, peaking real estate prices, and the prospect of rising interest rates. 'The risks are now greater than they were a year ago, while the potential upside over the coming year is perhaps less attractive than it has been for some time.'

In the first quarter of 1993 the Hong Kong market rebounded by 16 per cent, reflecting 'acceptance on the part of international investors that regional economic growth is almost guaranteed and that China will be the economic train that pulls Asia along a golden growth path well into the next century. We have been long-term advocates of this thesis, but now that it is universal wisdom we see some need to exercise caution.' Sofaer pointed to three issues of particular concern. First was the overheating Chinese economy, the lack of central control of bank lending, and the speculative fever evident in the real estate markets of both China and Hong Kong. 'Ultimately the price shall be paid in a much weaker financial system, undermined by loans made doubtful by a government-engineered slowdown. The only saviour may be the very substantial inflows of foreign capital, which may keep the juggernaut rolling along for some time.' His second concern was the likelihood of deteriorating Sino-American trade relations under the new Clinton regime; and his third the level of investment in risky China shares. 'Investor disenchantment, a fact of life in all emerging markets, is bound to prevail at some point over the next twelve months or so.' All in all, despite a PE of 11.5, 'we may be overdoing our caution here, given the obvious bullish future for an essentially capitalist China, but Hong Kong is now an over-owned market and I suspect that any black spots will result in serious selling.' Portfolio exposure was down to 18 per cent, at least partially hedged.

A quarter on, with the market up another 11 per cent, 'the hedges we instituted to protect the downside . . . have cost us several points in performance, but we believe the position was justified, and indeed recent events have borne out the thesis. The combination of serious inflationary pressures and speculative excesses particularly in property development in China has forced the government to act. The austerity measures recently announced spell tightening liquidity conditions in Hong Kong and, at the margin, curbing of further appreciation of property prices for the time being. Ordinarily, any market facing such negative short-term economic prospects would succumb to a sharp correction. In Hong Kong's case, it is not so easy a call . . . relief on the political front may well have a more inportant impact on the economy short term than a slowdown in China.' Nevertheless, exposure was by now further reduced to 10 per cent.

By the end of the third quarter, Hong Kong was up another 8 per cent. Sofaer's fundamental stance in mid-October was unchanged, but 'we are sensitive above all else to changes in liquidity conditions, and consequently we have increased our exposure from just 10 per cent to 16 per cent.' This was roughly the time at which Barton Biggs of Morgan Stanley came back from a trip to China marvelling at its progress and proclaimed himself 'maximum bullish' on Hong Kong, unleashing a tidal wave of US buying power. Talking about regional markets in general, Sofaer was now 'uneasy that the current re-rating owes more to the lack of growth elsewhere, combined with copious liquidity, than a profound appreciation of the fundamentals including the risks. Nevertheless, there is no denying that the outlook for growth in the region remains very positive and, barring unforeseen events, we expect valuations to continue to rise. We therefore plan to remain fully invested until the prospect of tightening liquidity becomes more real.'

By the year-end, the fund was 25 per cent net invested in Hong Kong, with Sofaer a 'nervous holder', largely because all markets had been bid up with Hong Kong remaining one of the cheapest in the region. A sharp setback ensued, with Asia falling away before the major markets, and the speed and magnitude of the decline caught him by surprise. The fund was not as badly hit as any of the major regional indices, but a 14 per cent loss was nevertheless a major blow to a portfolio managed for absolute returns. Having tried unsuccessfully to trade the bounces in these extremely volatile market conditions, a subdued Sofaer was saying by April that 'when the siren call to trade becomes irresistible, we force ourselves not to reach for the telephone until the urge passes.'

With the Hang Seng index down 24 per cent over the quarter to 9,030, Sofaer reckoned that a rating of 14 times 1994 earnings was 'much more in line with its five year average, and probably discounts much of the bad news . . . We are nevertheless keeping a watchful eye on events in China. We have been sceptical about the management of the economy and the soothing announcements from Beijing about inflation, the pace of economic reform, and so on. Our fears concerning overheating are in fact increasing as unemployment in state industries undermines the resolve of the central government to slow investment growth. Investors should not underestimate the extent to which political and social stability in China is afforded legitimacy by economic success. Insofar as this success has been recognized by the outside world, all well and good, for it has also encouraged foreign investment into China and increasing political reform. However, the problems begin when growth in economic wealth fails to reach the agrarian sector which represents 70 per cent of the population, thereby creating discontent. The history of industrial revolution in the west (particularly where constitutional democracy was not well established) should serve as a restraint for those whose enthusiasm for China's economic potential is unbridled. Long term we remain sanguine, but clearly there are problems which, if not properly handled short term, will test the fabric of the country's social economy. If the worst does happen, Hong Kong will surely bear the brunt of any shock (therefore we shall continue to run hedged positions), although it will also be bearish for the rest of the region.'

Net exposure to Hong Kong, following the first quarter's fall, was down to 10 per cent. It was little changed in mid-year, as the markets continued to drift, but Sofaer was beginning to cover some shorts 'with the aim of playing a bounce should we gain greater conviction'. During the third quarter, exposure was doubled to 18 per cent to take advantage of the ensuing market rally, but cut back to 10 per cent again thereafter with Sofaer describing the market as problematic.

'On a simple level the market is obviously cheap, especially when compared with its regional rivals. Earnings growth this year should be around 18 per cent, with the same again anticipated for next year, completing a remarkable five year earnings streak. However, a review of the potential problems explains why valuations ought to be modest for the time being. Most prominent is, of course, the prospect of rising rates and the impact this will have on a market heavily dependent on property and finance earnings. Secondly, earnings are anyway likely to peak in 1995 . . . Thirdly, and no less important, is our long held belief that China's economy is headed for a hard landing. Despite repeated promises from the mainland that inflation is under control, the evidence suggests that the reverse is true – all the more unsettling given the credit restrictions in force for about a year. Our guess is that the authorities will be unable to navigate the economy skilfully enough to avoid foundering on the rocks of destabilizing inflation and unacceptable levels of unemployment, both of which must lead to ever increasing social unrest. Should fate dictate that conditions become so worrying at the same time as the leadership of the country comes up for grabs when Deng dies, political instability may then be added to the list of problems. While we do not underestimate Hong Kong's resilience, there are too many accidents waiting to happen for us to be long this market. We are long at present as we feel a meaningful rally in the US from oversold levels may help Hong Kong higher, but our medium-term outlook is not bullish and we would anticipate being net short the market over the next few months.'

STRATEGY AND TACTICS

Sofaer thus appears to combine a very consistent and unusually balanced long-term view with an ability to swing the weightings around very quickly on a much shorter-term risk-reward assessment. If he is unsure, he will sit tight. If he has a view, he will back it heavily, but remains very alert to indicators (including market behaviour) which are interpreted to confirm or to question the original thesis. When investments do not behave as expected, they are immediately reviewed, and may be sold if he lacks the conviction to continue holding. Sofaer will cut a losing position quickly, not worrying about the risk that it may rebound at a later date. He believes that the worst characteristic for a hedge fund manager is to be stubborn about his positions, and cheerfully admits to being 'notorious for changing my mind at the drop of a hat'.

The speed of reversal of losing positions, along with diversification, are the two hallmarks of the fund which Sofaer believes to underlie the low volatility achieved in recent years. (He has also operated without leverage since 1987, and on average has been only 80 per cent invested on a net basis.)

For example, as tension mounted in the Gulf at the end of 1990, he liquidated the bulk of the fund in order to preserve capital. By the end of the year he had 86 per cent of the Asian Fund in cash, and was up 9 per cent for the year, one of few Asian funds with a positive return for the year. He was then badly wrong-footed when markets surged following the Allied eviction of the Iraqis from Kuwait. Before the end of 1991's first quarter, he was 85 per cent invested. Having been almost bottom of the performance leagues in the first half of 1991, he had clawed back to the top by the end of that year.

Again, in the second quarter of 1991, he started with 25 per cent in Thailand, about which he was then 'reasonably confident', and slashed the exposure to 6 per cent by the end of the period, after the market fell 12 per cent. (By the end of the third quarter, the portfolio exposure was roughly the same, the market had now fallen another 12 per cent, and Sofaer was 'warming to the Thai market, where we have been light all year'.)

Often, however, U-turns are unnecessary, because Sofaer has started thinking about possible turning points well in advance, but waits for catalysts or confirming indicators to become apparent. For example, having been increasingly positive on Singapore for the previous six months, he commented in October 1992 that 'the news is that the economy has essentially gone ex-growth and therefore the market no longer deserves to trade at premium multiples. Certainly that is the perception; we are not prepared to accept just yet that it is reality . . . As we see it, the problems are not necessarily structural in nature. When shipping rates and office rents eventually pick up, the stock market will rally sharply, for inflation is low and liquidity remains enormous. Although we had planned to invest 10–15 per cent of our (Asian) portfolio in Singapore over the quarter, we have decided to postpone our action until reality has a chance of overcoming sentiment.'

In Korea, too, he has been remarkably consistent. He started following the market with increasing attention in mid-1991, although refusing to chase short-term rallies. A year after first mentioning it, he awarded it the wooden spoon for consistent disappointment, but set out the good news on the business and economic cycle and valuations, and started to build up exposure when the index was between 500 and 600, ahead of a very strong year-end advance following the presidential elections. By mid-1993, Korea accounted for 25 per cent of the portfolio, although it dropped back to 16 per cent thereafter. It was a disappointingly dull performer in the second half of 1993, but Sofaer kept reiterating that it was one of the more attractive in Asia in terms of economic fundamentals and valuation. It proved a relatively safe haven in early 1994, although it still lost ground in absolute terms, and exposure was increased to 20 per cent. When it finally took off, stock selection proved a minefield; the securities companies in which Sofaer had invested heavily were 'inexplicably poor performers, at one point falling over 25 per cent for the year'.

He now says he should have kept to his normal selling discipline. The Korean selections were cheap, Sofaer says, but over-owned; they were hit by selling on the part of locals who were raising cash to move into the blue chips preferred by other foreigners. Technical analysis would normally have allowed this mistake to be reversed earlier, and the damage contained.

The Korean experience has thus provided a complete microcosm of the complexities and frustrations of investment. Sofaer was absolutely correct throughout on a very large part of the picture, but the ride was far from smooth none the less. This episode also provides a good illustration of Sofaer's approach, which is to try to identify economic trends, to play them in such a way as to control risk while achieving attractive returns, and to remain at all times open-minded and questioning.

Chapter 11

Buying unloved stocks

Kerr Neilson of Platinum Asset Management

Sydney-based Platinum Asset Management is a new name on the investment scene, established only at the beginning of 1994 by Kerr Neilson, and backed by Soros Fund Management. Neilson ran the highly successful retail fund operations of Bankers Trust Australia (BT) for eight years from 1986, and five of his team of seven fund managers come from the former BT team.

After only a few months of operation, Platinum had US$300 million under management. The flagship closed-end fund, Platinum Capital, is listed on the Australian stock exchange, and has a global investment mandate with the flexibility of a conservatively run hedge fund. If undervalued investments cannot be identified, the fund will hold cash; derivatives of all kinds can be used to protect against risk. Two open-ended funds have a similar global mandate and philosophy.

Australia is not renowned for international fund management, and two of its largest insurance companies decided in recent years to move these operations offshore – AMP to London, and National Mutual to Hong Kong. BT Australia however, with a disciplined stockpicking rather than asset allocation approach, showed that the location need be no drawback. Over the five years to March 1994, Neilson's International Fund recorded compound annual growth of over 25 per cent, and the Pacific Basin Fund over 31 per cent, both in A$ terms – which put them right up near the top of the international league tables, let alone the much shorter domestic league.

Neilson started his investment career in London in 1973 with the Courtaulds pension fund, working for the highly respected John Evans, whose approach he describes as somewhat academic. After three years in England he decided there was no prospect of making any money and every chance of freezing to death, and headed back to his native South Africa, where he initially joined a fund

116

management company and then set up the research department for a broking firm. The prospects for South Africa, however, were dim – and in his view still are – so he moved to Australia and joined BT in 1983, despite misgivings about the strength of the trade unions.

During his tenure at BT, the firm had a reputation for taking aggressive bets, which originated when it was entirely out of the Japanese market for a year before the final collapse. Neilson says they did not think at the time that it was a big bet to stay away from a market trading on an average PE of 70.

SEEKING OUT UNLOVED STOCKS

Neilson seeks to identify stocks which the market has undervalued. He looks first and foremost for companies which are out of favour or neglected by the market. This may be because of an unfavourable short-term outlook for the industry, or because of recent mistakes by management, or because of sheer boredom with a company where earnings have been stagnating. Often, at the bottom of a share price cycle, the emphasis is all on the historic woes of the past; as people become more optimistic, the emphasis shifts first towards present performance, and ultimately to the blue sky potential, so that an earnings turnaround can be accompanied by a dramatic re-rating. Just as importantly, the downside risk of a bombed-out investment should be more limited than the risk on a share which is near peak pricing.

He also looks for companies where there has been a change in the operating environment which may significantly affect long-term profitability; for example, he suggests, changes in competitors' production capacity, technology, or government regulations, may all have such an impact.

He tries to assess the inherent value of the business, in absolute terms and relative to its peer group. Factors evaluated include the company's competitive position, changes in technology, the regulatory environment, and the quality of management. If and when the market price increases to reflect the estimated inherent value of the company, the stock is sold.

The creation of ideas is the key to the whole process, Neilson notes. This is inherently a random process. 'Identifying a potential opportunity can come from many sources. For example: scanning the Asian Wall Street Journal, a headline on changes in regulations regarding Japanese property taxes may raise questions about the potential benefits for Japanese house builders; an interview with the finance director of a large electronic consumer goods company may point to an emerging listed company competitor; and a call from a stockbroker or research analyst may highlight the turnaround of the profitability of a company and its industry.'

The development of themes can be helpful. When some fund managers talk of themes, they buy a group of stocks on the basis of a concept. Neilson thinks through concepts in order to point himself towards specific beneficiary stocks; and these stocks must then stand up to individual inspection. You have first to make sure you really understand the business, he says; *then* you factor in what other people think, but you never play the perceptions game on its own.

Cross-fertilization of ideas between markets is another source of ideas, and one advantage of a global mandate. Ideas which crop up in one part of the world can often be capitalized upon in another. As an example, shipping companies have been attracting some interest in the west and elsewhere; Platinum has been buying Japanese shipping companies at the same or lower valuations.

When it comes to the analytical stage, the company's annual report is the starting point, supplemented by all the secondary sources available. Company visits are critical, and he makes a particular point of trying to talk to third parties, not involved in either the target company or the investment industry – suppliers, competitors, customers, industry associations, and occasionally academics or industry specialists. 'The creation of ideas is the hard part. Sorting, processing and refining ideas are all of great importance, and need plenty of drive and tenacity to be implemented well.'

THE TURNAROUND OF TVB

One of Neilson's most classic purchases was the Hong Kong company Television Broadcasts Limited, TVB. During 1991, the market came to view TVB as a low growth company. It had once been a market favourite, but had fallen on hard times. It was reliant on Hong Kong advertising revenues which had been weak and, in the previous three years, profits had fallen. Not helping matters was a competitive thrust by the new owners of the competing station, which was poaching staff and driving up costs. There were additional concerns about the possibility of new competition from cable and satellite television, even though at that stage these new media were still far from being implemented. The staff themselves were demoralized, and did little to encourage enthusiasm amongst investors.

'The market had lost sight of TVB's strong franchise: TVB was still number one, and in advertising you just don't get the same proportionate revenue when you are number two. On critical analysis it was clear that the competitor was simply weakening itself by its predatory actions. Moreover, the market had underplayed two other important points. Firstly, in Southern China, where TVB's signal could be easily picked up, viewership had been growing strongly as televisions became more widely owned. Neighbouring Guangdong province had 60 million potential viewers versus Hong Kong's 5 million. TVB provided an avenue for advertisers to reach not only Hong Kong consumers, but also these consumers. This fact was not widely reported because of political sensitivities, but it could be easily confirmed by talking to TVB or advertisers. Secondly, TVB had perhaps one of the finest production studios in South-East Asia and a library of Cantonese language programmes.'

From the low, earnings doubled over the next two years, and the share price jumped by a factor of six over the same period as investors rediscovered and re-rated the company.

Peter Phillips of Fidelity also bought TVB at this stage (see p 15), on essentially the same logic, but waited for a catalyst – something which would change the market sentiment on the stock. He could afford to do so, since he was running a fund which was relatively small at the time. Neilson was buying on a much larger scale, and had 5 per cent of the BT Pacific Basin Fund and 3 per cent of the other eligible funds in this one medium-sized company, which at its low would have been capitalized at US$270 million. BT's gain was therefore more like three times, as it had been accumulating throughout the low period, and left 20 per cent or so on the table for the buyers when it exited – which now had to be by way of a placing, as its stake was then worth around US$100 million.

Neilson does not wait for evidence that the market consensus is about to change, nor worry unduly about identifying a catalyst which might cause this. It is often only practicable to accumulate a large position by doing so when everything looks bleak, and it may not pay to be too attentive to timing. However, he would not nowadays buy an asset play without an earnings story. He would have done so in 1983–85, when a falling inflationary bias was leading to the realization of assets hoarded in the 1970s, and the realization

119

of value for shareholders – but that was a big thematic overlay at the time, and no longer valid in today's conditions.

TVB at its low was a good example of the type of plays Neilson's team is looking for now: sectors and industries which the market misunderstands. Hopewell was another such company. Neilson built up a big position in 1990, when the company's popularity was low and its entrepreneurial proprietor Gordon Wu written off as a talker rather than a doer. The need for Wu's 'superhighway' linking Hong Kong and Guangzhou was self-evident; the economics of the project, and Wu's ability to deliver, more contentious. Neilson took the view that Wu was actually getting quite a lot done in China, and was playing a relatively astute game with the banks. Sentiment did indeed change, shortly thereafter.

Interestingly, Neilson bought in again at around $5.50 during 1993, and sold at $7.20; he not infrequently comes back to stocks which he thinks he understands, and will trade them when he believes they are mispriced.

JUDGMENTAL CALLS

The search for unrecognized value is not just a quantitative exercise. Discussing a competitor's research department full of backroom number-crunchers, Neilson does not think this will work well in Asia, where you need a qualitative understanding of the company, the business environment, and managers and key shareholders. He has successfully played various patrimony stocks in the Malaysian market on the basis of impending privatizations and other deals. If he believes he is on to a story early, before it is discounted in the market price, and sees a reasonable degree of downside protection – which in these cases may be a function of local market conditions, for which you therefore need a good feel, rather than classically favourable valuations – then he is happy to buy these stocks. He was an early buyer of UEM in 1988–89, on the story that it would be awarded the contract for construction of the North-South highway, despite concern that the scale of the project made the story too good to be true. Likewise, he bought Renong, with a downside calculation that it was already at a 30 per cent discount to the market value of its stakes in affiliates. In markets like this, judgment may be as important as analytical technique. Neilson says he is ardent about his investment approach, but it has to be flexible.

Neilson and his team often miss opportunities in specific stocks, and do not regard this as a problem. Their priority is to avoid losing money, and to find a reasonable number of winners. What distinguishes them from 'maintenance managers' is focus. A maintenance manager will try to keep track of all major stocks in his universe at all times and may claim to know a company when in reality he can only describe it, without having a grasp of the key factors. Neilson's team tries to zero in selectively on opportunities which are particularly promising, and think them through much more carefully.

How has his own investment thinking been refined over time? He says that, reading back over his old research, it is not bad but far too tentative. He used to say that the PE relative could be revised up a little, when he should have recognized a major bargain and gone for it. Experience has taught him to be decisive.

EMERGING MARKETS – FUN WHILE THEY LASTED

Emerging markets were 'a gift from heaven', but there are now few left, in Neilson's view, and after a huge re-rating in both Asia and Latin America he believes that game is almost over.

Neilson was an early buyer of Thailand, buying stocks in the mid-1980s on PEs of around five. He now laughs about having tried to be too clever, buying stocks like Metal Box on even deeper value when he 'could just have bought Siam Cement and the stocks all the other foreigners bought' – but the strategy worked pretty well. (Many foreigners also bought the banks, by analogy with countries like Hong Kong and Singapore; these underperformed the market by an unnerving 70 per cent during the four years 1986–89.)

Likewise, he was early into Indonesia, at a stage when he remembers fourteen listed stocks of which seven were traded and only four or five available to foreigners. He says they could have just argued that foreigners were going to buy the infrastructure story and played the market on that basis, but wanted to understand the companies first; information was inadequate, but the companies were very cheap. There is clearly a trade-off; a less complete picture may be acceptable if the valuation is sufficiently low.

Neilson was early into most markets, and, like Marc Faber (see next chapter), tended to be very early out. He was very successful

121

in Latin America. When he could not buy Chile for the mutual fund because of restrictions on foreign investment, he went to Colombia instead – wandering in amongst the exploding bombs, he says, to find a very promising economy and ridiculously cheap stocks.

In Argentina, he nearly missed the boat, having visited in September 1989 as President Menem came in, the stabilization plan was introduced, and the local stock market surged. He managed to buy some of the leading stocks, but 'turfed them out far too early'. He looked for more tangential plays, and spotted a reportedly well-run brewing company with a dominant position in Argentina, Uruguay and Paraguay. This company, Quilmes Industrial or 'Quinsa', was owned by a foreign company which was said to be listed in Paris and Luxembourg. Neilson went through every page of the French company handbook looking for a company with Latin American assets, and discovered a share which had not participated at all in the euphoric re-rating of the Buenos Aires market. Moreover, the holding company decided to obtain a separate listing for Quinsa, and distributed Quinsa shares to existing shareholders, many of whom sold their new allotment. Quinsa could then be bought for US$30 per share, capitalizing the company at US$100 million. Taking into account net cash of US$25 million, this valued the brewing and soft drink bottling capacity at less than US$10 per hectolitre, less than a quarter of the estimated replacement cost – and the company had other interests and an entrenched market position. The stock eventually went to US$460, a rise of over fifteen times. Neilson still owns some.

In Argentina, either Kerr Neilson or Mark Mobius were usually the first investors to visit each company. Having a Bankers Trust business card was an advantage, Neilson recalls, because companies were used to bankers. When he said he would like to buy shares, however, the companies knew he was a fraud; who would want to do anything so stupid?

He has just come back from the Russian Far East, where he has been casting a cynical eye over what may be one of the last great emerging market stories, but was an early buyer nevertheless. 'Profits don't mean a lot when you are paying nothing for the electricity. Balance sheets are shot, and working capital has been destroyed by inflation. The companies have spent no money on equipment for years, and the workers are untrained when it comes to modern systems. The investment banks and the country funds are in a frenzy to get set up. They bandy about crudities such as cost per megawatt or per ton or per line without knowing the profile of likely production, its true cost, and indeed the new companies' enormous capital replacement needs . . .

'My sense is that the pricing of companies will go well ahead of realities within the next four to six months, and then the penny will drop about the depth of the problems. Much of manufacturing industry will be eliminated, jobs will be lost, and despondency will set in. Of course there are plenty of entrepreneurs who will do good things in the service sector (mafia permitting, and this is very real), but the economy needs more than this. It is not improbable that Russia may become like Brazil from 1980 to 1993; lots of unfulfilled promise . . . The Russian Far East may however fare better. With a population of only eight million and all the advantages of a North-East Asian location, natural resources, and encouragement from its aggressive neighbours, it could escape the pains of industrial restructuring which is likely in the Russian industrial heartland.'

In general, however, emerging markets have now in Neilson's view become too fashionable. 'Buying something when it is unfashionable is the key. Now everyone is talking Mexico and everyone owns it; how can you make money when everyone owns it?' Coming from a greater knowledge base than most emerging market investors, he is also cynical about elements of the current story, especially in South American markets. 'You need to question the ideas of the herd. The Hong Kong property market is a classic – people don't want to believe that it is the end of the game.'

De-rating is a possibility many people are overlooking. 'Singapore lost rating in the mid-1980s. Japan will lose rating as the Japanese become net users of their own savings – and anyway, it is no longer as high growth an economy as people think.'

YOU HAVE TO BELIEVE . . .

In order to manage money successfully by stock selection, Neilson maintains, you have to be convinced that you can ignore the indices. If any doubt exists, then you will creep back towards the indices. He makes the analogy that many western manufacturing companies have failed to implement just-in-time systems successfully, because the participants intuitively just *knew* that they had to have inventories – and that belief in itself created the failure.

Chapter 12

A historian's long view

Marc Faber of Marc Faber Ltd

Faber has style. A ski racer in his youth, he remains a flamboyant character. He plays to the press, who call him Dr Doom; his monthly newsletter, always an excellent read, is called 'The Gloom, Boom and Doom Report'. He wears a pony-tail, in defiance of the expectation (in Asia, especially) that investment managers should look conventional. His book, *The Great Money Illusion*, written in a hurry after the 1987 crash, was dedicated 'to many beautiful and kind women whose names are better kept confidential'. His office is eclectic. Nineteenth-century oil paintings of Hong Kong and Macau mingle with Korean paintings, an amazing collection of Mao memorabilia (including one white alabaster statue with a red scarf tied round its neck), an ancient horned gramophone with old Chinese records, soft fluffy yellow toys and a china polar bear, bottles of XO brandy and cases of Grolsch beer. He has a superb library of first editions of works on economics and stock-market cycles – in a variety of European languages, being a multilingual Swiss – and a collection of a quarter of a million Mao badges.

What he says is usually impeccably well argued, but it is the delivery which makes him so sought after as a speaker: he is a master of rhetoric, and of vivid everyday examples, and the very dry sense of humour and the heavy Swiss accent provide an irresistible mix. (He describes his own writing as 'Swiss-German pidgin English', but is actually one of the most articulate and grammatical people I know.)

A recent survey in the *South China Morning Post* polled public figures in Hong Kong with the question, 'Have you ever taken cannabis?' Cannabis is illegal but not uncommon in Hong Kong, and is freely available in many countries around South-East Asia. Most people said no, or refused to be quoted. Faber was as usual more straightforward and more confident: 'Naturally, I have smoked a lot of marijuana, but for breakfast I prefer omelette of Balinese mushrooms.'

It is amazing how much vitriol the mention of Faber's name can generate – mainly from traders with a limited sense of historical perspective. He is well aware of this reaction. Back in 1987, he wrote: 'No one likes a party spoiler, and as long as the stock-market orgy goes on the pessimists are shunned almost as badly as AIDS carriers.' The more intelligent professionals around town give him considerably more respect – even when they don't understand the detail of his operations. Some assume that he says one thing and invests differently. Other people assume he is a simplistic and publicity-seeking contrarian. A large number think of him as 'Dr Doom', the congenital pessimist. He plays up this image, or is at least amused by it and lets it run.

THE HONG KONG CALLS

He was indeed very bearish on Hong Kong ahead of the 1987 crash, and is bearish on it during 1994. It is often assumed that he has been bearish throughout; in fact he called a buy in the emotional aftermath of the Tiananmen Square massacre in 1989, when stocks fell back almost to their 1987 crash lows. (He wrote a report just eleven days later, concluding that the poor political climate and investment environment were of a short-term nature, and that 'true contrarians should buy China plays such as Tian An and Luks', which were then totally out of favour.) Going back further, while Faber issued repeated warnings during 1980 and 1981 that a collapse was imminent (the Hang Seng index eventually fell more than 60 per cent, and the loss in US$ terms was about 75 per cent), he wrote a buy recommendation for Hong Kong in October 1983 when the Hang Seng index was 758. The market immediately rallied to around 1200, fell back again one more time in mid-1984, and then started an unbroken advance. By the peak in October 1987, the index had more than quintupled from Faber's recommended purchase level.

To many Hong Kong residents, Faber is a maverick contrarian who is bearish on Hong Kong because he wants to spoil everyone else's fun; for all the city's cosmopolitan attributes, its investors (and even more so its newspapers) can be very parochial in outlook.

Relatively few people appreciate that he has made many spectacular calls on the long side. While he failed to get back into Hong Kong after the 1987 crash, he invested heavily and early in Latin America, Sri Lanka, and Bangladesh, where the performance has been even better. He bought Vietnamese debt at 12 cents in the dollar (it has recently been trading at 70), and is a major holder of North Korean debt. He is a very conservative investor, although the consultants now so prevalent on the institutional side of the investment industry might find it hard to fit him into their models: in mid-1994, he had 10 per cent of his Iconoclastic International Fund in Russia. He takes many such aggressive bets, although always with a small percentage of the portfolio, and only where he considers them relatively safe. Meanwhile the global stock-market risk, which he has for some years considered extreme, is hedged with shorts on major indices and selected US theme stocks.

He tends to short faddish stocks much too early, he says: many double or triple after his first sale, before eventually collapsing – but nevertheless he maintains that his shorting activities have been generally profitable. 'If we look at all the stocks that have come out in the world, the majority of companies after their new issues have gone below their issue price, and there are more companies that fail than companies that succeed . . . In the share market, because most people are so much conditioned to go long shares, and to believe in fantasies and concepts that never materialize, the shorting opportunites are actually very good. In the US you don't sell at a premium, you sell at the market price. And if stocks don't pay any dividends the cost of shorting is lower than the cost of holding shares long, because the margin requirements are lower.'

In 1993, for example, telecommunication stocks had become targets for heavy thematic buying worldwide; Faber thought the concept had driven prices to absurd levels of overvaluation, and went short.

He has commented in the past that emerging markets have been much more profitable for him than the US market, but continues to follow the US market in detail because of its importance for liquidity flows in the emerging markets, as well as because of the short-selling opportunities there. I suspect, too, he enjoys tracking the inefficiencies and excesses of the world's most developed market.

126

TRICKY CROSS-CURRENTS AT SECULAR TURNS

Faber believes that the yen is at a secular turning point, but cautions about the uncertainty of timing in such situations, and goes to some length to emphasize 'how long it can take to reverse a well-established trend. Furthermore, at major turning points, markets tend to be extremely volatile and are therefore very tricky for the leveraged players.' He gives as an example the four years it took for the reversal of the US bond market in 1980–84. 'I shall never forget the secular low for bonds in the early 1980s, because so many speculators and professionals correctly identified the approaching bull market in bonds, yet they were wiped out in the 1983/84 corrective phase.'

Faber keeps stressing the timing uncertainties, the patience required when making the major calls, and the sort of risk-reward ratio he is looking for. It is amazing how many 'professionals' in the industry then pour scorn on his recommendations on the basis that they have not come good in the short term, or that he has said the same thing before. He comments wryly: 'When a boom or a mania is in full swing, warnings are always ignored. Characteristic of a full market cycle is that at a major market low the bulls are totally discredited, having been bullish too early, while at market peaks the warnings of the bears are ridiculed because their forecasts have almost inevitably been wrong for some time. Warnings are ignored because at the peak of every market the majority of well-known and seemingly knowledgeable experts will find arguments supporting a further advance. A mania is a mania, and the experts are caught in it just as the public is.'

And again: 'In the world of investment management, it is far better to fail very badly in a conventional way and lose a great deal of money for your client than to lose a little in an unconventional fashion . . . It takes courage and a strong belief in oneself to resist conforming to the beliefs of the majority and to follow one's own investment policy independently. For these reasons, I understand why most fund managers prefer to do what everyone else is doing so as to avoid being out of step with the majority.' Most institutional managers, of course, do not have the flexibility to deviate too much from their peer group, even if they theoretically have room to do so under their mandate. 'A money manager who does not buy while the market is going up will be regarded by his clients as an idiot,' and institutional tolerance for such maverick behaviour is very limited.

His case on the yen is based on an expected recovery in Japanese consumption and imports, a rise in overseas travel, a probable rise in commodity prices, the outsourcing of Japanese manufacturing industry (so that, firstly, Japanese companies will export to the west from their overseas subsidiaries and not from Japan, and secondly, Japan will itself be importing more from these offshore plants), purchasing power parity, and a slowdown in portfolio inflows.

A WORLD EQUITY BEAR

He is extremely wary of the major world equity markets, on grounds not just of valuation (PEs, yield gap, market capitalization versus replacement value) but also of time elapsed, cycle theory, the high proportion of assets now held in equities, and the leverage of key players. He has considered global equity markets overvalued since 1987, and argues that a secular turning point has been characterized by a long rolling top in which Japan topped out in 1989; Korea and Taiwan and many European markets in 1990; and a number of major US sectors during 1991–93.

After a recent 'bull-bear debate' over lunch at one of Hong Kong's five-star hotels, attended by an audience of two or three hundred, I congratulated him on a virtuoso performance – as entertaining as it was well-argued and punchy, if also decidedly scary for those of us who make our living in the financial sector. Faber growled, 'Ja, but did you see the number of people there? There are far too many people interested in financial assets.' Back in 1987, he was already grumbling about the flood of newcomers into the industry, and estimated then that the average market experience of brokerage employees was about four years. (Now, in Asia, it is probably more like two years.) 'Short the industry which the majority of Harvard Business School graduates want to join!'

Faber has drawn attention to the dangers of the stampede into emerging markets. 'During the mania, the less people know about an investment theme, the more enthusiastically they tend to endorse the idea. Take, for instance, a dentist. If a Merrill Lynch salesman tried today to sell him an investment in a new dental clinic three blocks down the road based on an almost unlimited profit potential, he would have reasonably good knowledge about the merits of such a scheme. If a Morgan Stanley salesperson sold him the concept of investing in a dental clinic in Shanghai, being a dentist he would probably still have some idea about the potential of such an investment, but obviously with less certainty than in the first case. Consider now the Smith Barney salesman who wants to sell our dentist a whole China Fund based on the unlimited future riches that will be earned by foreigners from the one billion strong Chinese population. What knowledge does the dentist have about such an investment? Rest assured, the Smith Barney salesman has the best chance to make a successful sale, because during a mania, the less investors know, the more credulous they are.'

Faber himself tends to be very early into markets and very early to get out. He bought shares in Korea in 1978 (well before foreigners were officially allowed to do so; but he took cash up to the country, and dismissed concerns about getting the money out again since he was buying for the long term). The Korean market went nowhere until 1985 – over seven years – and the won declined 50 per cent against the dollar; the payoff finally came when the market soared seven-fold between 1986 and 1989. He bought Taiwan in 1980, and waited patiently until the market finally took off in 1985. Recently his patience has barely been tested, because of the increasing number of brokers and funds interested in emerging market investments: Faber has made a remarkable number of prescient calls, for markets which have then surged dramatically within one or two years. He bought Philippine stocks in 1985, Singaporean and Thai in 1986, Chilean in 1987, and Argentinian in 1988. He recommended Brazil in late 1990. Six months later, when Brazil had risen 150 per cent in US$ terms, but was, he thought, still very cheap by Asian standards, he recommended Peru 'for the most venturesome investors'. He visited Bangladesh in early 1992 and, while appalled at the poverty and economic mismanagement, found 'a ray of hope' in the small private sector, and some very cheap stocks. The Bangladeshi market rose 120 per cent over the next two years; Faber was selling as foreign investors became very enthusiastic in the first half of 1994.

When buying into a country for the first time, he tends to make repeat visits, build up a network of trustworthy advisors – this is easier, he points out, when one is early, and the new business is appreciated – and then buys some of the major stocks, relying on local advice to a large extent for the selection. He always tries to look at charts, however, whether or not they are available. 'You can ask someone to give you the trading range of a stock for the last ten years. Then mentally you can see roughly how the chart looks; it doesn't matter that it's not drawn on a day-by-day basis. If the stock has been basing for ten years then maybe there is some attraction to it.'

THE LIFE CYCLE OF EMERGING MARKETS

In 1992, Faber wrote a report on 'The Life Cycle of Emerging Markets' which analyses the psychology of each market phase, and also clarifies his own philosophy. He likes to invest during 'phase zero', defined by the following characteristics: long lasting economic stagnation or slow contraction, flat or falling per capita incomes, little capital investment, unstable political and social conditions (strikes, high inflation, continuous devaluations, terrorism, border conflicts etc), depressed profits, no foreign direct or portfolio investment, and capital flight. Symptoms of 'phase zero' are: little tourism (unsafe), hotel occupancy 30 per cent, run-down hotels and no new hotels built recently, curfews at night, little volume on the stock exchange, stock exchange has been moving sideways or moderately down for several years, stocks ridiculously undervalued in real terms, no visiting foreign fund managers, negative press headlines, no foreign brokers establishing offices, no country funds launched, and no recent brokerage research reports. Examples he suggests include the Philippines in the early eighties, Argentina throughout most of that decade, Sri Lanka prior to 1990, and communist countries for most of the post-war period. The risk of buying in phase zero, Faber admits, is time: a catalyst is required before the outlook and the stock market start moving (phase one).

There can actually be other risks: I recently mentioned that I was nervous about an impending trip to Vladivostok in the Russian Far East, where a prominent Hong Kong lawyer had just been shot dead. That is when you find the good bargains, he reassured me. 'There were no foreigners in Peru when I first went there; it was much more dangerous than Vladivostok is now. But of course I have the advantage,' – gesturing to his chunky build, jeans, and crumpled T-shirt – 'people think I am the gangster! In New York also. I walk down the street, and all these people are crossing to the other side.' (It was a Saturday, I should add. People dress down to dead-scruffy in Hong Kong on a Saturday. It makes you feel you're not working, even though you are in the office, and is a gesture against the conformity of the week.)

Faber tends to exit in phase two, when large inflows of foreign funds propel the market to overvaluation: symptoms of this phase include hotels full of foreign businessmen and portfolio managers, many new hotels under construction, very positive international headlines, an avalanche of thick country reports from brokers, brokers opening local offices, and the launch of country funds. Phase three includes the end of the boom and the cyclical top; phase four is a low which is assumed to be a new buying opportunity; phase five is a serious downturn, with corporate profits, stocks and real estate all falling sharply, and speculators pulling out of the market. Phase six is when deep pessimism takes hold, and no one is interested in stocks.

He admits that he almost always gets out prematurely, and has always tended to underestimate how far prices will rise. 'Why does he do it?' marvelled one competitor, of Faber's exit timing in more far-flung markets. 'It's as if he can't bear having anyone else on the beach. As soon as the market is "discovered", he picks up his ball and doesn't want to play.'

The opportunity costs of pulling out early can be large. After the 1987 crash, the Hang Seng index bottomed at around 2,000. It peaked in 1994 at 12,200. Faber admits to having missed an opportunity here. As it turns out, China boomed after 1987, and so did Hong Kong, Tiananmen in 1989 notwithstanding. During the six years from 1987, index earnings tripled. By the 1994 peak, however, the market was unquestionably over-blown on a historic PE of 20; this may not sound too outrageous for a growth economy, but is historically high for Hong Kong, which lives with political uncertainty, and especially so for a property-dominated market.

Faber however shows little grief over missed opportunities, and will continue to err on the side of caution. 'While during the early part of phase three the markets soar almost vertically, it is also a high-risk zone, for two reasons. While in phase two almost all stocks rise, in phase three the advance becomes much more narrow as the market breadth deteriorates. Many stocks begin to decline long before the market's final high. Furthermore, it is impossible to predict when the market will turn down and how sharply it will fall during the initial sell-off. The highs reached during phase three are frequently milestone highs, which are often not exceeded for eight to fifteen years or more.

He points out that the reason that the magnitude of market movements is so unpredictable is a positive-sloping demand curve.

131

For a normal commodity, such as fish, if prices go up, consumers buy less. In a financial market, if prices go up, investors buy more. This makes the markets extremely volatile, and hence potentially rewarding. The result, however, is that prices rise much higher than people dream possible on the upside, and equally fall much further than expected in a decline.

He comments that many busy fund managers who travel to Asia only visit the big cities and the smart hotels, leaving no time to visit outlying parts of the country, and consequently they have a very limited understanding of the full picture. Faber himself is both well travelled and compassionate: he worries about the extreme wealth disparities in Asia and the possibility of future social tensions, appreciates Tibetan Buddhism and deplores the predicament of that country, and concluded his article on Bangladesh by recommending a visit:

'In Bangladesh, you cannot fail to see the effects of an inefficient and corrupt government, misguided economic policies, and an extremely disorganized and chaotic socialism all kept alive by the "donor countries" under the auspices of such organizations as the Asian Development Bank and the World Bank whose loan officers stay in luxury hotels and give away funds to corrupt government officials. You will probably also be angered that such mismanagement has been possible for so long, and that it has all been paid for by taxpayers in the western world! A visit to Bangladesh will also reveal the advantages of free markets, open competition, and a capitalistic system in fostering economic progress and prosperity. Finally, I may add that the Bangladeshi are friendly people and, having seen their poverty, you will again appreciate the many achievements our western civilization provides, such as social mobility, health care, sufficient food, law and order, education, and at least some measure of social justice.'

Faber wrote his book, *The Great Money Illusion*, in the weeks after the 1987 crash. It gives the impression of having been dictated and left unedited and this may have denied it some of the respect it deserves, but the immediacy of what is essentially a diary at a time of momentous change makes it especially interesting. This was a conscious decision. Faber decided that 'the advantage of buying old books is that one gains insight into how events were perceived at the time and not how we look at them today.' Accordingly, although 'every possible book about economics and the stock market had already been written . . . and one can find many books about the

1873, 1929 and 1973 crashes, most of these were written years after the event and therefore fail to capture the mood of the moment: the excessive greed and carelessness and, after the crash, the panic and fear and the atmosphere of *sauve qui peut*. By writing a diary, I could seek to capture snapshots of investors' behaviour and expectations, as well as of my own reactions and observations at the time.' The result is an idiosyncratic book, which together with the current newsletters should be essential reading for all emerging market investors.

GROWTH AND CAUTION IN CHINA

Back in 1987, Faber was already predicting that, long-term, around the year 2000, 'the emergence of economies such as Russia, China and India will have an impact on the world's economy similar to the opening up of the American West in the mid-nineteenth century.'

He is very bullish about the long-term prospects of China, but cautions that 'growth will be highly cyclical, depending largely on the intensity of foreign direct investment flows. Boom periods will be followed by busts brought about by a slowdown in the inflow – or even an outflow – of foreign capital. As is common in emerging economies, the principal casualties of such busts will be foreign investors.' He is 'confident that in ten years' time Shanghai will be Asia's most important commercial and financial metropolis besides Tokyo', and is very positive about the north-eastern provinces, which 'are rich in resources and will benefit over time from increased trade within the region and investment from Japan and South Korea', while warning that Hong Kong may be marginalized as other cities develop.

'Investing in China, however, is not without problems, and all too often, foreign investors' expectations of potential returns are far too high. A bureaucratic maze, constantly altering rules, regulations, and tax laws, a weak currency, and a poor legal infrastructure can lead to much frustration, as well as losses, on the part of foreign direct investors. In particular, we believe that the various China funds, mostly run by over-educated western business school graduates, who grew up being taught to "play fair" and "by the rule" on tennis courts, golf courses, football and cricket fields, but lacking

133

practical experience in gang warfare and street fights, are totally ill-equipped to succeed in China's jungle capitalism.'

In February 1993, Faber wrote as follows: 'Investors from all over the world are lining up to invest in China. Most of them have no idea about China's economic, social, and political structures. They have read the headlines of one of the many magazines featuring cover stories on China, and now firmly believe that easy money will be made by investing in China funds. Most of these are nothing more than blind pools of money. To the student of economic history, the current China mania has many similarities to John Law's Mississippi scheme, for which he established a company that was to be given the exclusive privilege of trading along the Mississippi River and in the province of Louisiana; or to the South Sea Company to which the monopoly of England's trade to the South Seas was given by an Act of Parliament. Then, as now, investors had become credulous, and since they knew virtually nothing about the New World their imagination about future profits ran wild. We have no doubt that as China opens up, many fortunes will be made. We only doubt that the overseas China fund investors will make them.'

By July 1994, he reaffirmed his caution. 'Although stocks in China have declined by over 60 per cent from their highs, they are, in my opinion, not particularly attractive. Most listed companies are still majority state-owned, with poorly paid and mediocre management having practically no share ownership in their companies. Consequently, managers of Chinese companies are more interested in personal gain and quick speculative profits than in their business's long-term performance. The large current and future supply of Chinese equities, at a time when demand from overseas has been cooling, will likely keep prices from rising much in the near future. Only when Chinese equities sell at five times earnings, and at significant discounts to their asset values, will we be tempted to take the plunge.'

Faber has been bearish on Hong Kong property for some time – notoriously so; this does not make him popular in a property-obsessed and property-dependent city. He was certainly early in his caution, but also consistent. In December 1993, he was recommending shorting the Hang Seng index along with emerging market telecom plays, and wrote: 'Property prices in Hong Kong soared not so much because of the China-related boom but because interest rates fell and stayed strongly negative for several years. As a result property developers who held large land banks were able to reap extraordinary inventory profits for several years in a row. In fact, investors have become so accustomed to these inventory profits that they now regard them as recurring. But this is a fallacy. As developers gradually sold their developments based on the cheap land they were holding, they had to replace it with a more expensive land bank. Therefore, unless Hong Kong real estate prices continue to double every three years (not likely from the present level), developers' profits will inevitably come under pressure. Finally, when the real estate market in Hong Kong turns down and when real interest rates swing from negative to positive, the recent regular earnings increases in Hong Kong's real estate industry (largely based on the aforementioned inventory profits) will give way to some nasty profit declines!'

Faber himself has no present plans to move out of Hong Kong. 'If any business will survive reasonably well in Hong Kong, I would say it's going to be the financial field . . . for a lot of other businesses I would be less optimistic about keeping my base in Hong Kong. Anyway I am just too lazy to move! And Hong Kong is a very free city, which is also acceptable to me.'

RUSSIAN BARGAIN BUYING

He was an early bull of Russia, and in February 1994 wrote a detailed report on the attractions of the market, calculating that the traded price of privatization vouchers and the equity available to the voucher holders at auction valued the whole of Russian industry at US$5–6 billion – compared to a market capitalization for Hong Kong at the time of over US$300 billion. 'The incredible undervaluation of Russian assets also becomes evident if we look at the market capitalization of individual companies: Surgutneftegaz Oil and Mining Company (the largest oil company in Russia), which produces about 2 per cent of world oil output . . . has a market capitalization of about US$170 million! Uralmash and Permsky Motors, each of which employ over 30,000 people, are valued at US$7 million and US$4 million respectively. Gum Department Stores, a leading retailer in Moscow (its main store, which it leases, is right next to the Kremlin, but it owns freehold another fifteen stores in Moscow) is valued at about US$24 million . . . whether a sustained uptrend will get under way any time soon is doubtful, and will obviously depend on a visible political and economic improvement.

But the potential is certainly there for Russian equities to rise by 10 to 20 times.'

He has a philosophical approach to the many uncertainties over the ownership of assets, the tax regime, and so on: he is buying an option, he says, and the option is in perpetuity, because Russia cannot now go back to a state enterprise system. The option may become worthless, but he considers the risk-reward ratio favourable. 'Or, again, we bought into the Port of Vladivostok. Again it's capitalized at about US$25 million. Exactly how they own the land, and whether they have to pay for a lease, that is still a debatable issue, but it's an option on the whole port facilities of Vladivostok. If Vladivostok develops, and the cargo volume increases, then that port will be worth one day as much as the terminal sites here in Hong Kong, so I am quite happy to take these options.'

Over the following few months, an increasing number of brokers and emerging market investors took up the theme. By late summer, the path to Moscow and St Petersburg was becoming well trodden, an increasing number of Asian based investors were visiting Vladivostok, the international press and the screen services were beginning to provide coverage of the new Russian financial markets, and several country funds were being rolled out. Prices were already a multiple of those paid by Faber on his early investments.

The February 1994 report included a fascinating analysis of 'the paradox of inflation', pointing out that for foreign investors, 'hyper-inflation economies do not produce a high price level but an extremely low one, as the depreciation of the currency (due to massive capital flight) tends to exceed the domestic inflation rate. I personally remember three instances when stocks in high inflation economies became dirt cheap: the Philippines in 1985/86, Argentina in 1989, and Peru in 1990. In the Philippines during the early 1980s, high inflation and poor economic, social, and political conditions under the Marcos regime had driven down stock prices and the value of the peso. By 1985, the Commercial Stock Index was down from its all-time high in 1980 by 76 per cent in dollar terms. The Mining Index had declined by 94 per cent, and the Oil Index by 97 per cent. The market capitalization of the six largest companies (Benguet, San Miguel, Philippine Long Distance Telephone, Atlas, Philex, and Ayala) had fallen to only US$340 million, and the market capitalization of the entire Philippine stock market amounted to less than US$500 million. PLDT was selling for less than US$40 million and at 1.7 times earnings. San Miguel had then a market capitalization of only US$60 million, which was less than the value of the company's 75 per cent interest in its Hong Kong listed subsidiary. (Recently the market capitalization of PLDT exceeded US$4 billion, while San Miguel's market capitalization stands now at US$4.4 billion.)' Moreover, 'the Weimar hyperinflation provided the best buying opportunity for German shares in this century.'

Besides Russia, he can currently spot few opportunities in the equity markets, where most stocks are trading at a premium to replacement cost, and is more interested in direct investment. So far he has invested in a hotel project in Vietnam — the China Beach Hotel in Danang — and in New Zealand apartment buildings.

He is also the Hong Kong distributor for Grolsch beer, although this involvement goes back several years. 'I saw the beer in Australia once, and I noticed that it didn't give me a headache the next day, so I thought that this is a good product! So I wrote to them and we got the agency, and now it's expanded quite a bit . . .' He has learnt a lot, he says, about business in the real world, outside the cosy field of fund management; but while the beer itself doesn't give him a headache, presiding over its expansion does.

Faber currently has about $120 million under management, of which only $18 million is in the Iconoclastic International Fund, the balance being in discretionary and advisory accounts. His track record as an independent fund manager dates back only to 1991 (before that he was a broker, first with White Weld, and then with Drexel Burnham Lambert). The returns in the fund have been respectable rather than spectacular, compounding at 17 per cent per annum since launch. Given that Faber has yet to be vindicated on his major cyclical assumptions for the US market, this is a decent performance, and his caution will at some stage prove to be well founded.

Chapter 13

Painstaking analysis

Richard Lawrence of Overlook Investments

Most of the other managers featured in this book have excellent long-term track records, and vehicles through which the public can invest. Richard Lawrence has neither. His single fund was established in 1992, and is at present closed to new investors. His approach is however so disciplined that it is interesting to explore his philosophy and his success to date.

Lawrence would be the first to admit that he has invented no new theory of investment. In explaining his approach, he goes back to the American classics. He cites Benjamin Graham, John Neff, Warren Buffett, Peter Lynch and his fund manager father among the investors who helped to shape his thinking, and learnt 'bits and pieces' from all of these different philosophies. He does not want to be characterized as a 'growth investor' or as a 'value investor'; like Neff, he tries to buy good companies at a low price. He applies the most stringent of the classical US value investment techniques, in order to 'de-emotionalize' the investment decisions, and yet manages to find extraordinarily good companies, with growth prospects greater than most US investors would ever dream possible.

Lawrence studied economics at Brown University in the US, and then spent two years working as a financial analyst in Venezuela, and a further year travelling round South America. On his return, he joined the brokerage-cum-fund management firm of J. Bush & Co, which he describes as a great training school. The firm focused on cheap growth stocks, and Lawrence headed up the research team in New York from 1981 to 1984.

He moved to Hong Kong in 1985, and became a founder employee of F.P. Special Assets, a listed company which was formed by Bob Meyer to invest in undervalued assets throughout the Asia-Pacific region equities, real estate, or venture capital. Meyer had been one of the founders of the First Pacific group, a few years earlier. The new company became involved in an eclectic range of deals; it bought real estate, took over existing companies, started new ventures, contested the decisions of public companies, and bought an interest in a contingency fee in an Australian lawsuit. Bewildered stock-market investors could never quite figure out what the company was all about. In 1991 most of the assets and the stock exchange listing were sold; an unlisted successor company remains in existence. The compound annual growth rate achieved by investors in the two companies was an impressive 32 per cent from 1986 through mid-1994 (NAV plus dividend). Lawrence says it was 'a great university of investment: the university of Bob'.

Lawrence then set up his present company, Overlook Investments, and spent a year investing his own money before his present fund was established. At this stage he was renting an office from Marc Faber, who was the first outside investor in the fund, and remains an advisor. He moved into his own offices in 1994, but still runs what is now a US$83 million fund with one analyst, an accountant and a part-time clerk – four people in all. He likes to minimize people-distractions within the office, in the interests of an investment focus which he himself describes as 'almost possessed'.

SUPERIOR BUSINESSES

He looks for superior businesses, which he believes to be 'very special and uncommon'. Key elements are:

- superior long-term growth in earnings per share
- a proven record of self-financing growth
- an ability to generate free cash flow
- a high return on equity
- a strong, largely debt-free balance sheet
- strong market share
- pricing power in the core business
- stable management structure
- management integrity, and a commitment to the interests of minority shareholders

– and then a bargain valuation. He concentrates on shares with the following characteristics:

139

- PE less than half of the long-term EPS growth rate
- PE less than half of the long-term return on equity
- high asset backing, as reflected in price-to-book and price-to-net-current-asset ratios
- a valuation in line with that of private businesses.

Thus, for a business with a return on equity of 20 per cent and a sustainable annual growth rate of 20 per cent, he would hope to buy at a price earnings ratio of 10 or less. This would be a classic growth stock in the US; in Asia, he has found a fair number of such companies which are not considered by the market to be growth stocks, such is the level of expectations. In general, he finds that most businesses in Asia grow between 5 per cent and 25 per cent a year; 30 per cent is unlikely to be sustainable on a per share basis.

He uses the ratios as guidelines, rather than as absolute requirements, and the details can be flexible. Whether the PE ratio should be based on historic, current or prospective earnings, for example, is a question on which he is not rigid. Similarly, he is not sure what weight he would attribute to the various different valuation measures in a quantitative system, and he believes it would be a mistake to lay down hard and fast quantitative rules.

He, does, however, monitor the aggregate valuation of the portfolio, and draws comfort from having these figures within the benchmarks. When we talked in October 1994, the portfolio had a dollar-weighted return on equity of 20 per cent, expected earnings-per-share growth of 23 per cent, and a prospective PE of 8 – remarkable figures.

The price-to-book ratio was 1.8, so for the portfolio as a whole the PE times the price-to-book ratio comes to 14.4, well within Benjamin Graham's suggested limit of 22.5. (Graham's rule of 22.5, recommended for defensive investors, corresponds to a valuation of 15 times earnings and 1.5 times book value.) What is extraordinary, however, is that such low valuations are combined with expectations of such attractive growth. Lawrence believes that the stocks he has selected, being shares of businesses with innately superior characteristics, should as a group be trading at a significant premium to more commonplace shares; instead he has managed to acquire them very cheaply.

Overlook Investments is not yet well known, even in the financial community. Lawrence's ability to find an entire portfolio of forty or fifty stocks on such valuations will come as an eye-opener, even to many experienced Asian investors.

Many of the shares in the fund are illiquid. For Lawrence this is not necessarily a deterrent, as he tries to take a three-to-five year view, and does extensive research ahead of each purchase. The average capitalization of the companies in his portfolio in October 1994 was just over US$200 million. (He has the figure at his finger-tips, on a two-page portfolio summary spreadsheet which incorporates all the statistics he considers vital. The average age of his earnings estimates, for example, was just over two months at the time of our discussion.) As of April 1994, he estimated that the majority of listed companies in Asia had market capitalizations below US$350 million. His fund can therefore choose from a large number of companies too small for the larger players, although he does not limit his search to these.

THE SEARCH, AND RELATIONSHIP-BUILDING

In scanning for opportunities, Lawrence uses paper sources only – company handbooks and a certain amount of broker research. He is dismissive about electronic databases, which tend to be out of date and inaccurate, and which therefore throw up too many statistical anomalies.

He devotes a lot of time to financial modelling, emphasizing cash flow projections for the next two to three years, and the implications for the balance sheet three years out. He often sends these numbers to the companies concerned, and likes to discuss the projections with the management.

Once a company has been identified as potentially interesting, on the basis of the numbers, personal visits are of vital importance. Lawrence regards company visits as absolutely fundamental, and says you cannot possibly understand a company adequately just by looking at the financial statements. There are no companies in the fund which he has not visited personally, and he keeps in regular contact thereafter; he or his analyst will usually visit each of their principal holdings every three or four months. With a specific question, they sometimes make contact by telephone, or through a local broker if there is a language problem. However, Lawrence tries to build long-term relationships, and emphasizes the importance of eye-to-eye contact.

Although he is among the most quantitative of the managers featured here, he would not dream of buying a company on the strength of numbers alone, and like other investors stresses the power of controlling shareholders in the Asian markets and the importance of their track record with minority shareholders. He estimates that he does one hundred and fifty to two hundred visits a year. Initially, of course, most were to new prospects. Now that the fund is settling down, around 40 per cent of visits are to existing holdings. The visiting schedule can be disrupted by marketing, so he makes a point of opening the fund to new investors only occasionally, and keeping his attention focused on investment all the rest of the time. (He also makes a point of running only one fund, the Overlook Partners Fund, known as Top Fund. He runs no discretionary accounts or side funds.)

He will cut a position quickly if he decides he has made a mistake but, other things being equal, he would prefer to buy and hold his investments indefinitely. This preference is reinforced by tax considerations, since the fund is a limited partnership and US citizens are taxed on the realized capital gains. He sometimes sells a stock if its performance proves very disappointing, or if it makes a diversification move which reduces its attractions. He will stick with a good stock until the valuation becomes extreme, but also tries to keep the dollar-averaged valuation of the portfolio within acceptable limits, so may sell a highly-rated stock to lower the portfolio PE. Again, he has no firm rules on how far individual or aggregate valuations can be stretched. He sold two major holdings as the market surged in late 1993, realizing gains of 250 per cent on one (a Malaysian stock) and 319 per cent on the other (one of the Korean holdings).

More recently, he has been selling a Philippine stock which is now trading at over twenty times earnings but had also disappointed, diluting its capital, missing its earnings projections, and diversifying into an unrelated business. It is not necessarily a bad stock, he argues, but there are many more attractive options in Hong Kong, Indonesia, Korea and Thailand on single-digit PEs; and if he did want to have a stock in the portfolio on that high a rating, is it the best company he could buy at that multiple?

Lawrence avoids kneejerk reactions, and went to visit this company before taking the decision to sell; he has been concerned about the company and monitoring the situation for several months. Conversely, however exciting a new idea, he will not buy a huge amount of a stock immediately. He will buy a little first, and build up the position as he gets to know the company better and his confidence increases. He doesn't worry that he may pay a slightly higher price in a few months' time; if it is that good a company, it will probably still be cheap anyway. This takes the pressure off the decision making; not too much is riding on any one purchase or sale.

He has not tracked his portfolio turnover, but guesses that it has been around 20 per cent. He says he has made many mistakes, but none of them has really hurt, because the valuations on purchase have been sufficiently low. Moreover, because of the cautious approach to building up positions, he has made no serious mistakes in his top fifteen holdings. (The portfolio is reasonably concentrated, with 80–90 per cent in thirty-five stocks.)

RISK CONTROL PARAMOUNT

Lawrence says he is not aiming for top performance, or indeed for any particular rate of growth, and is just trying to invest his own money and that of his partners in a very conservative fashion. If you protect the downside, he argues, the upside looks after itself. Nevertheless, he achieved a return of 73 per cent in 1993 and has held his own in the much more difficult first three quarters of 1994 – which is more than respectable. (In 1992, with his small personal portfolio, he managed a return of 68 per cent in much more difficult market conditions.)

These returns are particularly impressive given that he had an average cash balance of 37 per cent during 1993. This was mainly because of the timing of portfolio inflows, which he takes his time to invest. For most of 1994 he was more fully invested, and at times lightly geared.

He is not interested in hedging market risk, which he reckons just contributes to the already-adequate wealth of the American investment banks. He does not trade, and does not spend time attempting to fine-tune execution.

Korea has had the largest market representation in the portfolio since inception, with Hong Kong for most of the period in second place and Thailand third. Lawrence has no preconceived ideas of the appropriate geographical weighting, so this has just happened to be where he found the opportunities – which is of course partly a function of the time spent searching in each country, although naturally he looks where he thinks the prospects are best. Korea was a particularly fruitful hunting ground during 1993, generating a return of 81 per cent on that portion of the portfolio.

Korean companies provide the greatest accounting detail in Asia, although Lawrence comments that they are falling behind on accounting policies. The inconsistencies however provide tremendous scope for a fundamental investor. While many of the larger groups have aggressively chased market share and sheer size at the expense of minority shareholders, others are conservatively run and offer outstanding value. Conveniently for foreigners struggling with the unfamiliar script, Korean companies report in a standardized format, and Lawrence is now sufficiently familiar with Korean accounts to read them without a problem.

Examples of the stocks which Lawrence has uncovered make fascinating reading. I cannot improve on his own account, so readers are referred to the extracts from his quarterly reports to partners, given in Appendix C. Of the six stocks which he has so far described in these reports, three are from Korea, two from Hong Kong, and one from Thailand – broadly reflecting the geographical spread of his investments to date.

I have also reproduced in Appendix D some of Lawrence's examples of what to look for in company accounts, which are drawn from Korea and provide a vivid insight into the value of fundamental analysis – and indeed of the Chartered Financial Analyst (CFA) qualification, which he commends as the best possible training for any aspiring investor.

Chapter 14

Cheap stocks in Hong Kong

Cheah Cheng Hye and V-Nee Yeh of Value Partners

Somewhat similar to Richard Lawrence, both in their quest for small undervalued companies overlooked by the market and in the short track record of their present fund, are Cheah Cheng Hye and V-Nee Yeh of Value Partners.

Where they differ from Lawrence is in focusing on Hong Kong, where small companies have historically been treated with some suspicion by the fund management community. On balance this scepticism has been well justified, but Cheah and Yeh believe that there are bargains amongst the rubbish, and that their local knowledge and connections enable them to pick their way profitably through the minefield.

Yeh believed in 1994 that a long period of underperformance by Hong Kong industrial shares might finally be reversed, because of growing foreign concern about the property cycle and the potential for this to weigh heavily on property and bank shares. Perceptions of the industrials, on the other hand, could hardly become less favourable, and certain stocks offer prospects for multiple expansion as well as an earnings increase. In developed markets such as the US, cyclical stocks tend to have a high PE at an earnings trough, as the market discounts the recovery potential. In Hong Kong, a cyclical stock reaching the bottom of the cycle often has a very low PE, as the market has become disillusioned by years of falling earnings. 'With an improvement in the industry cycle, not only do earnings advance, but frequently the PE ratio increases as investor sentiment turns bullish. Patient and astute investors are therefore offered more bang for their buck, and are rewarded twice for being prescient once.'

Cheah is Malaysian, but has spent more than half his life and most of his working career in Hong Kong. He was a financial journalist for twelve years, latterly at the *Far Eastern Economic Review* and the *Asian Wall Street Journal*, and moved into the securities industry only in 1989 when he joined Morgan Grenfell to set up their Hong Kong research department. Once there, he decided to focus on value investments, which in practice meant covering the second and third liners. This generated some popularity, little commission, and a profitable line in proprietary trading. More importantly, it gave him confidence and the beginnings of a track record: a client account which he managed from July 1991 through to February 1993 rose 100 per cent, compared to a 58 per cent gain for the Hang Seng index.

Yeh is vice-chairman of his family company Hsin Chong, but his interests have always tended more towards finance than to that group's core businesses of construction and real estate. He studied law in the United States, and then spent six years in corporate finance and capital markets for Lazards in New York, Hong Kong and London. He returned to Hong Kong in 1990, and even since Lazards days has co-managed Hsin Chong's pension fund (worth about US$30 million in September 1994) and the group's liquid assets (usually rather larger). The performance of the pension fund, which is more formally monitored, has been exceptionally good. The compound annual return over the seven years to September 1994 was 26 per cent, and over all shorter periods to this date the compound growth has been significantly higher.

One of Yeh's great coups was to initiate and structure the leveraged buyout by the family of Hsin Chong International Holdings. The privatization offer was made in January 1991 when the Hang Seng index was 4,455, and was on sufficiently generous terms to achieve a record 99.6 per cent approval rate from minority shareholders. By June 1993, all acquisition debt had been repaid, and the residual asset value was estimated to be significantly higher than the original offer price. Yeh claims this as a triumph for fair dealing, having rejected advice that they could have pared a few percentage points off the price; the market took off rapidly thereafter, so any delay might have cost them the deal, whereas in the event all parties were satisfied and the buyout a great success. The deal taught him not to cheese-pare in business or stock-market dealings.

Having met when Cheah paid a company visit to Hsin Chong, the two began to exchange investment ideas, and Value Partners was formed in February 1993. Initial assets of just over US$3 million had grown to about US$70 million by October 1994.

Value Partners has focused mainly and increasingly on Hong Kong. Initially they were enthusiastic about Korea, and at the end of 1993 had 15 per cent of the portfolio there, but their experience has been much less satisfactory than Richard Lawrence's, and Cheah candidly admits that they underperformed badly in the other Asian markets. Likewise, they lost money dealing in futures, an activity which Cheah at least has now foresworn, and they have determined to concentrate on undervalued stocks in Hong Kong, where they should have a comparative advantage. (At the end of the third quarter of 1994, 80 per cent of the portfolio was in Hong Kong, but they still had 9 per cent in other Asian equities.)

EXTENSIVE CROSS-CHECKING OF MANAGEMENT CREDENTIALS

Like every other Asian manager interviewed, Value Partners emphasizes the vital importance of management. Cheah and Yeh draw upon all available resources to cross-check the integrity and credibility of the principals of any company in which they invest. They generally avoid newly-listed companies, preferring instead to pick up bombed-out earlier issues which have weathered a few down-cycles, where further share price downside is considered to be limited and any illusions have already been laid to rest.

While they have no prescribed valuation limits, they look for ideas by screening companies by price-earnings, dividend yield, and price-to-book ratios plus return on equity, and maintain their own spreadsheets for this purpose. They have no systematic press files, and limited input from brokers, but maintain a comprehensive library of annual reports and announcements, and base their decisions on these original sources plus their own research and contacts.

Learning from experience, they have pruned the portfolio, trying to concentrate on investments where they have most knowledge and experience, and real conviction. The number of holdings has been reduced from over fifty, and they now think the ideal would be thirty to forty. They like to have individual holdings of 5–10 per cent of the portfolio, diversified by sector, and have several bets of such size.

Winton Holdings is among the largest. This taxi financing company is one of Richard Lawrence's favourites too, and his description can be found in Appendix C. Before making this investment, Yeh satisfied himself about the sustainability of Winton's extraordinarily high margins. The company provides a valuable interface between taxi drivers, who might not ordinarily know how to present an effective case to a bank for financing, and banks who might not ordinarily know how to appraise such individuals. A barrier to entry therefore exists, in the form of knowhow and a reputation built up over more than twenty years. Winton also deals in taxi licences, and offers the convenience of one-stop shopping. Effectively, Winton was borrowing at 1–2 per cent over the Hong Kong Interbank Offer Rate (HIBOR) – 7 or 8 per cent – and lending at a floating rate which would be double that on a loan held to maturity, but in practice achieving 22–23 per cent due to early repayments. The default rate had historically been extremely low: of the order of 0.5 per cent. Clearly therefore the company was happy, but what of other parties? From the investor's standpoint, all this would be to no avail if the margins were unsustainable. Yeh therefore modelled the returns on taxi investment and labour from all angles – that of an investor-driver, an investor employing one or more drivers for the shifts, and an employee driver – and concluded that the current economic structure made sense for all parties and was probably therefore stable. He had also looked into government policy on transport and taxi licensing.

This is where contacts come in. Cheah and Yeh use a wide range of sources – competitors, suppliers, customers, bankers, and government officials, amongst others – to check both the credentials of individuals and the prospects for specific businesses. Yeh notes that Hong Kong is a small place, that most people in the territory have been involved in a number of different businesses, and that often one is assessing a family rather than an individual – all of which make the process easier. They try to cross-check from as many angles as possible, and look for inconsistencies between the information received from the target companies and that from other sources.

ENTREPRENEURS AND BUSINESS BUILDERS

Both Yeh and Cheah are cynical about the quality of many local companies. Yeh suggests that the US approach of buying a good company and holding it for five years is often inadvisable in Hong Kong, where there are many good entrepreneurs but fewer good business builders. The entrepreneur often takes a two-to-four year view, and invests too little to build effective barriers to entry. The nature of many businesses in the region is also inferior, he suggests; many are effectively commodity businesses, based on low labour cost, and the better businesses are often already highly rated blue-chip companies. Reinvestment risk is therefore a key consideration, as the entrepreneur shoots off at an unpredictable tangent, diverting company cash flows into the latest venture. All too often, therefore, 'you can share the trials and tribulations, but not the fortunes'.

Accordingly, many of Value Partners' bets are cyclical turnaround stories, where the shares are trading below book value, there is little or no remaining institutional following, and an immediate earnings rebound is in prospect.

Their largest holding, Fountain Set, is a classic of the genre. Fountain Set is the largest local dyer of knitted cotton fabrics, which was listed in 1990. Earnings per share for that year were flat; the following year they fell by a third. This is par for the course among Hong Kong new listings. Fiscal year 1992 saw little improvement, and investor enthusiasm was by now at a low ebb. Earnings rebounded to a new high in FY93, but this was by now presumably regarded as a fluke as it attracted little interest. By 1994, a major four-year expansion into China was on the verge of completion, and dollar sales would, on Value Partners' estimates, have doubled in the four years since listing. The investment included computeriz-ation to cater for the just-in-time purchasing systems installed by many retailers, a change which in conjunction with other economies of scale had helped to squeeze out smaller competitors. Earnings per share, previously dented by the rising depreciation and financing costs associated with the expansion, were set to double over the next three years, in Cheah's view. Meanwhile, the share price at $1.20 represented only 6.3 times historic earnings and 70 per cent of book value.

Cheah has been following Fountain Set since listing, and has great confidence in the story. He has, indeed, been investing in it for the best part of two years already, and while the fundamentals may have been in place the share price has been going nowhere. Patience is a virtue which the partners recognized at an early stage, but Cheah is beginning to share more of his ideas with the press and other analysts to assist in recognizing value when it comes through.

This willingness to become proactive was illustrated with knitwear manufacturer Novel Enterprises, which represented 5 per cent of the portfolio at the time of a privatization announcement in November 1994. Value Partners had held the stock in small size since 1993, and tipped the company in the Hong Kong press in April 1994, estimating the PE at 7 and the discount to net asset value at 44 per cent. Novel's managing director Ronald Chao used to sit on the board of Hsin Chong International, and was therefore familiar with Yeh's orchestration of the Hsin Chong buyout. Value Partners was instrumental in persuading the Chao family to take their company private.

Value Partners' third largest holding, QPL, also illustrates the philosophy well, in that the fund has bought for a cyclical upturn and not for the long haul. The QPL management has ventured into property in the past and not done well. If the core business of assembling integrated circuits prospers as expected in the next couple of years, past form would suggest that the company may diversify into some other new venture.

An analysis of the Hong Kong portion of the portfolio, produced in August 1994 (a couple of months before our meeting) showed an estimated current year PE of 7.9, an expected dividend yield of 5.9 per cent, price-to-book of 1.6, an average return on equity of 23 per cent, and a three-year forward growth forecast of 32 per cent per year. Needless to say, these figures are very much more attractive than the market averages.

SOVEREIGN DEBT AND OPTION PRICING

The fund also has 6 per cent in defaulted Vietnamese and North Korean debt. At current market prices, Yeh is up 50–80 per cent on his cost, but is holding on for considerably more. He is hoping for Brady-style restructurings in both countries, although he may sell earlier if the market price goes to an acceptable percentage, or if he thinks there are better opportunities in Hong Kong. He has studied past restructurings, can reel off the figures for present accrued interest, and thinks of the debt as analogous to an option with the exercise price declining as interest accrues. He points out that while the holders of a defaulted bond are speculating on the event of restructuring (or on secondary market sentiment in the meantime), holders of an interest-paying security are speculating on the non-occurrence of a default.

Yeh bought 30-year Australian zero-coupon bonds for the pension fund in 1991, on a yield of 11–12 per cent. In similar vein, he considered that purchase as an interest rate option which in the worst case would increase 33-fold in value over thirty years. In 1994, he is neutral on the direction of the global bond market, but yields of 7–8 per cent, or even 9 per cent, are insufficient to interest him. He is an occasional buyer of bonds, therefore, in special situations.

While the debt analysis is cogent, Value Partners does not appear to be as disciplined about its company analysis as Richard Lawrence's Overlook Investments, nor about its asset allocation or portfolio monitoring. A direct comparison is however unfair. Cheah and Yeh do far more analysis than most other fund managers, are better placed for the intangible but invaluable networking and cross-checking of the companies in which they invest, and in Hong Kong – and to a lesser extent southern China – they are playing on home ground.

Yeh also says that they leave a huge margin for error. He reckons that if you need a complex equation to justify the investment, that margin is probably inadequate. What they are looking for is very simple, he says: very limited downside risk, management integrity, a catalyst for change, and preferably an exit strategy.

Value Partners' performance to date has been respectable. Broadly speaking, in the first eighteen months of operation, even though absolute rather than relative returns are the yardstick, they matched the Hang Seng index with significantly lower month-to-month volatility. They missed the final surge in the index in late 1993 (unsurprisingly, since it was driven by massive flows of liquidity into the large-cap stocks), and suffered correspondingly less in the subsequent downturn.

The pension fund, although exceptionally successful over time, has been much more volatile. (Yeh manages it in a similar style, and again it is predominantly Hong Kong based.) In 1990, for example, it fell 12 per cent, while the Hang Seng index plus dividends rose by a similar amount. This was mainly attributable to heavy purchases of HSBC, at a price equivalent to HK$20 per share. The bank slid steadily throughout that year, before embarking on the straight-line rebound which took it to a peak of HK$130 over the next three years. This helped the company to record a return of 117 per cent in 1991, comfortably outpacing the 49 per cent return on the accumulation index.

A characteristic of Value Partners' target companies is that the share prices may remain dead for long periods of time, before the value suddenly begins to be recognized, and the timing of this change is unpredictable. Yeh hopes to see a 'conveyor belt' pattern, in which such individual events occur with some frequency. Inevitably this will not always happen, but meanwhile the downside risk should be relatively limited.

The jury may still be out on the attractions of Hong Kong smaller companies as an investment arena, but Value Partners is unusually well placed to succeed within it. Very often, such companies went public at the top of the previous cycle; the number of industrial listings has increased greatly in recent years. Investors at large often find it difficult to distinguish the cyclical element in the subsequent collapse, and may end up with a haphazard judgment on management competence, credibility, and the historic treatment of conflicts of interest. Smaller and industrial companies are usually covered by very junior analysts, who cut their teeth for a year or so and are then promoted to greater things. Many of the more experienced investors cannot focus on such companies because of their size – which would eliminate medium-sized funds, let alone commission-driven brokers. Information given by companies is of very variable reliability. While regulation has improved over the years, there is little practical recourse on this score – let alone on the diversification risk, which Yeh pointed out, or even on outright fraud. Assessing the people is therefore critical and few investors can match Cheah and Yeh's network of contacts for this purpose; many of those who could have easier ways of making a living. One can only wish Value Partners well.

Chapter 15

Seeking alternative angles

Charles Fowler of John Govett

Charles Fowler is the only fund manager featured for a chapter of this book who has never lived in Asia, although he thinks he travels enough to compensate. He also has the longest track record of any featured manager with a single fund: he has been running the Govett Oriental Investment Trust since 1983. Performance is impressive: his three funds feature regularly near the top of the league tables, and he is unusually adroit in dealing with both Japan and the rest of the Far East.

Over the ten years to September 1994, the Govett Oriental Investment Trust was the top performing closed-end fund in the Micropal universe, compounding at over 23 per cent annually in US dollar terms – enough to multiply your money by a factor of eight during that period. Over shorter periods, it has generally led its peer group, in a universe which includes Japan, probably helped by a greater bias towards the other Asian markets. (In the third quarter of 1994, the fund had only 27 per cent in Japan, down from 34 per cent earlier in the year.) More interestingly, though, it has generally performed very creditably against the whole range of regional funds, despite being one of the larger entities at around US$1.3 billion.[1] Internally, the group analyses the impact of its own stock selection in every market against the local index, and in recent years has managed to outperform in most countries.

---

1 The open-ended Pacific Strategy Fund, which is about one-tenth the size, has done even better since inception in 1987. This fund, formerly run by Charles Fowler, is now managed by Peter Robson.

ONLY SO MANY GOOD IDEAS

Fowler sometimes takes quite aggressive bets. He loaded up on Singapore and Malaysia during the last few months of 1992, and by early 1993 had some 37 per cent of the fund in these markets, a decision which proved absolutely correct. He reckons that he has only a few good ideas every year, so that it is appropriate to back them heavily, albeit to an extent commensurate with the risk.

He tries to invest on a six to eighteen month view, and is always looking for situations where the market is getting things wrong; he also believes that this timescale allows the flexibility to buy more interesting stocks.

In the autumn of 1992, there was deep gloom overhanging the Singaporean and Malaysian markets. Singapore was said to be in a growth cul-de-sac, having lost its entrepreneurial flair and its productivity edge, and earlier bulls of the market had been worn down after four years of sideways movement in the index. In Malaysia, there were concerns about inflation and the current account; 'the economists as usual had got the wrong end of the stick, underestimating the importance of capital goods imports and therefore grossly overstating the problems on the trade account. People always underestimate how far Singapore and Malaysia have moved up the scale of value-added, keeping well ahead of Indonesia and China. All of the capital investment undertaken over the previous few years was just about to come on stream.'

In Singapore, 'the regionalization package was largely hot air, but nevertheless catalytic. The economy was not ex-growth, as the market thought, but about to enter a period of strong sustained growth.' Govett picked this up partly because of the electronics companies, which it follows closely because of its SESDAQ fund. These companies were all very small, and the SESDAQ* market is much less liquid than the main board, so the companies were at the time little monitored by other fund managers, and Govett's research at the company level was invaluable. Company order books were lengthening fast, and this fitted in with input obtained from Japan and from the group office in San Francisco. Despite the light representation of the electronics sector in the stock market, it is hugely important to the local economy, and this turnaround was therefore of great significance.

---

* Singapore's small company market, modelled on the US NASDAQ.

Fowler says this is the real value of visiting small companies. He is not convinced there is a 'small company effect' in Asia, and that small companies necessarily perform better in terms of earnings: there is some evidence to this effect, but he considers it inconclusive. However, small companies are less researched. When they are researched at all, it is often by the most junior analysts, who may fail to pick up the significant points at the company level, and fail to recognize significant inputs for the broad macro picture. There are therefore real investment anomalies to be found, and visiting these companies helps one to understand what is going on in the real economy.

LOOK FOR A DIFFERENT ANGLE

Fowler reckons, moreover, that if you are covering the markets from a distance, you have to try to give yourself an edge by approaching things from a slightly different angle. It is important to get input from as many sources as possible, he believes: if you get several insights from different people, you often come up with an original investment idea.

Doing something different was part of the logic of setting up an office in Singapore, in 1989, rather than making a late entry into Hong Kong. With the recent liberalization of fund management rules, this finally looks like an astute commercial decision, but meanwhile there is clear evidence that it has given Govett an edge in those markets.

Similarly, Fowler says that input from the direct investment side of the business has been invaluable. A stake in First Pacific Land, for example, gave him a seat on the board of that company for a time, and a useful education in the mechanics of large property developments and consortium deals.

The group's overall orientation is towards value investment, and smaller companies. Fowler uses these inputs to drive the asset allocation decisions on a top-down basis, and at the same time provide for aggressive stock selection. These days he tends to leave the stock selection to other members of the team (now eleven strong, between London and Singapore), but still visits a lot of companies, and can talk at length about some of the more successful turnarounds.

In picking stocks, he looks for value, ideally in combination with a long-term concept, blue-sky potential and the likelihood of positive

155

surprises. He also looks at liquidity, earnings momentum, and technical factors, but says the emphasis of the mix will vary from time to time and from market to market.

DON'T WAIT FOR THE CROWD

Fowler was early into a number of emerging markets. He bought Philippine stocks in 1986, in the last days of the Marcos regime when Aquino's supporters were flooding the streets after the rigged election. Had he been really brave, he says, he would have taken Toby Heale's advice and bought ahead of the election, but he moved in 50 per cent higher and still did well. He started buying Philippine Long Distance Telephone at $1.50, and eventually accumulated several per cent of the company at an average price of $2.85. He started to sell from $30 upwards; the stock recently reached $70.

A little later, he bought a large stake in Taiwan, ahead of the market's major explosion. The Formosa Fund attracted sufficiently little interest on launch that Govett was able to secure a significant stake in the management company along with its investment in March 1986. The index at the time was just over 1,000; over the next four years it went to 12,000. Fowler very prudently chickened out at 7–8,000, for a five-fold profit on the fund, and the market collapsed to about 2,500.

Similarly, he was among the earliest foreign investors in Indonesia, being one of the buyers of Jakarta International Hotels in 1988; he quadrupled his money on this one. He was similarly early in Sri Lanka, where he bought into Asian Hotels alongside David Crichton-Watt (see p 83) in July 1992; and more recently in India.

In recent years, with fewer new markets to explore, the key calls have been in the more established markets. He loaded up early and heavily in Singapore and Malaysia during late 1992, and then sold steadily through the second half of 1993 as those markets became increasingly overvalued, reinvesting in Korea and Taiwan. Those markets performed adequately if not sensationally in 1993, but more importantly held up relatively well in 1994. Exposure to Japan was increased in early 1994, to about one third of the portfolio, but run down again subsequently.

Curiosity, confidence, and decisive bets: it seems to work.

Chapter 16

The herbaceous portfolio

Angus Tulloch of Stewart Ivory

One of the most dedicated stockpickers in Scotland is Angus Tulloch. He heads the small team of four who run the Asian and emerging markets funds of Stewart Ivory, one of the fortunate companies still ensconced in the elegant houses of Edinburgh's Charlotte Square. There are limits to tradition, however: Tulloch is not dour.

As he embarked on a recent trip to China, his son requested that he should bring back a panda. He returned with a panda suit, changed into it on the plane, and persuaded staff at Edinburgh airport to broadcast a request for William Tulloch to report to the meeting point to collect his panda. His family, unfortunately, were late. He therefore ended up sitting in the waiting room, in his panda suit, reading the *Financial Times*. A large crowd gathered. William was not impressed by his father's antics: pandas, he thought, should be on all fours. Tulloch's efforts were not entirely wasted: a prospective client was far more amused, and invested a million pounds in the fund.

NAV PLUS DIVIDENDS: THE MEASURE OF ENTREPRENEURIAL SUCCESS

One of Tulloch's long-standing arguments is that the markets focus too much on earnings, whereas an Asian entrepreneur will focus on appreciation in the net asset value of the company, plus dividends. This is a fair observation, and a useful extension to the conventional ways of thinking about investment. Much investment theory of course has been developed in the United States, where real estate is much less important as a component of business and of the stock market than it is in Asia, and the true value of a business is a function

157

of its future cash flows. The difficulty in Asia is that book values often lag far behind current market values of the assets, so how possible it is to evaluate the historic record of an individual company on this basis depends on whether the company is regularly realizing assets and booking its capital gains, or alternatively and less commonly revaluing its assets.

Asian entrepreneurs, he argues, have a philosophy which can be simultaneously very short term, and very long term. When choosing the site for a brewery, they will automatically pick a location with long-term potential for an extraordinary gain, recognizing the dramatic transformations which can occur over a period of decades in a particular economy or city. Accordingly, he looks for growth, not necessarily in earnings, but maybe in net asset value or cash flow. He tries to take a three to five year view, rather than one or two years. While he looks for value, he considers it well worthwhile to pay up for quality and management integrity.

Tulloch's largest holding for some years has been the Malaysian conglomerate Perlis Plantations, which in mid-1994 accounted for 6 per cent of the New Pacific Fund and 7 per cent of the Emerging Markets Fund; it is one of the few holdings common to both funds. Earnings have been relatively lacklustre in recent years, and the company is not viewed with much enthusiasm by brokerage analysts – but Tulloch reckons that annual EPS growth has been of the order of 12 per cent and NAV growth around 17 per cent; the dividend yield is about 2 per cent. His comment in a recent report was that: 'Interests comprise a mixture of strong cash generators (principally flour-milling and sugar-refining) which have been used to finance the purchase of initially low-yielding but potentially very rewarding assets (hotels, plantations and property). Perlis is typical of many Chinese-controlled companies in focusing more on long-term net asset value appreciation than short-term earnings growth. Consequently, extraordinary gains (usually tax-free) are a regular feature of the company's results.'

Another unusual name which has featured in the portfolio for many years is the Singaporean company Trans Island Bus Service (TIBS). Tulloch bought this company when it was on a PE about half that of the market, and its cash flow multiple one quarter; at one stage he owned 10 per cent of the company. The holding has been trimmed back to 7 per cent after a quadrupling of the share price in the last few years, but Tulloch remains an enthusiast. The buses are depreciated over eight years, he points out, compared to a fifteen year norm in the UK. Earnings growth fluctuates because of the timing of price increases, but the company's very strong cash flow has allowed it to diversify into other businesses ranging from packaging and waste disposal to leasing, and most recently a bus manufacturing joint venture with Mercedes Benz in China. 'The key to evaluating TIBS is its success in growing net asset value. We expect the historic compound NAV growth rate of 20 per cent per annum to be maintained through the disposal or listing of group assets over the next five years.'

A SOUND ATTITUDE TO ACCOUNTANCY

The interest in transport goes back to a spell working for a bus company. Tulloch graduated from Cambridge with a degree in economics and history, and spent a few years in accountancy, which he treated with an appropriate and unconventional irreverence. (He spent most of his final examination paper composing 'An Ode to Cheer up the Examiner', composed to the tune of 'Hark the Herald Angels Sing'.) The subsequent stint at a 'nationalized, bureaucratic' bus company taught him how an industry should not be run. He subsequently joined Cazenove in 1980, spending three years in Hong Kong researching Malaysia, Singapore and Thailand before moving to London to run the Australian desk in 1984, then into fund management in 1986, and back to Scotland in 1988 to join the independent firm of Stewart Ivory.

Another of Tulloch's favourite stocks is Saha Pathana in Thailand, which is trading at a discount of over 50 per cent to estimated net asset value, based on the value of stakes in affiliates and industrial property. Stewart Ivory started accumulating the stock in 1993, on the basis that the various group businesses were of high quality and only temporarily troubled, and that the stock was cheap; a ruling that associates should be equity accounted came as a bonus, and is expected to double the reported earnings in 1994. With recovery under way, the stock is estimated to be on a current-year PE of around 10, with sustainable growth of the order of 15 per cent thereafter.

Tulloch says his principal mistakes have been made with recovery stocks, and he has now decided that distance is a disadvantage in this limited category, since local investors are better placed to pick up any deterioration or discrepancy in the story. (In general, he is a

159

firm advocate of the argument that distance conveys detachment.) In a dynamic region, the opportunity cost of waiting for recovery or takeover can in any case be high. Moreover, the prevalence of family-controlled companies limits the scope for release of value by predators.

He does not worry unduly about country weightings, which tend to arise from the stock selection and can differ dramatically from the indices, but does try to ensure reasonable geographical and sector diversification.

The team members generally visit their most important regional markets (Hong Kong, Singapore, Malaysia) three times a year; Thailand, Korea and India twice; Indonesia and the Philippines at least once. Tulloch makes a point of trying to visit new or potential emerging markets early; he went to Vietnam in 1990, and in late 1994 has just returned from Myanmar, now vastly changed from his last visit in 1983. Between them, the team have visited 70 per cent of the portfolio in the last twelve months; they emphasize visits to the small and medium-sized companies, which they find less researched and more informative.

An interesting checklist of 'What to look for in a company', which he drew up at the request of his colleagues, is included as Appendix B. While there may be nothing there which is totally original, the list may be of interest both to new analysts and to more experienced investors who are new to Asian markets, since there is a clear emphasis on the issues which crop up most regularly in the region.

THE BEST, THE WORST, AND THE MOST INTERESTING

The internal quarterly review discipline at Stewart Ivory is unusually constructive. Tables are drawn up to show the ten top-performing stocks, the ten worst-performing stocks, and the impact of country weightings against the benchmark. A paragraph has to be written on the single best-performing stock, the single worst-performing stock, and one stock selected by the manager, with conclusions or lessons drawn. Each investment director makes a ten-minute presentation, and fields fifteen or twenty minutes of questions from his colleagues in different markets.

Tulloch says he pays more attention than most people to risk; and that he always tends to outperform significantly in flat or dull markets, but to underperform in bull markets, which make him very nervous. This makes sense: he does not chase the themes which can take popular companies to unsustainable valuation levels, and the less popular companies in which he is invested do tend to be much less volatile. Long-run returns, nevertheless, are respectable.

Over the five years to September 1994, the Stewart Ivory New Pacific Fund achieved compound growth of 23 per cent a year in US dollar terms, against 13 per cent for the MSCI Pacific Index. A couple of recent bull market years with growth in the 30–35 per cent range have dropped the fund down the league tables. It would be churlish to complain about these rates of growth, as risk levels rose with the markets. Like many of the more conservative fund managers who know Asia well, Tulloch was becoming cautious on Hong Kong well before Barton Biggs led the final surge of US investment into the territory in late 1993. On a risk adjusted basis, funds like this one and the Cazenove Pacific Fund, which have been uncharacteristically far down the league tables during the more exuberant periods, move sharply up the rankings.

THE HERBACEOUS PORTFOLIO

Tulloch is fond of a gardening analogy, a traditionalist's version of modern portfolio theory. He learnt from Lord Faringdon at Cazenove to view his portfolio as a herbaceous border, and wrote the following explanation in early 1993:

'Gardening is an art, not a science. A herbaceous border should be much more than a symmetrical expression of what flowers are currently in vogue. Variety – be it in or out of fashion – is the essence of success. Plant exploration has an important role to play, as newly discovered seedlings could be tomorrow's Chelsea Show triumphs. These, in moderation, ought to have a place alongside sturdy shrubs, hardy perennials, and regular blooms. Whatever the weather, colour must always be found. Above all, gardening should be creative and fun.

'The New Pacific portfolio owes much to the influence of this approach. We too aim for balance and avoid taking excessive positions in individual markets, sectors, or stocks. No one market presently accounts for more than 30 per cent, or stock for more than 5 per cent of the fund's value. Ten countries and fifty companies are

161

currently represented. Over half the portfolio is invested in recognized regional "hardies" – Brambles in Australia, Fraser & Neave in Singapore, and Swire Pacific in Hong Kong are examples. Less well-known medium to smaller companies with proven track records – Cifra in Mexico, Crusader Oil in Australia, Shaw Brothers in Hong Kong, and Trans Island Bus Services in Singapore – are also strongly represented. Finally, we always make room for a selection of publicly untested "exotica".

'Many of the latter holdings result from subscription to new issues in the less mature and currently unfashionable markets of Indonesia (eg Dynaplast and Nipress) or Thailand (eg Bangkok Dusit Medical and Srithai Superware). Access to such issues in more buoyant times is rarely available. Such companies are chosen primarily on growth criteria – all are in the process of expanding capacity – but careful attention is also given to their balance sheets. As much as possible, we use our local contacts to check out management integrity prior to subscription and make a determined effort to visit the companies when in the relevant country. This investment category will never comprise more than 10 per cent of the fund (now a little over 5 per cent) and individual holdings, at cost anyway, will rarely exceed 1 per cent of the total portfolio. Here we hope to find tomorrow's star blooms. Here also we might experience our greatest disappointments. We operate a particularly vigorous weeding programme in this part of the herbaceous border, having no hesitation in discarding seedlings which disappoint on to the compost heap.

'With a substantial premium being placed on liquidity, smaller companies in the region have tended to be ignored by international investors over the recent period. One of the advantages of a specialist fund is that by holding a relatively large number of stocks, it can afford to carry a limited spread of younger companies. Thus the New Pacific Fund is particularly well-placed to apply this green-fingered guru's herbaceous border approach to portfolio management.'

Chapter 17

New blood in the United States

Anthony Cragg of Strong/Corneliuson

Experienced Asian managers are still in short supply in the United States. Their ranks have been strengthened by the arrival of Anthony Cragg, now running Asian and international funds from the relaxing lakeside environment of Strong/Corneliuson's office in Milwaukee. As a newcomer, he is also attuned to the differences in approach between American and Asian managers, and to the adaptations which sometimes prove necessary.

The sudden explosion of American interest in Asia and emerging markets has outpaced the availability of fund managers with experience in these markets. The problem is bad enough in Asia and the UK; in the US it is acute. The solution, all too often, is to take an experienced domestic fund manager and give him international responsibilities. Cragg sees significant drawbacks to this approach: such managers try to impose a US blueprint on international markets, which he believes inappropriate. 'What you need to do is to marry the analytical, quantitative US style with international awareness. That marriage is critical. You cannot pretend that all these markets are little Wall Streets. We've seen a lot of problems where people approach international markets in that very simplistic way.

'There is tremendous depth of expertise in the US; there is a discipline which is applied here, which typically wasn't applied in the international markets. But having said that, a lot of these disciplines rely on historical earnings and other numbers which simply aren't available. Many of the companies didn't exist ten years ago, and certainly for most you can't get numbers going back ten years. The very immaturity of the markets is sometimes hard for Americans to fathom.'

An entirely quantitative approach is inappropriate, in Cragg's view. 'Even today we get brokers telling us that they've screened a particu-

163

lar market to find stocks which come out well on price-to-book and price-to-cash flow, and here are the top ten on these criteria. But anyone who's been covering these markets for five minutes can run down the list and say, the guy who runs that company is a crook, this other company is in big trouble, and cross off 80 per cent of the names on first sight. You need to be aware of the local context. We will look at the rankings, and then apply judgment; you don't have to buy a job lot.'

PRECISION IMPRACTICABLE

Detailed comparisons of one company against others in the industry become trickier in international markets. Cragg finds that American analysts often want to do very precise calculations, concluding perhaps that a company would be fair value at 14 times earnings, so that it would be cheap at 12 times and expensive at 15 times. 'Often in an Asian context this is completely irrelevant. When we first invested in Advanced Info Service in Thailand, it had at the time a virtual monopoly of one of the fastest-growing businesses in one of the fastest-growing economies in the world. What on earth could you compare that to? What PE are you prepared to pay?' Global industry analysis he therefore finds to be of limited use.

One reason why rating comparisons cannot be too precise is the unpredictability of earnings in many international markets. 'America is an exhaustively analysed market where earnings estimates are honed to a high degree of precision. If the consensus earnings estimate on a company is 15.8 cents, and an analyst comes out with a forecast of 15.2 cents, that can be big news and hit the price. In Asia, you rarely have numerical analysis of that precision. Moreover, it is often wrong to get too upset about deviations from forecast: if the number comes in this year at 13 rather than 15, that doesn't mean that next year it won't be 19. When you are on a fast growth curve, there are hiccoughs along the way, and it is often wrong to get too hung up about those hiccoughs.'

Volatility is much greater than in the US markets, and again can be disconcerting. 'If you wanted to buy a stock when it was $15, and the next morning it is $16.25, the domestic investor's reaction is that the opportunity has been missed. In international markets, you cannot be put off by that sort of move. Similarly, if a stock suddenly falls 10 per cent in an efficient market like the US, that almost always means you have to look at it again, nine times out of ten it is the precursor of some real bad news. In the international markets it may mean absolutely nothing: the price may have dropped because of a clumsy foreign seller, a silly domestic rumour, or just a weak market that day. You can't afford to worry, you just buy more and average down, but this volatility can be quite unsettling for a US-trained investor.'

The importance of the key people is another feature of Asian investment which he finds himself explaining at length. 'American investors are used to public companies and professional directors; they are less used to family companies and the interplay of personalities. In Asia, you have to be aware of the undercurrents. You have to recognize that the public company is often only the tip of an iceberg, and know whether it is a good tip or a rubbish tip.'

Cragg's own approach has changed as a result of exposure to American methodology. 'You become more disciplined, more finicky, hopefully without losing the instinct and the guts which you do need in international markets.'

STOCK SELECTION ADDS VALUE

He is a confirmed stockpicker. 'What can we add at the macro level? We all get the same macro input, the same interest and inflation information. Whereas at the micro level we can have knowledge ahead of the pack. I don't mean inside knowledge, but we may have visited a company, we may talk to better analysts, we may just know the company better than the crowd. So you can get your nose ahead on the company level; I think it's very hard to on a macro level. We look at about forty markets around the world, and invest in thirty. There are very few at any one time which fall into the extremes where you must avoid the whole market, or where you just have to get in regardless of which stock you buy. In most countries, at most times, there are stocks in which you can make money, and stocks in which you can lose money. So I won't put 20 per cent of the fund in Thailand, or get completely out of Japan; we'll take bets, but we take company bets rather than country bets.'

He describes his stock selection as 'picking out the eyes. You do not need to have an opinion on every stock in the universe. If we're going into Finland, we don't need to analyse the top twenty stocks as you would if you were running a country fund, we can just pick

165

one like Nokia which makes sense to us. It is huge in mobile phone and telecommunication markets all round the world. It could be that there is another Finnish stock which is better than Nokia; that doesn't matter. I don't need to look at every Finnish stock, and nor do I need to have a firm view on the Finnish economy.'

His time horizon is 'as long as possible. We've still got cash coming in all the time. What we desperately want all the time are core holdings: stocks which we can buy, go on buying, and then buy more of, with a steady robot-like progression upwards. This should be possible in Asia because we still have structural growth; it's not like a mature cyclical market where you have to catch the last bit of the wave.'

SPOTTING THE CROSS-BORDER LINKS

Picking up cross-border connections is one of the advantages of running a global fund. A number of Australian companies are in the portfolio for their international exposure. Accor Asia Pacific operates hotels in Vietnam, China and Indonesia; Coca-Cola Amatil has the Coke franchise for a large part of Eastern Europe and all of Indonesia. Anzoil has potentially interesting oil and gas assets in Vietnam. Cable and Wireless in the UK is of interest primarily for its stake in Hong Kong Telecom, although it has important assets in Australia and Eastern Europe; it used to be thought that Cable & Wireless was cheap if it was capitalized at less than a billion pounds more than the value of its stake in the Hong Kong company, but today you pay only £650 million at the margin for a portfolio of businesses valued at anywhere between three and six times that. The case for another UK company, Trafalgar House, is the other way around: it is partly owned by the Jardine group, which has given it an edge in Asian business, and a recent large contract in Indonesia. CDL Hotels in Hong Kong has worldwide assets which are not fully appreciated by local investors.

Cragg maintains that 'to be a successful fund manager you have to be extremely bloody-minded, and more than a little arrogant. You have to be able to go off in one direction and say, that's what I'm doing, I don't care if everybody in the world disagrees. Time and time again, that is when you make the money. Now, if you are the domestic fund manager who has suddenly been made inter-national, you're not about to go off at a tangent, against the conventional wisdom. You've already got your head on the block, so you won't want to sharpen the executioner's axe at the same time. The people who do that must have some track record and experience.'

He has been consistently cynical on prospects in China, for example, and in 1993 was swimming against a strong tide of enthusiasm for the China theme. He believes the tendency towards consensus amongst US fund managers is if anything increasing, because so many are deriving all their input from a very narrow range of sources, principally the US investment banks.

He tries himself to talk to far more people, from a range of backgrounds, 'from second-line Malaysian brokers to friends in Thailand and journalists in Hong Kong; you can't be spoon-fed by a few international gurus. Some of the best people to talk to are outside the financial sector; journalists, or company executives. These contacts are impossible to build up instantly. There's no phone book in which you can look up "little Thai broker"; no directory of "One Thousand Good People to talk to in the Far East"!' He finds that many of the brokers are very inexperienced, and relates being introduced to an 'Indian specialist' who sheepishly admitted that he had yet to make his first visit.

Having lived in both Hong Kong and Japan, Cragg sees these as the two extremes of economic society. 'In one the whole emphasis is on the individual; in the other the whole emphasis is on the company. The Japanese operate very badly as individuals; the Chinese operate very badly as part of a large company. Even if they are running a big public company, they see it as a private company which happens to have gone public.'

His knowledge of Japan dates back to a three-year stint teaching English in Nagoya after coming down from Oxford, where he read English literature. In 1980, he joined Gartmore, working first in London and then in Hong Kong, before setting up the Tokyo office in 1984. A stint in London followed, setting up the international asset management operation of Dillon, Read, before the move to the United States in 1993.

He warns that Asian entrepreneurs are adept at supplying the stocks which the market wants, playing on the enthusiasm of naïve new investors. 'China was such a strong drug, it was like honey to bees, a lot of companies blew up that angle. It becomes a question of supply and demand.' If investors want companies with China exposure, China plays will be supplied – just as Hong Kong electronic companies came to the market in the early eighties to capitalize on investor demand.

Experience helps, he reckons, giving him a bank of impressions from a couple of thousand company visits over the course of his career, an awareness of patterns of development in emerging economies, and growing confidence. Another British fund manager commented that 'it is very easy to be silly in Asian markets' – selling Singapore after the Pan-Electric scandal, selling Hong Kong after Tiananmen Square, buying China concepts on euphoria. Cragg inspires confidence as a safe pair of hands.

Chapter 18

Emerging markets

'How would you have liked the opportunity to invest in Europe during the Industrial Revolution? Or Japan after World War Two? This type of fundamental economic change has been occurring for some time in the countries known as developing nations.' This is from Templeton, in a typically compelling marketing pitch. Get in on the ground floor, the firm urges.

The widespread acceptance of market economics, of foreign investment, and of the utility of stock markets has been one of the most remarkable phenomena of recent years. Richard Chenevix-Trench of Barings thinks this step 'so profound that even visionaries can only guess at the implications'.

New opportunities have opened up all over the globe, as one market after another has opened the doors to foreign investors. At the same time, many existing markets which had fallen from grace due to incompetent economic management have been spectacularly rehabilitated. Stock-market infrastructure has been improving by leaps and bounds, even though in many markets there is still considerable scope for improvement. Mark Mobius of Templeton observes that the number of emerging markets in which Templeton could invest increased from six in 1987 to twenty-five in 1993.

The amount of new money which has flooded into these markets is extraordinary. According to Jardine Fleming,[1] foreign investment in emerging markets now accounts for one-third of all cross-border equity capital flows, and 'the question investors should be asking themselves is not whether they can afford to have an exposure to emerging markets, but whether they can afford not to.'

Definitions of emerging markets vary widely, although there is a growing consensus that an emerging market is a stock market of

1 'Dollars Sense', October 1994

169

a low to middle income economy, as defined by the World Bank (per capita GNP of US$8,356 or more in 1992). This classification takes no account of the level of development of the stock market itself. This is convenient for investment managers seeking to invest significant amounts of capital, as it includes well-established stock markets such as Malaysia. Other managers broaden the scope further. Templeton for example includes Hong Kong and Singapore in its emerging market universe, even though these are high income economies, on the basis that they offer exposure to adjacent developing countries.

MARK MOBIUS

Mark Mobius has done more to popularize emerging market investment than any other man on earth. His presentations of the long-term conceptual case for emerging markets are succinct and persuasive, and he is a master of the soundbite. He has become known as 'the Indiana Jones of emerging market investment', and cultivates the image, posing in suitable hats and trenchcoats in recognizably esoteric corners of the globe. As a magazine pointed out recently, if you were going to invent a guru, you might come up with a figure like this: eccentric, strange clothes, bald head (other press coverage tells us he shaves it every morning), a couple of doctorates, iron confidence, and a jet-setting schedule (we are now told he does most of his sleeping on planes, and Templeton has just bought him a Lear jet). The latest press photograph shows him gazing in visionary fashion over a crystal ball.

On top of all this, he was in the right place at the right time. Templeton had the foresight to set up a fund for emerging market investment in 1987. This was perfect timing. Few other large-scale emerging market funds have been established quite as long, and in the United States especially, Templeton secured an advantage of several years.

The performance of Mobius's flagship, the Templeton Emerging Market Fund, has been excellent. It achieved compound annual returns of 30 per cent in the seven years from inception in February 1987. This is a tremendous return by any standards, and comfortably outpaced the IFC composite index.

EARNINGS GROWTH AND RE-RATING

A large part of the return of any emerging market fund over this period, however, would have come from re-rating. Based on IFC figures, the historic PE for Asian emerging markets had risen to 33.3 in February 1994, compared with about 18.6 when the fund was started, a rise of 80 per cent. Latin America was on a historic PE of 20.6, compared with 4.7 at the outset, a more than fourfold re-rating. The composite index by February 1994 was on a historic PE of 26.8, compared with 9.4 seven years earlier, an overall re-rating of 2.8 times. If the stocks in the Templeton fund experienced a comparable re-rating, that would imply underlying earnings growth of the order of 12 per cent per annum – which is good, but less than sensational, particularly since it relates to a period during which corporate profits in many countries staged a spectacular rebound as the underlying economies were reformed and deregulated.

This calculation should be treated with caution, as index compilers have serious problems in emerging markets, a topic covered in chapter 20 on investment issues. Nevertheless, the IFC's ratings seem to be of the right order of magnitude, and Templeton has no argument with the calculation. Where it may be unfair is that the index composition has changed dramatically. The number of companies in the IFC's total emerging market universe has doubled in the last seven years, and many new companies have come to the market – and presumably been added to the indices – at a premium. This would account for part of the re-rating, and imply that underlying earnings growth had been somewhat higher.

In practice, of course, markets opened up and were 'discovered' at different times. Fund managers like Kerr Neilson, Marc Faber, and Mark Mobius, who were able to roam the world in search of the next chrysalis, were able to ride a succession of exhilarating rebounds and re-ratings, catching the best of one market and moving on to the next.

The danger now is that expectations for emerging market returns have become overblown. Once ratings stabilize, growth in share prices becomes dependent on growth in corporate earnings. The base figure for corporate profit expectations should be similar to that for nominal GDP, unless the profit share of GDP is changing, or the companies of interest are unrepresentative of the market as a whole. The profit share may change because of variations in interest rates or taxation, or because of structural change in the returns on labour and capital. As badly managed economies restructure, profit improvements tend to be dramatic. As markets develop, the listed companies become more representative of the whole private sector. Privatization of state-owned assets may generate productivity gains. This period can be spectacular. The question is whether, for emerging markets in general, the exceptional restructuring rebound in corporate earnings has now run its course.

Jan Kingzett of Schroders thinks there is still a long way to go. Returns on equity in Brazil, for example, are shockingly bad, and could treble before reaching a normal level.

As so often happens, the number of emerging market funds is proliferating after a period of exceptional historical performance. The underlying story of recovery, reform and growth is a sensationally good one, but as always investors should be wary of overpaying for growth. The weight of new money may itself continue to push the markets higher, although offset to some extent by a growing supply of stock from privatizations and new listings. However, investors are now being lured in with marketing statements such as 'Asia's emerging economies and stock markets can only go upwards from here.' As the cycle matures, there will be increasing vulnerability to disappointment.

PROBLEMS OF SIZE

Apart from the diminishing (although still very positive) returns available in each stock market, there are clear signs that size is an impediment to performance in emerging markets. In the UK, Stewart Ivory has produced a table of one-year returns by emerging market funds up to mid-1994, which shows an almost perfect negative correlation of returns with fund size; admittedly the relationship a quarter later was less clear-cut. Likewise, the newer Templeton open-ended funds have been notably duller performers than the original closed-end Emerging Market Fund. The new funds have higher levels of cash, but it also seems likely that size has had an adverse impact on Templeton's ability to select and monitor the stocks.

The inflows of funds must have been extraordinarily difficult to cope with. Much of Mobius's historic track record was laid down when managing a fraction of the present total. He started in 1987 with US$60 million. By late 1992 this had become US$1.4 billion;

by late 1994 it was US$7 billion, up five fold in two years, and spread over twenty-six funds. Other firms, such as Scudder, experienced a similar build-up.

STOCK SELECTION INCREASINGLY CRITICAL

At the same time, stock selection is becoming more critical. In the early stages of stock-market opening, no great sophistication was required – you could buy the bank, the brewery, the cement company and the telecommunications share in each market, and wait for them to quintuple. As the ratings become higher and average returns more sedate, discrimination becomes more critical – doubly so as the amounts invested increase, and with them the effective cost of initiating and unwinding each position.

This suggests that it may be wise to concentrate emerging market investments with fund managers who either have well-established research networks for these countries (for example, Schroders or Fidelity, and in Asia Jardine Fleming), or are unusually small, adept, and agile.

Jan Kingzett points out that emerging markets are a stockpicker's dream, and that the big index components are often the least attractive investments. He dismisses the idea that there is anything different about emerging markets; Schroders thinks in terms of a continuum of economic development. The places you end up in are different, he says, but the decision making process is the same whether you are in the US or Japan, Brazil or Thailand. It may, however, take local knowledge to understand some of the peculiarities and pitfalls of specific markets, and it is the combination of a strong local analytical network with experienced fund managers which puts the firm in a strong position. Schroders maintains that stock selection adds value consistently, year in and year out, and the less developed the market the greater the potential for outperformance. Kingzett finds it bizarre that some firms devote tremendous effort to analysing whether to buy BP or Shell, which is extraordinarily difficult, and yet fall for the argument that asset allocation is the sole key to emerging markets.

The best managers of large emerging market funds agree that one of the keys to success is to concentrate on what is important and not get too distracted by small sideshows. 'We have fantastic prospectuses coming in every day,' Kingzett says: 'every time you turn around, someone has just secured special access to Uzbekistan, or launched a new Mongolia fund, or spotted a whizzo new convertible in Papua New Guinea. There is a huge variety of attractive opportunities which could treble, but most of these are too small, and can just take your eye off the ball. Botswana may be great fun for intermediaries, but it's irrelevant to all but the smallest funds.'

Richard Chenevix-Trench suggests that it is also advisable to concentrate on countries which have some strategic importance to the world, and are therefore less likely to fail. If Eastern Europe or Russia were to run into difficulties, for example, the OECD economies would have a major problem, so there is a vested interest in ensuring that they succeed.

Schroder stockpicking focuses on the long-term beneficiaries of domestic economic growth: companies with a strong market share, a clear growth path, good management and a sustainable competitive advantage. Their philosophy is to let the regional growth do the work, fill the portfolios with the more predictable high-quality companies, and avoid trying to trade in and out of markets in which transaction costs are very high. It works very well; Kingzett's fund, although now amounting to almost US$1 billion, has been near the top of the performance lists since its 1992 launch.

Andrew Economos, now running the Tiedemann/Economos Global Emerging Growth Fund, a US$100 million hedge fund, used to have similar constraints, but is now adopting a much more active approach. The sheer size of the liquidity flows had resulted in a two-tier market, in which the relatively neglected smaller companies had become significantly undervalued relative to the index stocks. He is now trying to zero in on specific sectors and research them in far greater detail than before. Within a quarterly sweep of two or three weeks through a particular region, for example, he may now spend three days in one country trying to understand thoroughly all four of its cement stocks. He describes his approach as both top-down and bottom-up, and is disciplined on both fronts. His core portfolio accounts for about 70 per cent of the fund, and is intended to be held for several years; the remaining 30 per cent is actively managed, on a timescale of three weeks to three months, and overall portfolio turnover is around 350 per cent. Economos says that the fund is both unleveraged and conservative, and is experienced enough to understand emerging market risk. In the abstract, one would say that the risk inherent in this style is very high, but for a talented individual running a small fund, the anomalies and opportunities in these inefficient markets remain huge. While trying to cover a huge range of markets, Economos is very focused on investment. He is also very highly regarded, so his performance will be interesting to watch.

THE BIGGEST RISKS ARE NOT ALWAYS THE MOST OBVIOUS

Overall, the intrinsic risks in emerging economies are probably lower than perceived – individual countries may be very risky, but collectively much less so. Richard Chenevix-Trench believes that international investors probably worry too much about events within these countries, and not enough about the foreign flows of funds. What happens when there is a rush for the door?

Marc Faber has been one of the shrewdest chroniclers of emerging markets over the last couple of decades. Apart from his analysis of the life cycle of emerging markets (see p 130), he has produced a fascinating account of the lessons to be drawn from the great emerging market of the nineteenth century, America. (The full article is reproduced in Appendix F.) Describing the booms and busts of that era in infrastructure, property, and stock markets, he makes the following observations:

- Vicious cycles can take place within long-term growth industries
- Severe financial crises can occur for a number of reasons, including excessive speculation, and not necessarily because of a general or lasting downturn in the real economy
- Warning signs were frequently ignored because of the promising backdrop of industrialization
- Stock prices can fall long before the economy turns down or profits decline, simply because monetary conditions deteriorate
- Foreign investors throughout the nineteenth century were latecomers to each investment fad. They bought American canal, railroad and industrial stocks at or near the peak in each cycle. When prices were low and business conditions depressed, foreigners were usually absent, having burnt their fingers in the previous boom.

'People who in the nineteenth century would have bought American canal and railroad shares (most of which failed) are now buying

China infrastructure funds and telephone companies in the remotest regions of the world,' Faber wryly comments. 'Investing in rapidly growing emerging economies, like that of the US in the last century, is much trickier than it appears to the casual observer.'

Mark Mobius makes the same point: 'Many investors think the tiger is a tame animal.'

Chapter 19

Direct investment

When some of Asia's top equity managers are struggling to find value in the listed securities markets, now much more highly rated than in the past, it is no surprise that increasing attention is being focused on unlisted investment.

Some of those considering it, however, are well-connected individuals – such as Marc Faber and David Crichton-Watt – who are thinking of individual deals with partners whom they know. Institutionalized direct investment is relatively new in Asia, and sceptics abound.

Historical figures are scarce, since few if any funds have been through a full cycle and returned all funds to investors. Comparisons are tricky, but it is probably a mistake to assume that if direct investment represents a worthy diversification in developed markets, then it must necessarily be better in an emerging market.

Many direct investment funds highlight the returns achieved on the realized portion of the portfolio, without taking into consideration unrealized investments, cash balances, or hefty management fees. Cynics argue that direct investment funds are highly rewarding – for the managers – and that the historical returns have been lower than those available in the public markets. 'Higher fees for lower returns at higher risk and less liquidity', one sceptic summed up.

It is probably fair to say, however that many listed shares have been re-rated to a greater extent than the private deals available in the same markets. Anil Thadani, the managing partner of Schroder Capital Partners, observes that in the early eighties, he could buy businesses in Thailand on very attractive valuations of three to five times earnings. At the time, public markets were not much more expensive – perhaps four to six times earnings. Now, he says, he can still do deals on four to seven times earnings, and may go up to a multiple of eight in exceptional cases, while listed companies may be two or three times as expensive.

177

Moreover, the managers of most direct investment funds believe that they should be able to achieve net returns to investors in the range of 20–30 per cent per year. Michael Kwee of Prudential Asia expects that the effective return on their first fund will eventually prove to be in the high twenties, net to investors; but cautions that it may be more realistic to expect a net return in the low twenties on the second fund. He thinks that they will achieve fewer big hits (one of their first was the Taiwanese computer company, Acer), but that there are now more good diversified bread-and-butter deals available than hitherto.

CULTURAL DIFFERENCES

Historically, one of the problems of direct investment in Asia has been cultural. In Hong Kong and South-East Asia, capital is abundant, and good projects can often be privately financed without recourse to institutional sources. The entrepreneurial nature of the large conglomerates enables them to pick up a disproportionate share of new deals, and fledgling companies may seek to bring in partners with helpful connections, rather than neutral outside financiers. The formality of some western organizations can also be a deterrent.

Direct investment managers suggest that this is changing, and that there is a new generation of entrepreneurs who do not necessarily have family money, would prefer to avoid being sucked into large family companies, and are more attuned to western styles of financing. In countries like India, capital may be less readily available, and there are many highly competent managers without local access to finance.

Political uncertainty in Hong Kong has helped: at least one entrepreneur has sold out to Prudential and departed for a very long holiday, retaining an option to buy back his business after the transfer of sovereignty.

Meanwhile, mezzanine financing has been a mainstay of many existing funds. The companies like to persuade target companies that the presence and expertise of a blue-chip institution on the shareholder list will smooth the path to listing, and there may be an element of truth in that. For many companies, it just enables them to raise capital a year or two ahead of the listing, on terms worked back from those expected in the initial public offering. Funds which are restricted to unlisted investments can be at a disadvantage here, particularly in markets where IPO terms are regulated, as they have to exit on listing and are unable to participate in any re-rating in the aftermarket.

David Paterson of HSBC Private Equity Management emphasizes that it is essential in the direct investment business to be woven into the Asian business fabric. The Hongkong Bank parentage gives his company a useful information feed; it also gives them some ongoing leverage, as many businessmen would be reluctant to upset the bank. He is extremely cynical about the prospects of newcomers: 'People who parachute in get raped.'

ADDING VALUE

One way to secure above-average deals is to offer more than money. Most firms offer some sort of network of contacts; depending on the industry and the markets which are to be tackled, this can occasionally be of value. Access to technology may be a more compelling advantage.

One of the most interesting approaches to date has been that of Asian Strategic Investments Corporation (ASIMCO), which was set up specifically to pursue direct investments in China, and is run by Bill Kaye's partner Jack Perkowski. Its first fund raised was the China Automotive Components Group. New industries in the sights include breweries and cement, and the intention is to structure similar limited partnerships for these sectors.

ASIMCO's basic premise is that China, in order to achieve its economic development goals, will require a tremendous input of management knowhow and technology as well as capital, and that the United States is well placed to supply all three. The ability to supply management and technology can therefore be used as leverage to ensure advantageous equity participation. It is focusing on whole industries, rather than on individual companies, which should make it easier to build up a complete business picture, and the sectors so far chosen are clearly growth areas.

The total number of cars on the road in China in 1993 was only 1.4 million. Car production is forecast to increase rapidly, to produce about this number *per year* by the end of the century.[1] The automotive industry has been declared one of China's four 'pillar industries'

1 *Financial Times* figures.

(along with power generation, telecommunications, and natural resources), because of the need for improved transportation links, the assumed catalytic influence of automotive technology on the rest of the manufacturing sector, and its potential for job creation. While the major car assemblers have all imported foreign technology, and in most cases formed joint ventures with foreign companies, the motor components sector has been highly fragmented, with over four thousand small companies each making one or two parts each.

China Automotive Components Group, unlike most previous direct investment vehicles, has the ability to provide specialized, hands-on expertise. Senior executives have been hired from Chrysler and other multinationals, as well as from the Chinese automotive industry. In September 1994, six months after raising its first US$160 million, it had a staff of forty in Beijing: a few financial people, but mainly engineers and line managers. This group was negotiating the various joint ventures, from well over a hundred companies screened, and would go on to manage them. The three leading Chinese entities in the automotive industry were expected to come in as co-investors in the various projects.

In terms of lining up good investments, this approach makes sense. It does however depend on a few key managers. Some investors would prefer to back an established company, with a greater depth of managerial resources. American Standard recently tapped this pool of money for US$83 million to fund its expansion into China, and the Hong Kong company Siu-Fung raised US$85 million for a similar purpose.

The more critical questions may be whether the management group can remain useful to its investee companies and partners on an ongoing basis, after the initial transfer of technology and knowhow (ie, whether it retains any leverage); whether its expansion plans are excessive (there is now talk of raising another US$1 billion); and whether its exit expectations are realistic. China Auto Components Group is intended to be liquidated in eight to ten years, and its stake in individual joint ventures after three to five years. The mechanism is yet to be determined.

NEW MARKETS: CHINA AND INDIA

Anil Thadani, in a view shared by many experienced direct investors, is very cautious about committing his funds in China. His comment is that what is appropriate for the strategic investor is not necessarily appropriate to the financial investor. 'I believe that China is a fantastic market for strategic investors. I think that if you are a Pepsi-Cola, or a General Motors, or a Pizza Hut, you need to be in China today, because what is happening in China is for real. It is opening up, it is an enormous market, an enormous consumer market. You have to be there to establish your product, because the dividends will be there to come for years and years. But you have to have a ten, twenty, or fifty-year view, and be prepared to invest today for the future. A financial investor is totally different. I want returns in three to five years, maybe even six years. But I want real returns; I want to be able to sell the business, and get my money out, and give it back to my investors. In order to do that, there are certain things I must have.

'I must have a financial infrastructure in place. I must have reliable information: accounting information, and market information. Neither of those exist in China. There is no tradition of accounting in the country. We have seen numbers where the sales and the profit figure are the same . . . there are Chinese companies which say that when they have a dollar of goods sold, it is all profit, because they have no cost of goods sold, and labour is basically free. So you have to reconstitute all the numbers that you get. When you reconstitute numbers, you have to use assumptions. When you use assumptions, you bring in uncertainty, and that makes the deal less interesting. As regards market information: how can you do a survey of whether a particular product will work or not work? There is no mechanism.

'I need a legal infrastructure. I need to be able to rely on contracts that I enter into, because I am managing other people's money. I need recourse; when something goes wrong, I need to be able to go back and fix it. You can't always do that in China, so that scares me. And finally, I need capital markets. How do I get out? How do I raise more capital? What if the company needs money? Capital market, rule of law, accounting principles, marketing information: how can you invest someone else's money in China without those four? Yet, millions and millions of dollars have been given to inexperienced "dealmakers" to invest in China. Most of the people who have invested in China over the last five or ten years are not really smiling any more; they're beginning to wonder when they're going to see their money again.

'One of China's big problems is its sheer size. You do a deal with some provincial guy, he says he has the authority, and someone in

Beijing says no, you should have checked with me . . . so China is too big to handle. This will change: Chinese are very smart people, and they have asked every accounting firm and every law firm in the world to get over there and help them redraft, so a time will come when China will provide a great opportunity. But a country like China will produce dealflow for the next fifty thousand years, why do we have to be there today when it's much more risky, why don't we just wait and go there five years from now? What's the rush?'

He is now much more enthusiastic about India. 'You have an English-speaking population, people who have been educated like us, English accounting, and the rule of law; a fantastic pool of managerial and entrepreneurial talent, underemployed, available, begging to be employed – and now finally a government which welcomes foreign investment. For years I never went to India for business, because the government's attitude was totally unacceptable. But today India looks very, very attractive. The current government has done a wonderful job. They're not there yet, and I don't for a moment suggest that India is a bed of roses. It is still a minor nightmare. But when I compare the two, China and India, it's a no-brainer to me.'

Chapter 20

Investment issues

'ASIA IS DIFFERENT . . .'

One of the great alarm bells in any stock market is the statement, 'this time is different . . .' and the geographical equivalent should be treated with similar caution. However, some generalizations can be made.

Growth in Asia is higher than in the west, the confidence is higher, and what can be done in a short time is staggering. On the negative side, regulation is much weaker, and enforcement is worse. Investors are well advised to tread warily, and consider who is telling them anything, and why. Even more importantly, they should try to work out who is selling them stock, and why. Timescales can be different; details of investor lore and short-term investor psychology may be different. The real differences however are as follows:

1. Other players are not primarily institutional

They are mainly corporate, and retail. In Thailand in 1994, such players typically accounted for 60–70 per cent of trading, according to the daily breakdown. Foreigners typically represented 15–30 per cent, and the local mutual funds 5–10 per cent, with a final category of principal trading by brokers.

Jan Kingzett reckons that the typical Schroders competitor in an Asian market is a little old lady with a carrier bag full of notes. She is running her own money, not other people's money, and she's good. But she tends to be influenced by her friends and the newspapers, and she wants to make money in the next two to three weeks – or preferably the next two to three days.

The corporate players may however be more dangerous. They do, after all, have the benefit of inside information, and are often shameless manipulators.

2. They are driven by absolute, not relative, returns

The little old lady is less than pleased if she loses 10 per cent of her savings, regardless of whether the index is down 20 per cent. Unlike a pension fund trustee, she tends to think in absolute terms on the upside as well.

3. Entrepreneurial control

The controlling shareholders, who are rarely institutional and may be individuals or families, in practice have a high degree of autonomy. They may take the company in directions which to an outsider are irrational. They may do deals which the outside investors don't like. They may not distinguish very clearly between their public and their private interests.

4. Momentum players

The little old lady will buy after a bottom and into the rise. She does not have much of a handle on fundamental valuations of individual stocks. She does not have much of a mental framework of valuation – which is anyway made trickier by the absence of long-term bond markets in the region, so her benchmark may be the return on short or medium-term bank deposits, or on property. She does not tend to think in terms of a long-term savings plan which has such and such a percentage in equities; she will buy if she thinks they are going up, and sell if she thinks the market is dead.

She is, in short, a momentum player. Since most retail investors, many local institutions, and a fair number of foreign institutions are momentum players, volatility is unusually high.

Companies who effectively make a market in their own shares will tend in the long run to reduce volatility. They introduce a different risk. If you are buying, remember to think about who may be selling you the stock, and whether they know more than you.

5. The importance of property

Property is a more prominent part of the business scene in Hong Kong and South-East Asia than in western economies. Asian businessmen prefer to buy rather than rent, and banks prefer to lend against assets rather than cash flow. Many Asian individuals are active and well-informed investors in property. There is a school of thought that physical property is an investment, whereas shares are a gamble.

6. Liquidity, and how fast it can disappear

Heather Manners of Henderson thinks that continued marketability is the biggest risk of all. A corollary is that there is no safe haven in a major market decline, as institutional investors sell what they can. Blue-chip shares therefore come under sustained selling pressure, whatever their supposed defensive merits (frequently the prices are anyway too high for these to be relevant), and smaller companies may either hold their own on no turnover or collapse under the influence of any attempt to sell.

Newcomers should be aware of:

- Economic and business cycles, as distinct from secular trends
- The normal magnitude of such cycles, country by country
- The limitations of government statistics (what is mis-stated, and what they cannot know)
- The characters behind the companies
- Other market players (corporate, retail, local institutions, existing foreign investors, new foreign sources) – current stance, likely shifts, and flows of funds
- Accounting differences and deficiencies
- Transaction costs – which can be hefty, especially when dealing spreads are included
- Settlement difficulties and counterparties
- Registration delays and uncertainties (still a major problem in Malaysia in 1994!)
- Legal framework (US registered funds have problems in certain markets)

Whether foreign investors need to try to understand Asian politics is debatable. For some companies, political connections are vital;

185

foreign investors are at a disadvantage here compared with the locals. Some try to keep up, and some keep a disdainful distance. At the national level, locals usually take politics far more seriously than foreigners. (The issues tend to relate to stability rather than policy.) In recent years, this has presented outstanding buying opportunities, notably in Thailand and Hong Kong. A new consensus therefore is that politics can be ignored. This may not always be correct, but may still be a reasonable working hypothesis most of the time.

ASIAN COUNTRIES ARE DIFFERENT

Trading psychology is different from market to market. An enthusiastic reaction to bonus issues ('free shares'), and an emphasis on absolute prices rather than percentage movements, can be found in several markets. More importantly, the details of share price movements are often determined partly by market structure (board lots, registration periods, etc). Much of this affects dealing, rather than longer-term investment decisions.

Familiarity with the corporate environment, and the key players behind individual stocks, can be important, and requires experience. Liquidity conditions and stock-market development vary enormously. Martin Shenfield of Ki Pacific says that 'the most dangerous thing one can do is to view Asia as a monolith. We do not assume that an approach which is successful in one market will automatically work in another.' However, 'greed and fear will out, in any market. Japan is the ultimate proof of that. If ever there was anywhere which would have been culturally statist and consensual, it would have been Japan.'

Cross-border valuation comparisons are tricky. Asian retail investors act on the basis of historic valuations in their own market; a Hong Kong individual who owns Hang Seng bank will rarely compare it with a bank in Thailand. American investors, by contrast, like to make cross-border comparisons but have no sense of regional market history. An investor with both perspectives is therefore advantageously placed.

VOLATILE SENTIMENT

Marc Faber's 'Gloom, Boom and Doom Report' could not be more aptly named for the volatile swings of sentiment in Asian markets. I personally would not end on a note of doom, but gloom and boom are to be seen in rapid succession and glorious excess.

An active secondary market in share application forms is a fairly reliable sign of excess on the upside. In the last few years, such markets have sprung up in Indonesia, in various Chinese cities, and even in late 1994 in Thailand. The 1992 influx of hopefuls from all parts of the country into Shenzhen, for example, caused serious problems of crowd control. Some reports put the numbers in the millions; certainly there were hundreds of thousands. Police were tending the queues with electric cattle-prods, and there was at least one fatality.

By mid-1994, Hong Kong television was showing us pictures of the Shenzhen Stock Exchange morgue, with brokers asleep at their desks having seen no orders for several days.

A week later, the market had jumped 100 per cent.

Hong Kong and Singapore, of course, are mature institutional markets, and do not behave like this . . . Well, actually, they do, and so does the US market, but there are differences of degree. In late 1992, as Charles Fowler pointed out, Singapore was deemed to be ex-growth and quite irredeemably dull, a non-event in an exciting region. Two years later, the market is 50 per cent higher and it is once again a dynamic Asian hub.

At the stock level, I remember buying the Hongkong Bank (now HSBC Holdings) in 1990, on a day when it was described by a colleague as the worst-run bank in the world. It rose more than six-fold over the next three years. By the time it had risen four-fold, it was already being described as the best-run bank in the world.

MARKET CORRELATIONS

One of the arguments used in favour of investment in Asia is the low correlation between most of the individual Asian markets, and between Asian and international markets. The influx of global funds is however likely to change this. In particular, historic correlations between closed markets are likely to increase once they are open to cross-border flows. Correlations spike upwards whenever there is a sharp move in the US or Japan. That is, while markets may not be highly correlated from day to day or month to month (which is what the historic figures will tell you), a crisis in one major market can bring them all down together.

This does not, of course, invalidate all of the other strong arguments for investing in Asia, many of which were outlined in the introduction.

TOP-DOWN VERSUS BOTTOM-UP

Views polarize on this issue. The following attempts to summarize the arguments, most of which have been set out in earlier chapters.

Asset allocator arguments:

'Studies show that . . .' 70 per cent or 80 per cent of returns come from asset allocation.

Share price movements within a market are highly correlated, so stockpicking is pointless if you don't get the market movement right.

The market movements within Asia can be so dramatic that those returns dwarf the additional value added from stock selection.

Market movements are predictable, you just need to keep a close eye on domestic money supply and international flows of funds.

Stockpicker arguments:

The studies are invalid, most of them were done over very short time periods or under different market conditions.

The numbers may be correct, but we can't pick the turns, so it's irrelevant.

Market movements can be predicted occasionally, but stock selection generates superior returns year after year.

Companies give you a better, faster feel of the real economy than looking at official statistics; to call the markets correctly, you have to have this micro input.

Asset allocation is the lazy way out!

To some extent the differences are less extreme than they may appear, and many managers use a mix of both approaches. Many fund managers stress the importance of company visits in giving them vital input on economic trends, even though they then place their bets in the big index stocks. Others pick stocks which are positioned to benefit from identified trends and themes, rather than doing very detailed company analysis, but regard this more as allocation than stock selection.

Marketing imposes uneven pressures. Most institutional investors feel the need to present firm views on the big-picture backdrop, and may therefore spend a significant amount of time honing their view on the economy and the currency so that they don't get caught out under questioning – even if they have no great conviction on such matters, and would be better off concentrating on decisions where they can add value. The big picture is felt to be more interesting to clients, and a safer topic. Top-down allocators are less likely to be questioned aggressively on their individual stock selections.

Cynical stockpickers also claim that the top-down types focus on a few big issues in air-conditioned comfort, and are more likely to go home at a civilized hour, whereas bottom-up analysts contend with innumerable details and bone-shaking journeys. (Armed receptionists, primitive mines, and jungle breakdowns are all part of the training, although it has to be confessed that the big hotels in Asian capital cities present fewer hardships.)

The answer may be that the best strategy depends mainly on the stage of development of the market. If you have an undiscovered market where values of all common stocks are bombed out, then you can normally analyse macro-economic or structural reasons for the overall valuation to change and buy the larger stocks; correspondingly when these markets are undeveloped they are prone to euphoria, on which you may want to sell out entirely. We have seen many such markets in Asia, but the game has run for some years and is now played mainly in Africa and the states of the former Soviet Union. The key question then is whether you want to be there at all.

The other determinant is the market cycle. Individual markets which are more developed can still become spectacularly euphoric or excessively depressed, for identifiable reasons. Opportunities do, therefore, arise to predict market performance with some degree of certainty; this still happens more in Asian markets than in, say, the US. For most of the time, and in most of the markets, no such strong view is appropriate. In such conditions, stock selection is vital.

THE IMPORTANCE OF COMPANY VISITING

Even Peter Montgomery of Murray Johnstone, who thinks that stock selection is bunk, stresses the importance of getting out to meet local companies. He finds this essential to get a feel for the real economy. In 1990 he realized that an improving US book-to-bill ratio for semiconductors and previous capital expenditure by Singapore's manufacturing facilities would lead to a boom in exports of electronic goods, which are lightly represented in the market but represent the largest component of domestic exports – and chose to play it through the residential property developers, loading up with City Developments.

Elizabeth Tran of IDS comments that Japanese company visits have in recent years provided invaluable input on what is happening in South-East Asia or China. For several years, economists were worrying about the decline in direct investment by Japanese companies into Malaysia and other ASEAN countries, although this was in part because the earlier investments were already generating excellent cash flow and being ploughed back into expansion. 'Official statistics don't tell you enough, and may be unreliable. Governments normally publicize the investment approval figure rather than actual inflows, because the numbers are bigger.'

She observes, 'Mark Twain was absolutely right on statistics. Look at Golden Plus and the structuring of its Shanghai residential project. The Malaysian investment is routed through Hong Kong, so it's counted as a Hong Kong investment. The joint venture partner is a PRC national who is also routing his contribution through Hong Kong. So you have a Malaysia/mainland joint venture and it's counted as a 100 per cent Hong Kong investment.' So much for the statistics showing that Hong Kong accounts for a huge proportion of foreign investment into China.

Peter Montgomery also likes to 'develop a feel for the local fat cats – an increasingly important force over the last ten years', and to ask them about their own investment plans for the next few years.

When we spoke in the third quarter of 1994, he was about to head over to the Philippines to reassess that market, undeterred by its strong performance of the previous few years as there could be a major structural change under way. 'When you have Mr Quek, Mr Kuok and Mr Liem all putting money into the Philippines, that's telling you something. That's telling you there's a reasonable prospect of a return to an Asian rate of growth. And air-conditioner sales are up 30 per cent because the brown-outs have stopped.'

It goes without saying that all the stockpickers find visits essential. They like to visit several companies in the industry, both in the country and elsewhere; and to ask lots of questions about the competition, the suppliers, and the clients. 'Which companies do you respect?' is one suggested question. Visiting factories can be an eye-opener.

Most fund managers, however, cannot devote the time to deep analysis – building detailed profit models, for example. Overlook Investments and Value Partners are exceptional in this respect. One manager at a large stockpicking institution was candid: 'We say it's all very fundamental research, that we need to get there before the brokers, and find out things other people don't know. Actually it's all about getting a feel.'

MANAGEMENT

Developing an understanding of the business is one thing, and wandering around factories can be revealing. A feel for the controlling shareholders may be more important still. Integrity is a key consideration for most of the battle-hardened managers interviewed, and particular caution is warranted with newly listed companies with no track record in the public domain. Even the quality of historic numbers should be suspect for such companies.

Stephen Swift of Credit Suisse comments that there are many privately controlled companies in Asia which happen to have a public quote, and very few which behave as if they are answerable to the shareholders at large. This was brought home to him as a young analyst before the first oil crisis, when he was granted an audience with the great Tan Chin Tuan of OCBC. Swift enquired about their low dividend payout, and was sternly admonished: 'Young man, it is very generous of us to allow you to be a shareholder. It is a good company, you will do well if you hold it, and if you don't like our policy you can sell your shares.'

OCBC shareholders have in truth had little to grumble about over the years. Unfortunately, not all controlling shareholders are as scrupulous in their stewardship of shareholders' assets. Unpredictable changes of direction are unpopular with foreign investors. It can be irritating to build up a position in a lightly-geared manufacturing company, only to find it borrowing heavily for property investment in China. Deals with connected parties, such as relatives and associates, also cause suspicion.

Gavin Graham of Citibank reckons that 'the one final and basic test for stock selection is management, especially in places like Indonesia and Thailand where private and public companies are so intermingled. The price at which assets are shuffled from one hand to another is entirely dependent on the good offices of management and their desire to keep the minority shareholders happy enough to come back for the next offering. What is the track record? Has the management consistently legged over the minorities? If so, there is a very strong likelihood that they will do so again. You need to distinguish between companies you can trust, like Indorama, which makes textiles and will raise money on the equity market because it is a useful way of financing the expansion of production facilities, and those which see a stupid foreigner with a cheque book and calculate how much they can steal.'

It is sometimes unwise to count on entrepreneurs wishing to retain the goodwill of foreign investors as a class. For all but the largest companies, there may seem to be plenty more foreigners where the first victims came from. Embarrassment is not a factor; if they don't want to talk to you, they won't agree to see you. Some major companies have alternately cultivated investors, and refused to see them for years.

INTUITION

Several of the most successful managers stressed the importance of intuition for keeping out of trouble. Kathryn Langridge of Perpetual sold Atlas Industries just before it collapsed, within weeks of taking over her portfolio, after meeting chief executive Al Miller. She cannot now entirely explain the decision, except that 'you know, the fur on the back of your neck . . .' Instinct, she says, has kept her out of trouble time and again. In 1994, it is keeping her out of many of the racier Malaysian shares.

SUPPLY AND DEMAND

Asia's entrepreneurs are adept at supplying what the market demands, whether in the rag trade or in financial markets. If the fashion is for China plays, they will be repackaged and spun off from the existing operations. If investors call for telecommunication shares, a flood of such issues will come to market.

Few Asian entrepreneurs are preoccupied by building up one particular business to the exclusion of others. They are adept and adaptable deal-makers, and will readily take a turn and move on to the next idea. This does not mean that they will not invest in and grow their existing businesses; it merely means that they may not give them their undivided attention. If the market is offering them a high price for one business, they will sell all or part, and invest the proceeds in another venture.

Elizabeth Tran is cynical about the entrepreneurial mentality, and about concept stocks. 'Most controlling shareholders treat institutional investors as roast pig. As for fund managers who want to participate in the China boom, I ask whether they want to participate as a diner at the banquet, or as the dish in the centre of the table.'

SMALL COMPANIES

The merits of small Asian companies as an asset class are dubious. The research is inconclusive. James Alexandroff of GT, manager of one of the largest Asian smaller companies funds, is surprisingly negative. Over its short history, the GT Asian Smaller Companies Index has consistently underperformed the larger indices. Many small Asian companies are engaged in labour-intensive manufacturing, with no strong franchise, poor middle management, and a highly cyclical business. The service sector is relatively lightly represented. Optimists think that there may be periods of cyclical outperformance, towards the tail-end of the US economic cycle – perhaps in 1995.

The underperformance of small companies has been at least partly due to a relative derating, with the larger-capitalization stocks driven up in recent years by unprecedented liquidity flows. Many small companies have disappointed investors, but it is difficult to tell whether this is true of the sector as a whole. Reliable aggregate earnings numbers are hard to come by.

Where James Alexandroff, V-Nee Yeh and other small-capitalization managers agree is on the scope for stockpicking within the sector. Small companies are under-researched. Liquidity is too poor for brokers to dedicate experienced analysts to the sector. The research which is written may therefore be of low quality. Moreover, Ray Hood of Rothschilds points out that brokers rarely follow the best companies within the sector. There is an understandable bias towards companies which have plans to raise capital, and by definition this eliminates many of the most cash-generative businesses, which are self-financing.

Small companies at present are extremely interesting for cherry-pickers. As Richard Lawrence and Value Partners have shown, terrific bargains can be found – high growth companies at very low ratings. These gems, however, tend to be illiquid. It will take only a few more small-capitalization value investors in the market, and prices may be driven up to the point where the opportunities are less compelling.

INDICES AND OTHER PROBLEMS

Indices are one of the real headaches of Asian and emerging market investment. Issues include:

- Market access – some indices include partially open markets such as Korea, Taiwan, and India at full weighting; some include them at a percentage of the full capitalization weighting; some fail to include these (or fully open markets) until well after they have become entrenched in the institutional universe.

- Stock access – in countries like Malaysia and Singapore, some companies are subject to foreign ownership limits, some aren't, and the level differs from company to company. Trying to adjust for this frequently causes more problems than it solves, because it is very hard to estimate free floats for most of the other stocks. Trying to adjust for cross holdings is similarly problematical.

- Stock representation – global index compilers designing families of indices want to ensure that each company is included only once. Many companies however are listed in more than one market. HSBC Holdings, which accounts for 14 per cent of the Hang Seng index, has been taken out of the FTA and MSCI Hong Kong and Asian indices, and included in the UK. This may present a problem to fund managers who are measured against an index, but think that Hong Kong's largest bank should be included in an Asian portfolio.

- New issues – because many initial public offerings are small and/ or open only to local investors, some index compilers choose to include new issues only one year after listing. With large privatizations, sold both locally and internationally, sometimes having 20 per cent or even 40 per cent weightings in local indices, there is no right answer here – whenever they are put in, the index will be out of step with the majority of fund managers.

- Foreign board prices – in markets where foreign ownership is restricted, foreign stock often trades at a premium to local stock. The premiums can be both large and volatile. Using domestic prices may be unrepresentative. Foreign prices may however be less regularly available. In an illiquid company in Thailand, for example, it may be more appropriate to assess the foreign price by reference to the percentage premium last paid, plus the present domestic price, rather than by reference to the last traded foreign price – or it may not. Obviously index compilers cannot exercise discretion, and must therefore adopt some rules, which may sometimes fail to reflect market conditions.

- Offshore instruments – as far as I am aware, no major index has ever attempted to pick up offshore instruments such as ADRs and country funds, which may sometimes comprise the majority of international investment in a market, although Robert Fleming has for many years calculated the daily performance of Hong Kong shares trading in the London market.

- Accuracy – although the job of compilers may be complicated by the number and variety of new issues from the region's inventive corporate financiers.

- Timeliness and dissemination – there are some excellent indices which just aren't readily available, or only too slowly.

- Information – extraordinary confusion has occasionally arisen with reference to changes in the major indices, with major institutions unsure of and unable to ascertain the constituents.

The impact of different decisions on these factors can be huge. Genesis has published an excellent booklet on emerging market indices, which over the four-and-three-quarter-year period to September 1993 showed returns ranging from 42 per cent (the IFC Composite index) to 202 per cent (the MSCI Emerging Market Free).

In addition, individual funds may have constraints which prevent them from sticking too closely to capitalization-weighted indices. For example, many funds may have a single stock limit of 10 per cent; emerging market funds may have a single country limit of 15 per cent.

These complications are leading to a proliferation of indices. Some investors are still happy to select the index which seems easiest to beat, but confusion, if anything, is rising. An increasing number of institutions are compiling their own benchmarks, often by using their own weighted mixtures of appropriate local indices. There is also a trend towards absolute rather than relative return as a benchmark, which sounds sensible given the arbitrary nature of the indices, but may just increase the tendency to use the peer group as benchmark.

In terms of internal performance measurement, I like the suggestion by Michael Watt of Henderson Touche Remnant that actual performance each year should be compared with that of the starting portfolio. This would show the value added by active decision-making, as opposed to a buy-and-hold strategy. How many fund managers would be brave enough to test this publicly, or even internally?

THE VALUATION ANOMALIES IN CLOSED-END FUNDS

Closed-end funds in the United States are usually significantly more expensive than those listed elsewhere, even when structurally identical. These differences have persisted for years on end, but investors should at the very least be aware of them, and value-oriented investors will naturally wish to pick up the cheaper version.

For example, Stewart Aldcroft recalls that at one point in 1993 the Wardley China Fund Ltd, based in Hong Kong, was trading at a 45 per cent discount, while the China Fund Inc stood at an 18 per cent premium. The fund manager was the same, the choice of investments in Hong Kong and China was identical, and the only differences lay in the percentage weightings. The anomaly was mentioned in *Barrons* for three consecutive weeks without arousing any institutional interest.

Some observers suggest you should never buy a closed-end fund at a premium. I wouldn't be so rigid. Nevertheless, I am usually happier buying funds at deep discounts. 25–40 per cent discounts are not unusual, and over 50 per cent can be found on occasion. A discount at the higher end of the range tends to mean that the market is forsaken, and the shrewd investor may therefore benefit from a double-whammy – a market rebound accompanied by a narrowing discount, or perhaps a premium.

The launch of country funds – whether open or closed-end – often coincides with a peak in investor enthusiasm based on a strong market performance in preceding years. With remarkable frequency, the launch of a number of such funds marks the end of the bull run. (This is not necessarily the fault of the fund manager; funds may be launched on the basis of customer demand, or after years of negotiation with the authorities.) Similarly, funds tend to be wound up, or the objectives changed, at the wrong moment. By 1985–86, after a gruelling three year bear market, most if not all Singapore/ Malaysia funds had become regional funds. From the 1986 lows, the Malaysian market more than doubled, and Singapore almost tripled, in the space of eighteen months.

With a closed-end fund, the launch period may be the only opportunity for large institutions to pick up a sizable holding, but for private investors it often pays to wait, and to buy in the aftermarket.

SUSTAINABILITY OF ECONOMIC PERFORMANCE

Martin Dixon of TT observes that the differences between countries have narrowed. The Philippines and Indonesia, once thought to be basket cases, are now part of the economic mainstream. In the past, one might have bought the Philippines from time to time for an upswing, but never as a long-term investment. 'Now, the whole region, from the Philippines to Pakistan, is on a secular growth trend.'

Other investors fret that not every country can succeed with export-led growth. A number of experienced investors are sceptical about the Philippines, along with Pakistan and Bangladesh. The lack of land reform, continued dominance by an elite, and inadequate political maturity are among the core criticisms of the sceptics. Others complain that the Philippines has absorbed all of the worst aspects of the American legal and political system, and none of the best. Yet others wonder whether such countries, if competing head on with China and Vietnam in the export markets, can ever be adequately competitive. Elizabeth Tran observes that it is a question of probabilities: if there is a 70 per cent chance that the Philippines will catch up with the fast-track Asian economies, but the market is discounting 100 per cent, then the proposition is unattractive.

Another question is what might dent the growth consensus – the tacit agreement that economic development is the principal goal of society. Not all Asian individuals agree with the governments which argue that human rights are a western concept which should be subordinated in Asia to the greater good of commerce. However, both a respect for individual rights, and institutional checks on abuse of power, are entirely compatible with economic development. There is an observable trend in Asia for economic prosperity and the growth of the middle class to be accompanied by a growing appreciation of such freedoms. A 1992 Harvard study showed a positive correlation between economic development and democracy, with the causality in that direction (ie economic growth leading to more democratic government). Likewise, the growing environmental awareness at grassroots level in most Asian countries is moderate in nature: its proponents generally want continued growth, but with cleaner technologies.

A more serious concern is China's growing economic power and a widespread competitive build-up of military capability in the region. Marshall Auerback of Tiedeman Boltres Partners thinks it almost inevitable that the new economic powers will become more assertive. As they expand, and start exporting capital, that capital becomes exposed to the political risks of other countries, and will ultimately be backed up with military force.

The assumption that politics are irrelevant will not always be true. However, for the time being it is still a reasonable working assumption for overloaded managers who wish to concentrate their analytical efforts. Most of the political risk which may worry locals relates to individual countries and can be diversified away. Astute investors will remain attuned to the long-term regional risks, but for the moment they seem satisfactorily far away.

THE BIGGEST RISK

With most of this chapter devoted to risks of one sort or another, the last word goes to John Quinn of NatWest Investment Management. After protecting his capital from past downdraughts and failing to jump back in sufficiently quickly, he is convinced that 'the biggest risk in Asian markets is not to be fully invested at all times.'

Chapter 21

Fund management issues

GEOGRAPHICAL LOCATION

One of the extraordinary ironies of Asian fund management is the relatively high proportion of managers in the UK and the US who emphasize the importance of stock selection, and the relative scarcity of such managers on the ground in Asia. One of the key advantages of an Asian base, one would think, is that it is much easier to visit the companies. It is true that as the number of markets proliferate, the proportionate importance of your home market diminishes. When trying to understand Korea, a Hong Kong manager does not necessarily have any advantage of culture or local knowledge over his counterpart from Edinburgh. Nevertheless, being in roughly the same time zone makes communications and company visits easier, and the ability to make frequent short trips without jetlag and undue expense even more so.

Arguably, greater distance forces managers to focus more on ascertainable facts. Distant managers tend to emphasize their detachment, and suggest that they find it easier to avoid the emotional excesses which can result from getting too caught up in day to day events. Their portfolio turnover is therefore lower, they claim, and their investment philosophy more consistent. Moreover, as regular visitors to specific countries, they may be better placed than a resident to identify key changes. There may be an element of truth in this, although a combination of discipline and a local base would seem to offer the best prospects.

To some extent of course it depends on the type of fund. The Vietnam Fund could not operate as effectively as it does without its base in that country, and many managers of Indian equity funds are coming to the same conclusion. A manager of an Indonesian country

200

fund will have to try to understand all the important companies in the market, no matter how complex, and therefore needs to be on the ground a great deal; a global manager will tend to focus on a few companies which he can understand. When it comes to regional funds, the location debate warms up.

Surveys by Fund Research have shown inconclusive differentials in performance between the funds in their database run in the UK and those run in Asia. Grahame Stott of Wyatts is unconvinced; he believes there is a growing body of evidence to suggest that local fund managers significantly outperform distant competitors, not just in Asia, but worldwide. You only have to listen to visiting investors, marvelling at the most commonplace things, to realize how little they understand of business in Asia, he observes. Elizabeth Tran of IDS suggests that one need only look at the number of British and American firms setting up bases in Asia: the market has decided.

Many of the best of the distant managers have spent several years in Asia, thus achieving the necessary broad background understanding of the region. They may be able to compensate for distance with experience. Firms like Martin Currie and Tiger are starting to send people out to specific countries for a few months at a time, an approach which will probably pay handsomely.

Personnel stability may also be a performance factor. Many Asian fund management companies have been bedevilled in recent years by extraordinary levels of staff turnover, and the average experience of a fund manager may be no more than two or three years.

New technology may help to erode the drawbacks of distance. Peter Curtin of Warburg Asset Management in London is delighted with the impact of a video link to their Hong Kong office. Meetings are just as if they were in the same office, he enthuses: people look one another in the eye and concentrate, and it is incomparably better than a voice-only conference call.

Is there a distinctive Scottish style? It may be a myth, as the Scots themselves disagree, although they can rarely resist a swipe at the English. They have tradition on their side, having established the investment trust movement a century ago. Angus Tulloch of Stewart Ivory maintains that Scots are much more interested in companies than in glamorous money-shuffling. English managers will say the same, he maintains, but dry up if asked to talk about any individual company for more than half a minute, whereas Scots will have greater depth. Michael Watt of Henderson Touche Remnant reckons that Scots can be found buying phlegmatically in the bleakest downturns, well ahead of the English, and that the Scottish insurance companies make the investment trusts look very swash-buckling. Large numbers of Scots can be found overseas – dynamism, they say; driven out by cold, rain, mosquitoes and horseflies, accord-ing to the English. The myth, in any event, lives on: corporate financiers escorting companies on fund-raising missions warn their clients to expect their toughest grilling in Edinburgh.

The United States has a noticeably small pool of investors with experience managing Asian money. The choice of US-registered funds investing in Asian and emerging markets is also relatively narrow, and many of these funds have a very short history. Investors might give some thought to the advantages of the longer-established funds and fund management groups based overseas, which may in practice outweigh the perceived or actual safety margin accorded by SEC approval. The alternative is to select a US-based manager who has an individual track record in the international markets, and find out about that track record, which for regulatory reasons may not be publicized in the US.

Surveys of comparative performance between UK and Asia-based managers may also fail to pick up the small but highly significant group of individuals running money for sophisticated clients in funds which are not registered for retail sale. Some of the best managers fall into this category. They have the confidence and the track record to attract their clients on a private basis and work on performance fees, and they typically prefer to spend their time thinking about investments rather than in the mundane reporting and marketing which consume so much of the time for many managers in tra-ditional investment houses. Many of them, having cut their teeth in traditional investment firms, also have a keen appreciation of the deficiencies of indices, of traditional asset class restrictions, and of quarterly performance measurement.

An Asian base is almost certainly an advantage when it comes to dealing. While the quantity and quality of screen-based information on the more established markets has improved by leaps and bounds, making it possible to monitor executions there, real-time dealing becomes much more important in the newer and less transparent markets. Some managers reckon they need to be increasingly vigilant about executions because of the erosion of agency broking. Others fret that, being in a different time zone, they miss out on the most attractive lines of stock.

DISTRACTIONS AND TIME-WASTERS

Amongst institutional managers, it is noticeable that many of the best performers are those for whom marketing and administrative distractions are minimized. Some firms, recognizing this, have taken steps to protect some of their most talented and vulnerable individuals from excessive marketing demands; others have achieved a more structural separation of the two functions.

The importance of administrative systems is perhaps harder for the outsider to assess, but can be equally critical. Start-up fund management companies often grossly underestimate the problem. Even at larger companies, managers can sometimes be found spending a disproportionate amount of their day dealing with the confirmation and reconciliation of orders. Firms like Fidelity and Schroders which have separated investment decision-making from dealing, have automated mundane functions such as ticket-writing, and have streamlined the administration of multiple portfolios, suggest that it is hard to overestimate the importance of such improvements – particularly in markets where the administration can be very burdensome, and the pool of knowledgeable managers is so limited.

HEDGE FUNDS

The main distinguishing feature of most Asian hedge funds is that they are managed for absolute returns rather than against a stated or implicit index benchmark. Most of the funds run in this way and given incentive by performance fees are genuinely conservative; more so, in most cases, than conventional mutual funds. As in other markets, however, the term is ambiguous, and covers a wide range of operating styles.

For years there was little more that hedge funds could do, by way of either risk control or enhancement, but the range of options is gradually increasing. Many of the funds range into more liquid markets such as Japan and Australia, but in the rest of Asia there are still significant constraints.

Bond markets are undeveloped, for example, although there is much discussion about their development. Many of the currencies are either pegged (like the Hong Kong dollar), managed against a basket dominated by the US dollar (like the Thai baht), or not even fully convertible (like China's renminbi). Exchange-traded futures and options so far exist only in Hong Kong and Singapore, and the range of instruments available remains limited. The investment banks will create OTC puts and other synthetic shorts in some markets, but usually in limited size and at steep premiums. Finally, short selling is frowned upon by the stock exchange authorities in most markets, and stock borrowing facilities are limited outside Hong Kong.

Andrew Economos sums up the limited utility of derivatives in emerging markets as follows: 'very expensive, very illiquid, and often unreliable just when you most need the insurance'.

THE PETER PRINCIPLE AS APPLIED TO FUND MANAGEMENT

- The better you are as an analyst, the faster you become a fund manager
- The better you are as a fund manager, the more you get diverted to marketing
- The better you are as a marketing person, the quicker you become an administrator!

Out of deference to his former firm, I had better not reveal who explained this to me. It may be a universal rule, but is particularly true in Asia today.

There is, very clearly, a remarkable inverse correlation between fund management performance and other responsibilities. Many of the managers who made it into this book have the good fortune to work for firms which have successfully tackled this problem, and effectively shield their managers from excessive marketing and administration demands. Such firms also tend to have a real career path on the investment side, rather than requiring the ambitious to become general managers. These firms are still in the minority. Many of the other top managers in the book worked for firms of other types, and became independent to regain control.

INFORMATION, EXPLANATIONS, DISCLOSURE, AND MARKETING ABILITY

As an investor who appreciates being kept informed, but is reluctant to pester managers whose job is to get on with managing the money, the author's awards for written investor communication go to:

- Marc Faber, for vital historical perspective on world markets, an extraordinary range of insights on emerging markets, and a sense of humour.

- Michael Sofaer, for the prompt quarterly snapshots of his investment thinking. These are lucid and engagingly candid expositions of his mercurial, but always logical, shifts in asset allocation.

- Peter Everington and Jim Mellon, who launched the original Thornton topic papers explaining 'The Case for . . .' their latest fund launch, which may have been one-sided but were usually correct, and cut through the waffle to convey the essentials of an investment case in admirably succinct and memorable form. Recent Regent comments are in the same tradition, but the panache of the originals was hard to beat.

- Capital House, the current managers of the Thai-Asia Fund, for continuing the perfect investment trust monthly bulletin. This is a single monthly page, with everything one wants to know: latest NAV, price, premium or discount, and index; the same data annually since inception, quarterly for the last year, and in graphical form; top ten holdings, sector weightings versus the index, any transactions by the fund in its own shares, and a brief comment as to anything out of the ordinary. Nothing more. (Annual reports which arrive five months after the year-end go into the file, but are much less useful.)

- Foreign & Colonial Emerging Markets, along similar lines, for highly efficient weekly and monthly reporting of all the basics. Never underestimate how much confidence this inspires! On the other hand it is absolutely essential that this should not become a burden to the key fund managers; the essential thing is that the process must be automated.

- Michael Watt and the TR Pacific Investment Trust for showing the impact of stock selection in every market, by comparing the annual performance of the holdings in each country against that country's stock-market index. If they were then to show explicitly the performance of each country along with its relative weighting in the portfolio, the picture would be complete.

- Steve Silverman of Merrill Lynch (mainly on Japan), Angus Tulloch of Stewart Ivory (on the New Pacific), and Richard Lawrence of Overlook Investments, for public explanations of individual stock selections.

- Fidelity and Jardine Fleming, for efficient account administration and basic information; and especially Fidelity, for its educational investment in seminars for the Hong Kong retail public

- All those fund managers who reveal the cost as well as the value of their holdings, and the portfolio turnover. Very few of these are based in Asia!

On the other hand, some of the more competent managers are being upstaged by the more articulate, especially in the US. Sympathize, if you will, with the predicament of one of the most outstanding Asian managers who completed a competent 45-minute presentation in the US only to be told that he 'did not sound sufficiently *passionate* about his subject'. Why, only the previous week, Mark Mobius had been in town, and had really conveyed a *feel* for Asia; why, he had even told his audience what *food* they eat in China! Undoubtedly, this basic input had provided interesting colour for the novice interrogator. The fact that his present visitor had a much deeper understanding of Chinese cultures (in the plural), and of the immediate factors affecting the equity markets in the specialist area of which they were talking (Hong Kong and China), was quite lost.

The misunderstanding could well have worsened. The expert shrugged his shoulders and left. The novice asset allocator may well have decided to deal with Mobius, who is after all an experienced manager – but as a result of such fluency now has some US$7 billion under management, and has become a one-man global marketing phenomenon. Alternatively, the novice may have fixed on another of his more predictable and comprehensible compatriots; anything rather than one of these touchy locals! The new US fund managers in turn deal mainly with the new US brokers – for they speak the same language, after all. Thus are narrow information bases built, and thus is volatility exacerbated.

A plea to investors: have patience with fund managers who are new to US-style presentations, and with Asian fund managers whose first language is not English. Some of these people may speak fluently, but in an unfamiliar style. Try to understand what they are really saying. To rank these people on the basis of their oratorical ability is to reject some of the best investment managers in the world, and to narrow your investment choices unnecessarily.

VALUE OR GROWTH

This is one of the major areas of misunderstanding, because of differences in the jargon between Asia and the US. Asian investors want both. They want to buy a high-growth company which represents good value.

There are relatively few Asian investors who pay much attention to book values. (However, every Asian investor is interested in 'hidden assets' in the form of property.) Most Asian companies are growth companies, and in the fully open markets, at least, there are relatively few large-cap cyclicals.

Portfolios such as Richard Lawrence's show that there are many high-growth companies representing excellent value. Most investors pay significantly higher PEs than he does, but are still happy that their shares represent good value in relation to their growth prospects. Most Asians would probably understand the word 'value' to mean the economic value of the business and surplus assets, with reference to the growth prospects – not a formulaic numerical definition. In this context, Asian markets as a whole still offer excellent long-term value relative to more developed markets such as the US.

QUANTITATIVE MANAGEMENT

Some of the simpler value formulations may not be wholly appropriate for Asian markets; book values for example may be rapidly overtaken by asset price inflation, cross-border comparisons need to take account of the major differences in accounting policy, and companies have been known to change their core business several times in a decade. The mercurial changes in corporate direction possible with family-controlled companies in a lightly regulated environment may also invalidate numerical analysis in many specific instances. Limited marketability and tight control may distort share trading patterns. No wonder most fund managers dismiss quantitative analysis as 'garbage in, garbage out', and emphasize judgmental factors such as management integrity.

There are, as far as I know, few houses using a quantitative valuation approach to stock selection, although several are testing quantitative methods to refine their allocation methods. However, the huge caveats which a knowledgeable investor would place on many ostensibly cheap stocks does not necessarily mean that whole-sale purchase of such stocks would be unrewarding. A few big winners could offset the duds. There is some evidence to this effect.

At BZW in 1992, we took fifty of the leading companies in each of the four main markets, and went back more than a decade, ranking the companies at the end of each calendar year by PE, P/CF, yield, and P/BV. We then ranked the companies in quintiles – cheapest 20 per cent, next 20 per cent – and compared the perform-ance of each group over the subsequent year. In every market a simple low-PE or low price/cash flow strategy would have generated markedly superior returns with comparable or reduced risk. A high-yield strategy also worked well in Hong Kong. Price-to-book did not. The methodology was not perfect, because we had to work within the constraints of data availability, but the results of the PE and P/CF strategies were so strong and consistent in all four markets as to merit further investigation.

The conclusions we reached at the time, looking at the detailed rankings thrown up year by year as well as the aggregate numbers, were that investors were (a) reluctant to adopt a long view (even when they agreed with it, if the short term prospects seemed dull), and (b) inclined to huge swings of sentiment, overvaluing blue-chip stocks which had recently performed well, and undervaluing those which had been through a rough patch. The rankings subsequently proved a rich vein of ideas for contrarian cherry-pickers.

Looking at a list of the low PE or low P/CF companies at any time, an experienced manager may be able to distinguish good companies which are temporarily unfashionable, companies where the prospects have fundamentally changed, and companies where the accounts are particularly suspect or otherwise dubious. Quantitative firms say that the performance of a good automated stock selection system is often adversely affected by letting the fund manager pick and choose amongst its recommendations. When it comes to selecting lowly-valued Asian stocks, I suspect the judgmental overlay by a good contrarian fund manager would be beneficial.

QUARTERLY PERFORMANCE

Peter Pearson, who after a distinguished fund management career now runs a consultancy and head-hunting firm in London, observes that fund measurement periods have been shortening steadily for the last hundred years. The Scots in the 1870s measured their performance about every five years. By the 1920s this was down to two years. For decades thereafter, the key measurement was annual. Then quarterly reviews became standard. Now the emphasis is still theoretically on quarterly or longer performance, but in practice monthly or even weekly.

PERFORMANCE MEASUREMENT

Marc Faber suggests that the performance record of fund managers should be dollar-weighted by inflows, so as to show not the conventional measure of long-term returns for a single investor, but how much money has been made for the average current holder. This suggestion is unlikely to be adopted by marketing departments. It is not always the manager's fault that investors pile in at the wrong time, but the point is a good one, and especially valid today. Most of the returns which have been generated were made on a very much smaller scale. Most of the people who hold units in mutual funds today have bought them late, and achieved much less spectacular performance than the early birds.

Paul Matthews, of Matthews Capital Management in San Francisco, is astonished how few people understand the arithmetic of investment. If you're up 100 per cent one year and down 50 per cent the next, many people think that sounds fine – 'volatile, of course, but the manager makes a lot of money in a good year, so we'll forgive him'. In reality, of course, the investor would have made no headway at all. In the financial world, the conservative tortoise with a compounding strategy often beats the flamboyant hare. It would be unwise to laugh at Marc Faber for having achieved

17 per cent compound growth during tremendous bull markets; he may yet have the last laugh.

ASSET ALLOCATION

Benchmarking against indices based on market capitalization often results in fund managers chasing their tails. It seems likely, anecdotally and arithmetically, that asset allocation according to fixed percentage benchmarks – periodically reviewed – would prove superior. In this way, weightings in markets which had outperformed would be lightened, and weightings in the laggards increased – thus building in a tendency to buy low and sell high. In determining appropriate percentages, it might be worth considering 'stock-market earnings' (market capitalization divided by index PE) as a starting point.

STARS

Fund management stars are rare and unaccountable beasts, according to one manager whose firm tries to cultivate them and is large enough to have a few. Most are bad at training other people, he says. All are obsessed by the stock market, and may spend hours on end staring at the monitor screens – to what effect, lesser mortals do not know. They typically take only occasional big decisions, but then spend a huge amount of time fine-tuning. They spend far more time than the firm thinks they should on mundane details like placing their own orders (not always convenient for a large institution, from a compliance standpoint, apart from the administrative angle), and talking to brokers (being rude to them, ignoring them, complaining about them . . .). Ultimately, this firm concludes, stars are good at narrowing the universe, and zeroing in on growth companies in growth sectors which have a sustainable competitive advantage.

Not all of the managers in this book fit into this characterization. All, however, know where they can add value, and where they cannot, and concentrate on what seems possible. They minimize distractions. They are flexible, and they learn from mistakes. They are, in short, focused.

Chapter 22

Final words for individual investors

Most individual investors venturing outside their home markets are well advised to do so through funds.

Concept funds should generally be avoided. Historically, for example, it has often been less rewarding to invest in infrastructure than in the companies which will benefit from its completion, and this may well be the case again.

Buying other narrowly focused funds can also be treacherous. Individual countries are often made to sound most attractive when their economies and stock markets have been booming for some time – just as the party is coming to an end.

Reliance on pundits can damage your wealth, and it is worth bearing in mind that the individuals who are highly respected in, say, the United States may be less knowledgeable and sure-footed in their recommendations for distant markets.

Accordingly, the best bet for most distant investors is to buy a good regional fund, and let the fund manager allocate the portfolio as he thinks best. A diversified regional portfolio should be much less volatile than a single country fund.

When choosing a fund, the ideal combination is a good individual manager at a reputable house, but the key is the good individual manager. Styles differ, as this book has shown, but administrative and marketing responsibilities have destroyed many good track records, so the single most important thing is to choose a manager who has this side under control. Look carefully at fees and expenses, and at front-end and exit charges, since fund structures in Asia are occasionally piratical. Think about the size of the fund – if too big, it can make the fund manager's job much harder, but what is too big will depend both on the investment scope of the fund and on the style of the manager.

211

Trying to match indices in Asia can be a nightmare for the fund manager, and contributes little to investment returns. Many managers feel obliged to limit the extent to which they deviate from their benchmark index, if not to replicate it. Most also tend to benchmark the portfolios of their peers, to avoid being too far from the herd. Managers who are experienced enough to back their own judgment and withstand short-term commercial pressures will generally do better over time. It may be difficult for the individual investor to find out how their manager behaves in practice. However, there are some eminently experienced managers profiled in the preceding chapters.

In the long run, I would expect increasing market maturity and a lessening in the relative importance of new emerging markets – ie more stability in regional stock-market structure – to make market calls more difficult and stock selection increasingly important. In the shorter term, global interest rates and the international flow of funds may predominate.

This makes it hard to recommend a particular style for all purposes. The important thing is to choose fund managers who are solidly competent in their own style, know where their expertise lies, focus on what they do best, and have a good idea of the risks which their choices involve.

Long-term investors should always consider closed-end funds, if available at a discount.

Experienced investors who live in the region may have the insights to become successful contrarians, buying markets when they are most depressed and closed-end funds at deep discounts. The results of doing both at once are usually very satisfactory.

Investors who wish to pick their own stocks but have jumped to this chapter should go back and read the rest of the book. I hope they find it as illuminating to read as I did to write.

Appendices

Appendix A: Emerging markets

An extract from 'E Pluribus Unum', by Arnab Banerji, chief investment officer of Foreign & Colonial Emerging Markets, September 1994

WHAT IS AN EMERGING MARKET?

The term 'Emerging Market' was first coined by an affiliate of the World Bank, the International Finance Corporation (IFC), in 1981. The IFC uses the World Bank classification of developing economies based on GNP per capita. The IFC's definition of an emerging market is a stock market that exists in any developing economy, irrespective of how developed the particular market itself might be. The latest data establishes mean world income at US$8,355. An economy with a functioning bourse and a per capita income below this level is always classified as an emerging market. An economy that crosses this threshold may continue to be covered as an emerging market by the IFC for some time before it is reclassified as developed, so long as a material gap in per capita income between it and the developed world continues to exist. The importance of this gap in per capita income becomes apparent if the history of growth in the developed and developing worlds is compared.

GROWTH IN PRODUCTIVITY

Prior to the industrial revolution, the per capita income of the average labourer in Europe was very similar to that of his counterpart in the Middle East or Asia. Until this moment in history, economic growth in all regions had been an immediate function of population growth, the acquisition of new agricultural land, and to a limited degree a consequence of trade. Improvements in productivity tended to accrete slowly and nonsystematically. With industrial take-off, the picture changed radically as one western nation after another entered into a period of accelerated and generally sustained growth.

What is most significant is that this surge in growth was characterised by a massive increase in productivity. The present maldistribution of income around the world is primarily a reflection of current productivity differentials. During the heyday of the industrial revolution, it took Britain almost 60 years to double per capita income. Taking into account population growth, this translates into a GDP growth rate of around 1.8 per cent a year. Yet this growth rate was sufficient, by way of the magic of compound interest, to transform the UK into a world power in the context of other nations that were stagnating or showing minimal growth. From mid-Victorian times onwards, this lead started being rapidly eroded as other nations proceeded to first apply and then further develop the techniques and processes behind Britain's early industrialisation.

Starting from a similar per capita income base to the UK, it took the USA a little over 45 years to double productivity. Japan managed the process in 33 years, Brazil in 20 years, Korea in 11 years, and China in only 10 years. It would appear that the later a country started on the process of industrialisation, the shorter the doubling period for per capita productivity. It should also be noticed that this time compression is common to cultures as diverse as those of Brazil and China.

CATCH-UP

One reason for the approximately 50 to 1 difference in per capita productivity (and associated income per head) between the richest and the poorest countries in the world lies in their relative deployment of technology. For developed countries, further productivity increases arise mainly from the development and application of new technology. With productivity growth primarily a function of innovation, it is not surprising that amongst developed countries there is a tendency for growth rates to converge over the long term.

The GDP growth rate for the UK rose with the introduction of compulsory education from its Victorian level of 1.8 per cent to 2.4 per cent a year early this century. This is a growth rate around which the British economy has oscillated ever since. The post Civil War industrialisation of the United States was extremely rapid, though arguably catch-up with Europe was complete by the time of the First World War. In the 80 years since then, the US economy's long-term rate of growth has settled down to a remarkably stable one of around 2.6 per cent a year. The German economy has grown much faster than that of either the UK or the US for much of the last 120 years. However, the damage wrought by two world wars delayed per capita equivalence with the UK until the 1970s. It is interesting to note that the GDP growth rate of the former West Germany in the period 1979–89 was less than 2 per cent a year. In the same vein, many analysts see the Japanese economy having an underlying growth rate in the 2 per cent to 3 per cent range for the foreseeable future. Following catch-up it would appear that all these economies have been growing or are likely to grow at under 3 per cent a year. For developed economies it may well be that rates within this growth range reflect the boundaries of the economically possible.

For developing countries the challenge is not so much to develop new technology but rather to adopt and adapt technology already developed elsewhere. Bear in mind that the pool of technically trained manpower in the developing economies has more than tripled over the last 25 years and that this has occurred alongside the development of more efficient economic structures as a result of the collapse of communism and a general move towards the market. Freed of the need to invent the tools of growth, it is not surprising to see that the developing economies are capable of growing so much faster than the rate that the developed economies managed at the same level of per capita income.

AN ASSET CLASS

It may be seen from the IFC's classification of what is an emerging market that the definition has nothing whatsoever to do with the sophistication or openness of the country's bourse. Instead, by emphasising the per capita income gap between the emerging market and the developed world, each market's potential for catch-up is identified. Until recently, many of the countries covered by the definition lacked both a pool of trained labour and a commitment to market reform, making them unattractive to the investment community as a whole. Most developing nations have now addressed or are trying to address these problems, at last unlocking their potential for superior growth. It may be seen that this growth potential is qualitatively as well as quantitatively different from the basis upon which developed world growth is predicated. The emerged markets require innovation for further growth in productivity while the emerging markets are in the business of applying techniques and technologies already developed by others. They would grow even if all first world innovation came to a halt tomorrow.

In this context, while Chile and China have very different cultural traditions they are emerging markets because they are using similar economic policies to catch up with the developed world. By the same token, South Africa is an emerging market because not only does it have the requisite gap in productivity levels but it clearly possesses institutions readily capable of absorbing and applying developed world technology in order to grow. In the same vein, the former Soviet Bloc economies (the old 'Second World') are trying to copy and adapt First World techniques (such as markets) in order to close their productivity gap.

AN EMERGING CORE ASSET CLASS

On a purchasing power parity basis, the developing economies account for 43 per cent of global income but only 7 per cent of world equity market capitalisation. If the emerging market economies continue to use known techniques to catch up with the developed world in the manner suggested then, in twenty years' time, they may well account for around half of the world's equity market capitalisation. These markets will then no longer be considered a niche area of investment but will have emerged as a mandatory, core asset class.

Appendix B: What to look for in a company

Extracts from a checklist drafted by Angus Tulloch of Stewart Ivory

A. MANAGEMENT

Who controls the company?

How long has senior management been in place?

Depth of management? (One-man band, succession, etc.)

Has management a clear idea of goals and strategy?

Does management have a good grasp of sector trends?

Does senior management have a significant financial stake in the success of the company?

What is the track record for treatment of minority shareholders? (Asset injections, dividend policy, etc.)

What is the reputation for honesty and efficiency?

How is the company run? (Financial controls, targets for subsidiaries, etc.)

Has the company a conservative yet innovative culture? (Management aware of its limitations but willing to exploit new opportunities?)

How is management incentivised?

B. QUALITY OF BUSINESS

Does the company operate in a long-term growth sector?

Is the company well positioned in that sector?

Does the company have a competitive cost structure and sustainable pricing policy?

Does the company have an exclusive franchise and strong brand name?

217

Are there significant barriers to entry? (Capital cost, distribution networks, etc.)

How strong is existing and potential competition?

How vulnerable is the company's business to exogenous factors? (Changes in economic growth, domestic or international tariffs, currencies, government regulations, etc.)

How predictable and reliable is the company's earnings stream?

C. TRACK RECORD

Does the company tend to disappoint or to exceed expectations?

Does the company tend to be accident prone?

What has the company's growth rate been, in terms of profits (including extraordinaries), cash flow, earnings, and book net asset value, all in adjusted per share terms?

What have historical trends been for market share, sales, margins, tax rates and return on equity?

How has the company accounted for goodwill?

Has the company generated sufficient cash to finance growth in working capital?

What have historical trends been for working capital ratios? (Debtors to sales, stocks and work-in-progress to sales.)

What have historical trends been for debt-to-equity, interest cover, and net interest payments to operational cash flow.

D. OUTLOOK

What is the cyclical outlook for the sector?

Is growth momentum stable or increasing?

How do the company's near-term growth prospects compare with the market and the sector?

Is the company sufficiently well financed to survive in the long term? (Usual ratios but look at length of debt and currency exposure.)

Will future cash flow cover capital expenditure plans?

E. VALUATION

How do price to cash flow/earnings/book NAV ratios compare with the sector, domestically and internationally?

218

How do these ratios compare with the company growth rate and historical parameters? (Adjusted for inflation.)

How do comparative ratios of intrinsic value measure up? (Market
capitalisation to sales or to physical assets, current to peak earnings
ratios, etc.)

Does the company have hidden assets? (Brand names, undervalued
property, etc.)

Does the company have unrecognised future earnings potential? (Long-
gestation projects, conservative accounting policies, etc.)

F. THINGS TO REMEMBER

Predictable and sustainable growth is the key.

A premium for quality management, business, and track record is always
justified.

Brokers are paid to generate business, and to do this often sound
knowledgable about companies they know little or nothing about.

If a company transaction is too complicated to be understood, avoid
the company.

There is rarely only one cockroach in a cupboard.

The biggest mistakes are made by straying from your investment
philosophy.

Never look at book cost of an investment.

Do not be afraid to cut losses.

Averaging down on quality growth companies usually pays.

Value without momentum (eg earnings growth) can remain unrecognised for a long time.

Market psychology should be respected, but reality will always win
through eventually.

Patience will nearly always pay, so long as the ongoing business is
matching expectations.

Do not become too attached to, or too prejudiced against, a company.

The instrument should always be secondary to the company.

The more immature a market, the more it is prone to excess.

No matter how good the company, if it operates in a very cyclical
business, there will be a time not to own it.

Early timing is essential for both purchases and sales of illiquid stocks.

Analyse and learn from mistakes and successes.

Try to avoid instant decisions – especially after a good lunch!

*Note: like all good proverbs, some of these final maxims may be contradictory, but
they have the ring of experience and hard-won wisdom! CB*

Appendix C: Richard Lawrence's investment selections

Extracts from the quarterly reports to investors in The Overlook Partners Fund. (These excerpts have been lightly edited in the interests of current readability.)

SONG WOUN INDUSTRIES – APRIL 1993

Song Woun Industries is a manufacturer of high quality speciality chemicals in Korea. The major products include anti-oxidants, stabilizers for PVC, and polyurethane resins. Song Woun has established a successful track record of developing niche chemical products, and is presently expanding a line of water treatment products.

As most of you are aware, I am attracted to mundane businesses which have strong balance sheets. In the case of Song Woun the interest bearing debt to equity ratio at 31 December 1992 was 54 per cent, which is very low by Korean standards. The company has a consistent history of strong balance sheets and self-financed growth.

The company also boasts an admirable track record of growth. EPS have increased at an annual compound rate of 23.8 per cent since 1984. The company has experienced only one down year since 1984, that being the strike-torn 1989.

In terms of valuation the company fits the fund's parameters. The return on average equity was 16.6 per cent in 1992, and I forecast EPS growth to be in excess of 16 per cent over the next three years. I have purchased the partnership's position at a price of 8.6 times trailing EPS, and 7.4 times 1993's estimate. The stock sells at only 97 per cent of historic book value.

As with so many high quality Korean companies, the stock is difficult to source. The fund paid a premium over the local market price to buy part of the position, since the 10 per cent foreign limit was breached shortly after the partnership began to accumulate the stock. While that premium is not reflected in the net asset valuation we present, I am confident that this premium of less than 10 per cent will be maintained over time.

SHIN POONG PAPER MANUFACTURING COMPANY – JULY 1993

Shin Poong Paper is the type of company I attempt to uncover. The company competitively manufactures a product for worldwide markets, is in excellent financial health, and has a history of self-financed growth. The stock sells well below our benchmarks, with a PE of one half the EPS growth rate and one half the return on equity.

Shin Poong is a manufacturer of high-quality white cardboard that is utilized by a variety of customers as packaging for consumer products. The company is the second largest producer of cardboard in Korea, with a market share of just under 20 per cent. Importantly, Shin Poong has constantly upgraded the quality of its product to the point where today the company is just slightly behind the more expensive Japanese producers. Total sales are estimated to reach US$120 million in 1993, and the company has a market capitalization of US$80 million.

Unlike a number of Korean companies which sell products in protected domestic markets, Shin Poong Paper exports 45 per cent of production to Hong Kong for use in the export industries of southern China. Responses from Hong Kong based customers I have spoken to about Shin Poong have been positive about the quality and price. Shin Poong's price competitiveness has been underpinned partly by the rising yen, but also by its ability to manufacture in-house key components of its machinery that improve product quality and cost.

I was initially attracted to Shin Poong by its strong balance sheet. Net cash at 31 December 1992 represented over 40 per cent of market capitalization, based on the fund's purchase price. The company maintains a very aggressive depreciation policy: annual depreciation averaged 22 per cent of fixed assets over the past four years, and the accumulated depreciation of machinery was six times its residual book value at the end of 1992. This is not a company which has pumped up its net profits over the years.

Shin Poong Paper has compounded its EPS at 22.6 per cent annually since 1984. Remarkably, the growth was financed internally and was accompanied by a concurrent reduction in the debt-to-equity ratio. Future growth will come from a recently completed 25 per cent capacity expansion, and a recently initiated 40 per cent capacity expansion. These expansions will be financed internally by cash flow, cash balances, and the sale of a parcel of land where the company's old headquarters is located.

221

Sharply higher depreciation levels will slow the rate of EPS growth in 1993 and 1994, although cash flow will rise in line with capacity.

The stock is attractive on a valuation basis. Based on our cost, the stock was at 5.2 times trailing EPS and 4.2 times the 1993 EPS estimate; and at 3.2 and 2.8 times estimated cash flow per share for 1993 and 1994 respectively. The 1992 return on average equity was 22.3 per cent, and the price-to-book ratio as of 31 December 1992 was 1.06 times, despite my belief that the heavily depreciated book is significantly undervalued.

WINTON HOLDINGS – OCTOBER 1993

The consumer finance industry in Asia holds very attractive investment opportunities. Ever since I discovered that JCG Holdings, a Hong Kong public listed company, was making personal loans at a 2.5 per cent monthly flat rate, I have constantly searched the markets in Asia for investments in the broadly defined consumer finance industry. The attractions, besides the pricing, include low default rates, low cultural acceptance of personal bankruptcy, high industry growth rates, and high personal savings rates.

During my travels around Asia I have accumulated positions in a number of companies which meet my investment criteria. The largest investment is a Hong Kong listed company called Winton Holdings (Bermuda) Limited. Winton finances the acquisition of taxi licences in Hong Kong. It operates in partnership with Citibank, Wayfoong Credit, a wholly owned subsidiary of the Hongkong Bank, and a number of smaller Hong Kong banks. The partnership has a 33 per cent market share. Winton negotiates on behalf of the banking partners the loan origination, credit analysis, and terms and tenor of the loans. In addition to receiving fees for these services, Winton participates in the loans on a subordinated basis, and profits from their wide interest rate margin and early repayment of the ten-year loans. Since 1976 when Winton developed the business, loan write-offs have been next to nil, and the business has grown in excess of 20 per cent per annum. Importantly, the historical average yield to Winton has averaged 22 per cent per loan.

The taxi financing business, which generates over 63 per cent of the profits, is bundled in the public company with a number of medium-priced làrge Chinese restaurants. These are principally located in Mongkok, one of Hong Kong's busiest commercial and residential areas. The restaurants are well managed, profitable, and cash-flow positive. However, the mix of the financing business with the restaurant business is confusing for investors. This 'apples and oranges' approach has resulted in an attractive investment opportunity for the fund to acquire shares in Winton at under 6.7 times March 1994's net profit estimate of US17 million, and with a 9 per cent yield. (The fund already received its first cash dividend of 6.3 per cent in August.) Long term, I believe the interests of shareholders would be better served by spinning off the restaurants into a separate vehicle, although as far as I am aware no such plans currently exist.

After experiencing slower than normal growth for the year ending March 1994, which was triggered by concerns over a Governmental review of the Hong Kong system of awarding taxi licences, I eagerly anticipate fiscal 1995 and 1996 when Winton's historical growth rate should resume.

PACIFIC INSURANCE – JANUARY 1994

Pacific Insurance is one of the leading non-life insurance companies in Thailand, specializing in auto and fire insurance. The company has a cash flow positive business, honest and committed management, a bargain share valuation, and bright long-term industry growth prospects.

The Thai non-life insurance industry has very attractive fundamentals:

- less than 10 per cent of all cars have any form of insurance
- auto and fire premiums have grown at annual rates in excess of 25 per cent and 15 per cent respectively
- Thailand is one of the few countries in the world where insurance companies historically make consistent profits on underwriting
- Thailand is not located in a disaster zone like the Philippines, Japan, or parts of the US
- claim awareness is low
- litigation is not a dominant Thai characteristic
- Thai laws are geared in favour of the insurance companies.

In addition to these favourable factors, there was broad investor concern about two issues in mid-1993. First, there had been a number of serious factory and hotel fires, the most serious being at the Kader Industrial toy factory where 190 workers perished. Second, the Thai government passed a law implementing a mandatory Thai-style third-party insurance policy on all motorcycles for a ridiculously low premium of US$8 per policy. In the midst of these perceived problems, a number of Thai insurance stocks were selling at PEs of between 7 and 10 times 1993 EPS, and had experienced significant underperformance over the prior two year period.

After personally meeting with the management of eight insurance companies, I decided that first an effective reinsurance system and tight regulations limited the per claim exposure of the Thai companies to small percentages of their shareholders' equity. Second, I concluded that the Thai culture's desire for compromise would prompt the Government to adjust the motorcycle policy to alleviate the large loss potential. In fact, mandatory implementation of the motorcycle policy was postponed late last year, and most likely will be reintroduced in a few years with realistic pricing. Third, I discovered that Pacific Insurance was largely ignored but intelligently and competently managed.

Pacific Insurance is conservatively managed and controlled by Jiraphant Asvatanakul, the son of a Chinese family who moved to Bangkok from Shanghai. While the father originally founded the business, the financial performance dramatically improved after Jiraphant took control of the company six years ago. Importantly from my point of view, Jiraphant is building an infrastructure of people and systems which should allow him to produce consistent, high quality results over the coming four to five years and offset the challenge of Pacific's non-affiliation with any of the local banks.

Currently, Pacific Insurance sells at a reasonable 12.8 times 1994 EPS. The compound growth in EPS over the last five years was 55 per cent. Return on average equity will reach 25 per cent for 1993. After factoring in moderately higher loss ratios, I expect Pacific to report EPS gains of 20 per cent for the next three to five years.

SAMSUNG RADIATOR – JULY 1994

Samsung Radiator was founded in 1969 near Pusan, on the southern coast of South Korea. After 25 years of growth, Samsung Radiator has emerged today as one of the two dominant manufacturers of auto radiators. The company has a 50 per cent market share of both copper and aluminium radiators, and sells to all the major auto and commercial vehicle manufacturers. Despite the Samsung name, the company does not belong to the monolithic Samsung chaebol, but is a family-owned, conservatively managed business. The current president, Mr Ko Ho-kon, is the son of the founder and current chairman.

Samsung Radiator has very positive growth characteristics. The owners have a long-term track record of dealing fairly with minority shareholders. The shares sell at a deep discount to any realistic assessment of its true value and offer us a very attractive long-term investment opportunity.

Like many people, I am excited about the prospects for growth of the Korean auto industry. Over the past five years the compound growth rate in auto sales topped 16 per cent and the growth should accelerate with the improved domestic economy in 1994 and 1995. The business is ideally suited to the strengths of the Korean business community.

However, I have found it very difficult to uncover attractive investment opportunities in the Korean auto industry. Hyundai Motors, Daewoo Motors, Kia Motors and Asia Motors all suffer from very high debt burdens, and negative cash flow after counting the capital expenditures.

Reports of heavy unconsolidated losses at the overseas subsidiaries further blemish the attraction of these equities.

The auto parts companies offer more alternatives for investors, although many suffer from the same ills as the auto producers. Mando Machinery, Samsung Radiator's major competitor, is a typical example of Korean chaebol-related companies. In 1993, net interest expense totalled 67 per cent of operating income and 6.1 per cent of sales. Interest bearing debt to equity was 210 per cent. After-interest cash flow from operations covered capital expenditure only once in the last seven years. The 1993 return on equity was 5.2 per cent.

My initial attraction to Samsung Radiator was the balance sheet. The company's seven year track record shows that the company has never been heavily in debt since 1987 when the financial statements first became public and has self-financed above-average growth. In contrast to its competitors, Samsung Radiator has limited debt. Year-end cash, net of all interest bearing debt, amounted to 33 per cent of the current share price and more than 50 per cent of the fund's acquisition cost.

After a number of company visits to the head office in Changwon, a major industrial city near Pusan, and the regional office in Seoul, I am convinced of the bright prospects for the radiator business and Samsung Radiator's role in that business.

Like many Korean public companies, Samsung Radiator does not produce consolidated financial statements. Since the accounts of many private companies are available in Korea, David Devine and I have carried out our own consolidation of the balance sheet and income statement. In the case of Samsung Radiator the consolidated accounts significantly enhance the financial strength of the company and its earnings growth rate. Compound growth in unconsolidated EPS over the past seven years has been 34 per cent, while the consolidated results show compound growth of 41 per cent. This is particularly impressive since the consolidated balance sheet is stronger than the unconsolidated one.

While Top Fund purchased its holding at a lower valuation, the stock is still very attractive at the current price. Based on December 1993's consolidated earnings, the PE stands at an undemanding 7.6 times. The price to consolidated book value is 1.5 times, and the consolidated return on year-end equity in 1993 was 20.2 per cent.

I am delighted to report that the fund is currently the second largest foreign investor in Samsung Radiator. Like many of our Korean holdings, it would be almost impossible to source such a block of stock without an increase in the 10 per cent limit on foreign holdings.

I also remain excited by our other Korean holdings. The fund has been a buyer, not a seller, of Korean equities over the past several months. While undoubtedly we will experience periods of volatility while the North/South Korea reunification issue creeps its way towards an eventual solution, our Korean holdings represent solid long-term value for the patient investor.

YAOHAN INTERNATIONAL CATERERS –
OCTOBER 1994

I am delighted to inform our investors that the fund has successfully accumulated a large position at a bargain valuation in Yaohan International Caterers in Hong Kong, which should provide us exciting returns over the coming years.

Most investors know that my wife and her partners have built up a substantial retail business in Hong Kong and China called USA & Co. As a director of this company, I have experienced the extremely challenging retail environment in Hong Kong. In recent years, sales volume has been buoyant but the rising cost of people and space has generally outstripped the growth in turnover, particularly on a compounded basis. During my nine years in Hong Kong, the city has gone from being a cheap city to an enormously expensive city. This trend has not been friendly to retailers.

It was partially due to my direct experience in retail that I greeted Mr Glenn Chan, Managing Director of Yaohan International Caterers, with a fair dose of scepticism when I first met him early this year. And it was this same experience which convinced me that Mr Chan was an exceptional businessman, when I had the opportunity to fully digest and understand his business and track record. Glenn is an extremely experienced manager of stores and restaurants who was involved in the early success of Cafe de Coral and Maxims in Hong Kong in the 1970s. I find that Glenn treats his stores and restaurants like his own children, caring for them when they are sick and pushing them to achieve great results when they are strong. As shareholders, we could ask for no more of an effort on our behalf.

As of 1 September 1994, Yaohan International Caterers owned 21 restaurants under a variety of names and formats, and 38 cake shops and bakeries under the names St. Honore and Bread Boutique. In the most recent fiscal year ended 31 March 1994, the business generated over US$112 million in revenue and US$11.5 million in profit. This was the ninth consecutive year of increased sales and profits. As is often the case with successful businesses, Yaohan International Caterers has partly funded the growth in a creative and advantageous manner. In this case, the cake shops have collected over US$16 million cash in exchange for 'cake coupons' which the cake shop sells to brides at the time of their weddings as gifts for all invited guests. The cash cycle of this arrangement has helped Glenn Chan to self-finance the growth with a great deal of essentially free capital.

Yaohan International Caterers has produced a superb track record over

226

the past nine years with sales and net profits compounding at a rate of 26.3 per cent and 44.2 per cent respectively. Over the five years since the company went public, sales and net profits have compounded at a rate of 35.0 per cent and 25.3 per cent respectively. The return on average equity for the year ended 31 March 1994 was 32.7 per cent, which is particularly impressive since net cash equalled 50 per cent of equity.

Top Fund has purchased just under 3 per cent of the shares of Yaohan Caterers at a bargain valuation of 9.2 times historic EPS and 7.8 times our forecast March 1995 EPS. The stock yields 4.6 per cent on the historic dividend.

Glenn Chan has operated the company independently, but the Yaohan Group, a successful department store company from Japan, has held 51 per cent of the shares. While I am convinced of the high integrity of Glenn Chan and his ability to manage the company for its minority shareholders, I am leery of the Yaohan presence. Accordingly I welcome the recently announced transaction in which Glenn Chan has agreed to sell a number of profitable bakeries, which he owned privately, to the company at 6.5 times earnings, in exchange for an option to acquire an additional 8 per cent stake in the company. Upon exercise of the option, the Yaohan Group's stake will fall below 50 per cent. I am hopeful that by the end of the fiscal year, Yaohan's stake will fall further.

Appendix D: Accounting policies and information – opportunities and pitfalls

Examples from Richard Lawrence, first prepared for a presentation in Seoul in March 1994

Key areas of danger include: unconsolidated subsidiaries
depreciation methods
recognition of income
capitalization of interest expenses, R&D,
    and foreign exchange losses
guarantees

Example 1: the importance of the balance sheet
A Du Pont model comparison of Samsung Radiator and Mando Machinery

A key distinction is between size and profitability. Debt is often a treadmill, especially in a high interest rate environment like Korea. Watch out for megalomaniac companies!

Year end 31 Dec 92		Samsung Radiator	Mando Machinery
Gearing	total assets/equity	219.77%	370.59%
Asset turnover	sales/assets	95.93%	96.02%
Profit margin	PBIT/sales	8.54%	8.91%
Interest burden	interest/PBIT	−41.32%	78.93%
Tax burden	tax/PBT	11.83%	15.53%

Du Pont formula:
Gearing × asset turnover × operating profit
margin × (1–interest burden) × (1–tax
burden) =   **ROE =**   **22.44%**   **5.64%**

Broadly very similar businesses, the large difference in ROE lies in the different debt levels of the two companies. The greater debt of Mando gives it more assets, but the cost of servicing the debt more than outweighs the advantage of having more assets.

(A)	Gearing = total assets/equity	219.77%	370.59%
(B)	Return on assets	10.21%	1.52%
(A) × (B) = ROE		22.44%	5.64%
Overlook's target PE is half ROE		11.22x	2.82x
Actual PE on 14 March 1994		11.51x	34.50x

Example 2: rising profits and falling EPS – the effect of dilutive rights issues
A comparison of Shin Poong Paper and On Yang Pulp

Rights issues are usually dilutive to earnings per share.
Money raised through rights issues is often used to fund acquisitions from the majority shareholders.
Frequent rights issues show that companies are more interested in size than in earnings per share.

	Sales won m	Net income won m	Rights shares issued, m	EPS won
Shin Poong Paper				
1985	29,117	1,698	none	1,010
1986	46,238	2,958	none	1,759
1987	70,750	3,571	none	2,123
1988	78,553	5,978	none	3,554
1989	53,779	2,520	none	1,498
1990	68,389	4,571	none	2,718
1991	66,169	12,160	none	7,225
1992	71,004	12,225	none	7,265
Compound growth	13.58%	32.58%		32.56%
On Yang Pulp				
1985	23,383	295	none	670
1986	32,391	759	none	1,725
1987	36,700	1,258	360,000	2,516
1988	42,487	1,093	800,000	937
1989	50,668	1,143	600,000	653
1990	49,797	1,517	959,200	643
1991	46,354	2,012		637
1992	57,389	3,440	1,240,800	863
Compound growth	13.69%	42.03%		3.67%

Appendix E: The risks of conventional wisdom

Extract from an article by Marc Faber in the Asian Wall Street Journal, *October 1990*

Most investment managers prefer to fail conventionally rather than to succeed unconventionally. A successful country, a company with a well-established track record, a triple-A bond, are given strong preference over an unrecognized or unknown investment opportunity. So investors pay dearly for popular stocks or for perceived low-risk investments.

Conventional wisdom, crowd behaviour, and investment based on superficial analysis, however, frequently lead to catastrophic results. The lesson for today is that while it is quite likely that Asia will continue to flourish in the long term, history shows there are no assurances that today's economic centres will prosper the way most investors expect.

Following the Japanese surrender in August 1945, the Chinese Nationalist administration under Chiang Kai-Shek moved back into Shanghai. The Nationalists and the international community in Shanghai expected little trouble from the Communists.

From then until 1949, Shanghai was by far the most important and thriving industrial and commercial metropolis in Asia. Entrepreneurs and investors poured money into Shanghai's industries and businesses. The optimistic mood in Shanghai was also reflected in the booming performance of the Shanghai Stock Exchange.

Shanghai aside, the choices for potential investors in Asia appeared limited. Tokyo and Osaka may have rivalled Shanghai in terms of industrial might before the war, but after the Japanese surrender very few people gave Japan much of a chance. The Pauley report, published in December 1945, suggested that Japan should be given the lowest priority of any Asian country for US aid and financial assistance.

Taiwan had long been Japan's colonial breadbasket and was insignificant economically. Korea, annexed by Japan in 1910, had been repressed and a civil war was brewing that would leave the country bombed and divided.

231

Hong Kong and Singapore were thriving little port cities, but they had few industries in the mid-1940s. Hankow, Chungking and Canton were all much more important.

On the other hand, the conventional wisdom of 1946 found Saigon, Rangoon and Manila fairly appealing to the savvy investor.

Saigon was declared independent by Ho Chi Minh in August 1945, but one month later British and French troops entered the city and the Viet Minh retreated to the northern zone, where they retained control under Ho Chi Minh's provisional government in Hanoi. Once relegated to the north, the Viet Minh were not considered a serious threat to the south until the defeat of the French at Dien Bien Phu in 1954. But until the early 1970s, it was assumed that the US would prevent the Viet Cong from endangering Saigon.

Investors therefore remained quite confident about Vietnam. Even during the 1971–72 Hong Kong bull market, it was popularly believed that South Vietnam would be the next boom country. This was only one year before it fell to the Viet Cong!

Prior to World War II, Rangoon had been one of the richest and economically most important cities in Asia – much more so than Bangkok. Following the Japanese capitulation, Aung San and his associates won the elections for a constituent assembly and secured the agreement of most of the hill people for the establishment of a Union of Burma. The political climate soon deteriorated, but Rangoon still held economic promise.

The Philippines had been under American rule since 1902, and as a result Manila had become of political importance in Asia. The continued support and friendship of the US when the Philippines was granted independence in 1946 meant that the former colony, and Manila in particular, looked promising.

We can therefore assume that if a group of businessmen or portfolio managers had come to Asia in 1946 to invest, the bulk of such investments would have found their way into Shanghai, and some possibly into Rangoon, Saigon and Manila.

Ironically, even after the Communist takeover in 1949, foreign investment continued to flow into Shanghai as many overseas Chinese were lured back by Communist promises. Many local Chinese businessmen even argued that China had seen many revolutions and that the resulting chaos always provided a good buying opportunity! The rest is history.

By 1994, Shanghai, Rangoon, Saigon and Manila were all attracting renewed investment attention. No Asian cities which were popular in 1990 have fallen from favour – yet. CB

232

Appendix F: Boom and bust in emerging markets

Extracts from Marc Faber's 'Gloom, Boom and Doom Report', March 1994. (Tables omitted.)

Reading the international financial press, one might think that emerging market investing was a new phenomenon invented recently by the likes of Templeton, Morgan Stanley, Genesis, or Barings. One also gets the impression that the road to emerging economies is paved with gold based on the recent performance of these funds.

American business fluctuations in the last century provide an excellent historical precedent for today's emerging markets, simply because America was then the world's largest emerging economy. A study of past American economic cycles may thus provide some interesting insights into the current emerging market investment euphoria, and lay to rest some of the prevailing myths about striking it rich in emerging economies.

THE EMERGING AMERICAN ECONOMY IN THE LAST CENTURY

The US experienced rapid population growth and underwent a major transformation from a predominantly agrarian producer at the beginning of the 1800s to the world's largest producer of manufactured goods by the end of the century.

In 1790, the US was a nation of less than four million people dispersed over a huge land area (for comparison's sake, in 1800 Europe's population was about 180 million, India's was 190 million, and China's was 320 million). There were only seven cities with a population of over 5,000, and twelve with a population exceeding 2,500. The remaining population of 3.7 million was rural. During the first half of the century, the population grew on average by about 3.5 per cent per annum (largely because of immigration), but slowed to around 2 per cent in the decade preceding 1900.

By 1885, the US, which had hardly any industries at the beginning of the century, led the world in manufacturing, producing 28.9 per cent of the world's manufactured goods. Britain was second, with 26.6 per cent, and Germany third, with 13.9 per cent. America's rise to become the world's dominant economic power around 1885 is unique from a historical economic point of view. And today it is the dream of every emerging market investor to find another 19th-century America growth story.

However, America's road from extremely humble beginnings to an economic dominance and prosperity unprecedented in the history of mankind was not smooth and paved with gold (certainly not for foreign investors). Rather, it was strewn with nasty and frequently unavoidable potholes. Furthermore, the American route to prosperity was often controlled by all manner of bandits and extremely corrupt government officials who were very clever at robbing the naïve and credulous foreign and local traveller of his purse.

Economic growth in America in the last century was closely linked to the cotton industry (especially in the South), to canal and railroad construction throughout the continent (which opened the West), to the exploitation of America's vast natural resources (the gold discoveries in California), to the development of new tracts of land, and to the rise of the steel industry.

In the first half of the 19th century, the US cotton industry grew very rapidly and the prosperity of the South depended largely on good crops and high prices. While the US had produced hardly any cotton around 1800, its plantations supplied five-sixths of the world's cotton by 1860. For the South at least, the cotton industry was about as important as the oil industry is in the Middle East today, and certainly far more economically significant than the current agricultural sector in countries such as New Zealand or Australia. Just as the South's fortunes were very much tied to the price of cotton, so too were US manufacturing output (principally in the Northeast) and US imports. In the early 1830s, a cotton boom had a favourable impact on the entire economy. Between 1831 and 1836, income from cotton trade rose from US$25 million to US$71 million. But when cotton prices began to fall in 1837, the South's income and its ability to consume declined and negatively affected industrial production in the Northeast, as well as imports of luxury goods from Europe. The severe 1837 to 1842 depression was thus due, at least to some extent, to a 70 per cent decline in the price of cotton.

The reason for discussing the US cotton industry is that, although it expanded very rapidly in the first three-quarters of the last century (it was, without a doubt, a growth industry – by 1860 the US produced 2,300 million pounds of cotton, up from only 1.5 million in 1790), from time to time it bankrupted a large number of cotton growers who overpaid for land when prices were high. (The South's reliance on cotton and on cheap slave labour to grow it also led to the Civil War.) Furthermore, cotton fabrics were then as popular among consumers as VCRs, colour TVs and soft drinks are today. Emerging market investors should not overlook this point. That an industry is growing rapidly in the long term does not change the fact that when the market for its products deteriorates because of temporary oversupply or a deficiency in demand, prices fall, leading to painful consequences, not only for owners, but also for suppliers, and especially for creditors! Today, every emerging economy wants to grow through the export of manufactured consumer goods. But that does not mean that every industry will be successful year after year.

Consumer electronics, Nike shoes, soft drinks, and garments are today no different than cotton was in the last century, and will thus from time to time be vulnerable to periods of overproduction and price falls.

In view of the gargantuan appetite of investors to participate in infrastructure projects in emerging economies, a quick look at the construction of canals and railroads in the US during the 19th century is in order. It may also dampen some of the prevailing enthusiasm. Impetus for the canal boom, which lasted from about 1820 to 1836, was the completion of the 364 mile Erie Canal in 1824. The Erie Canal proved to be enormously successful, because it enabled grain from the Great Lakes to be brought to New York. It also linked New York to a hinterland of great economic potential and made it the financial and economic metropolis of the Union. The Erie Canal cut both the travel time and the shipping expense incurred on journeys from Detroit, Cleveland and Buffalo to New York to one tenth of what they had been previously. In 1833, the Welland Canal was completed, bypassing Niagara Falls and connecting the Great Lakes to St Lawrence. The completion of these two canals had a very favourable impact on New York as the route of trade and population growth shifted to that city. It also caused a wild canal mania as every city or state having two or more bodies of water planned or built canals in order to link them, hoping to duplicate the success of the Erie Canal. The 1820–1836 American canal mania did not fail to attract the attention of European emerging market investors, and the demand for American canal bonds and shares was so great that there were not enough issues to satisfy them (sounds familiar!). When the Morris Canal and Banking Company raised US$1 million, it could have obtained US$20 million, most of which was offered from England.

Hand in hand with the cotton and canal boom was a wild speculative orgy in real estate and banking shares. Between 1830 and 1837, 347 new banks were licensed, frequently led by men of very questionable background and no banking experience. These banks enabled speculators to purchase land in public sales at inflated prices on credit. Public land sales rose from 4.7 million acres in 1834 to 12.6 million in 1835 and 20 million in 1836, as prices for land in most parts of the East and South more than doubled (pale by Hong Kong standards). The Chicago land boom of the early 1830s has been well documented. Until then, Chicago had been a relatively unknown town and its real estate was much cheaper than land on the East Coast. However, the planned Illinois-Michigan Canal, which was to connect the Chicago harbour and Lake Michigan with the Illinois River which flows into the Mississippi at St Louis, began to attract great speculative interest in Chicago land. Upon completion of this canal, Chicago would become a major transportation hub. Within a few years, land prices soared by about 100 times. The construction of the Illinois-Michigan canal finally began in 1836 at about the same time as Chicago land prices peaked. Following the 1837 crisis, Chicago real estate plunged by 90 per cent, while it took ten years to complete the canal. (Construction came to a standstill during the 1837–1842 depression, as the State of Illinois, burdened by large debts and a poor economy, went into default – as did eight other states.)

How the American boom ended should be of some interest to emerging market investors: in 1836, British reserves fell by almost 50 per cent as gold flowed to America to purchase American securities. The Bank of England was thus forced to increase the rediscount rate twice, which led to a momentary panic in Britain and the closure of several banks. Higher interest rates in Britain (the call rate in 1837 rose to around 15 per cent) reduced the demand for American securities almost overnight, and this at precisely the time when the demand for money in America was at its highest. The sudden absence of foreign capital had a devastating effect on the US: all American banks had to suspend specie payments, and between 1837 and 1839 over 1,500 banks failed. The 1837 crisis was aggravated by a sharp fall in the price of cotton, which bankrupted many speculators and led to a sharp fall in the demand for consumer goods from the South. By the fall of 1837, nine-tenths of Eastern factories were closed. The 1837–1841 American depression, known as 'the Hard Times Depression', was extremely severe. It also had a very negative impact on Europe, especially England, because so much money which had been invested in American canals, banks, and real estate had become worthless. The slump in financial assets which followed the earlier prosperity was a consequence of rising cotton prices, excessive monetary expansion, and euphoric purchases of American securities by foreign investors.

While prior to 1837 the appetite of foreign investors for US securities appeared to be infinite, following the crisis the London *Times* wrote, 'The people of the United States may be fully persuaded that there is a certain class of securities to which no abundance of money, however great, can give value, and that in this class their own securities stand pre-eminent.'

From an historical economic point of view, the 1837 crisis and ensuing slump is interesting: the crisis was triggered by an event outside the US (the increase in the rediscount rate in Britain) which reduced the flow of money from Europe to America, leading to the first wave of bankruptcies among American banks. As well, the crisis and the subsequent depression (known in Europe as the 'Hungry Forties') were, for the first time, international in scope.

Recovery took place in the mid-1840s and accelerated thereafter mainly as a result of railroad construction which, as Schumpeter wrote, 'played a leading role in the process of economic evolution which produced the situations that developed into crisis'. A mini-boom in railroad completions took place in 1835, but in comparison to the canal craze it was insignificant and had little impact on the economy. However, after 1848, railroad construction expanded rapidly and stimulated the economy, bringing about the first railroad mania in the mid-1850s and the crisis which followed in 1857. (The economy also improved because of a gradual rise in cotton prices and an expansion of cotton production from 2.1 million bales in 1850 to 4.5 million bales in 1859.) One of the reasons for the pick-up in railroad construction in the 1850s and the attendant boom was the discovery of gold on Swiss settler Johann Sutter's property in California's lower Sacramento Valley. Gold production surged after 1847, which helped to finance the economic expansion and fuel a land and railroad construction boom.

The railroading of America led to a tenfold increase in the production of pig iron and a doubling of coal production between 1850 and 1856. Foreigners, who after the debacle of 1837 had left the US market vowing never to return, were once again eagerly buying US railroad securities and, for the first time in American financial history, speculative mining stocks in order to capitalize on the expected bonanza from the gold discovery. By 1853, 26 per cent of all American railroad bonds were held by foreign investors who focused particularly on the more speculative issues. One of the interesting aspects of the 1850–1857 railroad boom was that for investors it came to an end long before the 1857 crisis. The All-Inclusive index of railroad stocks topped out in December 1852, long before railroad construction peaked in 1856, this largely because capital transfers, which reached a high of US$56 million in 1853, declined to only US$12 million in 1856. The reason for the slowdown in overseas buying was the Crimean War (1854–1856) fought between Great Britain, France and Turkey on the one side and Russia on the other.

The Crimean War drained European liquidity and led to rising interest rates and less demand on the continent for American railroad securities, at a time when the railroads needed to raise a maximum amount of capital in order to finance their expansion. Simply put, there was a large oversupply of securities in the American capital market which depressed prices, even though business conditions in America remained strong until 1857 (it should be remembered that the Crimean War was, on balance, very favourable for America as agricultural product prices rose and industrial production was stimulated). However, emerging market investors should remember: stock prices can fall long before the economy turns down or well ahead of deteriorating profits, simply because monetary conditions deteriorate.

The catalyst for the 1857 crisis was the failure of the Ohio Life & Trust Company (which specialized in land and railroad investments and in commodity futures!) and the sinking of the steamer *Central America*, with its cargo of US$1.6 million in California gold off Cape Hatteras (gold shipments from California had always been a confidence booster and had provided some liquidity to the East Coast banks). The panic reached a peak in October 1857 when 1,415 banks and numerous railroads failed (the Mining Exchange in New York even closed its doors), and as the crisis spread to London and Paris where many American securities were actively traded. An interesting aspect of the 1857 panic is that it was principally a financial crisis and relatively little damage was done to the economy, particularly with respect to the South. While American cotton worth US$128 million had been exported in 1856, cotton export earnings rose to US$192 million in 1860 (the strong economic performance of the cotton growing areas at a time when the financial sector of the Northeast was in a crisis gave the South confidence that, in a conflict, the Northern economy would collapse – a notion which eventually contributed to the outbreak of hostilities and the Civil War). This is another point for investors to remember: a severe financial crisis can occur for a number of reasons (including excessive speculation, which was the case in the 1850s), and not necessarily because of a general and long lasting downturn in the real economy.

For emerging market investors, the lead-up to the global 1873 crisis and the depression which followed is also of interest. The end of the American Civil War (1861–1865) and the German unification which was achieved following the Franco-Prussian War (1870–1871) gave immense impetus to US and German economic development, enabling them to catch up with Britain and France, previously leaders of the Industrial Revolution era. This was especially true for Germany, whose economy was stimulated by the French War Indemnity. Max Wirth describes in *Geschichte der Handelskrisen* (published in 1874) how a new issue boom swept across Austria, Germany, and Prussia from 1869 to 1874, designed to finance railroads, new iron and steel works, real estate companies, and banks. In Prussia, 259 companies were established in 1871, and 504 in 1872, as against only 34 in 1870 and 225 since the beginning of the century (1866–1873 became known as 'the golden age of company promoters'). People felt extremely confident about the future, because the economy in Europe and in the US had been expanding rapidly in the late 1860s (between 1860 and 1873 German per capita consumption of iron more than doubled). Bullish sentiment in Europe was further boosted by the laying of the first transatlantic cable in 1866 (by Cable & Wireless) and by the World Exhibition in Vienna which was to open in 1873. Hyndman, a contemporary economist, writes in *Commercial Crises of the Nineteenth Century* (published in 1892): 'What made matters even worse was the foundation of all sorts of banking institutions, which had little else than stock-jobbing in view. The real object of banks and companies was quite lost sight of, and men were swept into the whirl of speculation without having any other desire than to gamble and to make money in the lottery of the share market. Mortgage banks and building societies gave an undue impetus to building speculations in the great cities, from which Berlin and Vienna still suffer. These building speculations were indeed among the most unsound and ruinous of all the businesses of the time. The price of land was run up to a purely fictitious level, and loans were made to cover the sites with houses to an extent which, when the crash came, rendered it impossible to recover even a fraction of the principal. The great object was to run up the houses in good, or what were likely to be good, situations, and put a rental upon them which in nine cases out of ten was never realized. To give an adequate account of this building mania in Berlin and Vienna would require a chapter to itself. But similar follies can be seen in London on a smaller proportional scale, and the speculative builder who, working on a small capital, must live continuously from hand to mouth, borrowing at usurious rates to complete jerry-built structures, is well-known here at home.'

In America, the most important event of the 1860s was the rapid territorial expansion towards the West Coast, which, aided by the construction of the great transcontinental railways (the first of which was the Union Pacific, completed in 1869), was accomplished in an astonishingly short time. The building of the transcontinental railways led to another speculative mania, largely financed by foreign investors once again. Between 1860 and 1873, railroad miles in operation more than doubled (the largest increase took place from 1870 to 1873). Foreigners, who held US$51.9 million in 1853, had increased their holdings to over US$260 million by 1872. But this time, the railroad mania was not confined to British or American railroad securities. Austria tripled her rail mileage in eight years, and Russia built 12,000 miles in four years. In addition, Latin American borrowers, especially Argentina, raised funds in London and Paris for a number of rail projects (by 1869 British investors held US$200 million worth of South American railroad construction bonds; these investments led eventually to the Baring crisis in the 1890s). The Suez Canal was completed in 1869, sparking renewed interest in ocean transportation and great optimism with regard to international trade and economic growth.

Reading contemporary accounts, one cannot fail to notice the parallels of the then prevailing optimism to the current upbeat mood about the prospects of so many emerging economies such as China, India, and Latin America. Then, as now, the sky seemed the limit, while risk considerations took a backseat. Everywhere, fraud, manipulation of stocks, government corruption, and all make of illegal or shady schemes were common practice, but no one took much notice, because as McCulloch pointed out: 'In speculation, as in most other things, one individual derives confidence from another. Such a one purchases or sells, not because he has had any really accurate information as to the state of demand and supply, but because someone else has done so before him.'

The end of prosperity came in May 1873 when the Vienna Stock Exchange was struck with a devastating financial panic which spread like wildfire to London, Paris, Vienna, Berlin, and then to New York.

Although the World Exhibition opened in Vienna on May 1, 1873, stock prices had already begun to drift lower in April and they totally collapsed on May 8 and 9. Within one month, most bank shares had been sliced in half and, according to a contemporary, 'die Wiener Boerse stand foermlich unter der Herrschaft des Schreckens'. In September 1873 the crisis reached New York. According to a German correspondent, American bonds could not have been sold in Europe 'even if sold by an angel of Heaven'. The leading and most prestigious American investment bank, Jay Cooke & Co (the equivalent today would be Goldman Sachs or Morgan Stanley), was forced to close its doors and went out of business. The investment community was stunned and a panic followed which brought the closure of the Exchange for ten days! Unlike in 1857, the 1873 crisis was followed by a deflationary depression that lasted six years (the Wholesale Price Index fell from 133 in 1873 to 91 in 1878). Most railroads under construction went bankrupt and in the years following the crisis, over 20,000 commercial and industrial failures were recorded in the US alone. America underwent the most severe depression of the 19th century, a slump which was almost as bad as the 1929–1932 depression.

There were many reasons for the 1873 collapse: the railway boom sweeping Europe and the United States which immobilized capital and strained financial resources, overexpansion of the iron and steel industries, overtrading in stocks, widespread fraudulent practices by stock promoters, corrupt government officials, and excessive speculation in real estate all contributed to the panic of 1873 and the ensuing depression which was felt throughout the world. Reading the works of contemporary economists, one notices that in 1869 some warning signals had become apparent. However, they had been ignored in the whirlwind of speculation as business conditions continued to look promising, because so many countries were in the process of industrialising. However, one factor concerning the collapse of the stock-market bubble in Vienna, Berlin, Paris, London and

New York should not be forgotten: a flood of new stock and bond issues came to the market between 1871 and 1873, and sooner or later, the supply of this paper had to exceed the demand of the investing public and depress prices.

SOME THOUGHTS

The 19th century was undoubtedly a period of rapid economic growth in Europe and particularly the United States, then the largest emerging economy. However, in examining historical economic literature, one cannot help being amazed at how much money investors repeatedly lost, and how violent the recessionary periods were. Foreign investors especially were taken to the cleaners again and again by ruthless and frequently fraudulent stock promoters, swindlers, and corrupt government officials. The most striking characteristic of foreign investors was that they were, throughout the 19th century, latecomers to an investment fad. They invariably bought American canal, railroad, and other industrial stocks at or near a peak in the cycle. When prices were low and business conditions depressed, foreign investors were usually absent, having burnt their fingers during the previous boom.

In the field of emerging market investing, nothing has changed, and to my surprise, nobody seems to have learnt from these past experiences, which I have tried – admittedly very superficially – to document. From time to time, investors seem to become far too optimistic about the prospects of a new region or the potential of a new industry about which they usually know very little. People who in the 19th century would have bought American canal and railroad shares (most of which failed) are now buying Chinese infrastructure funds and telephone companies in the remotest regions of the world. A few years ago, investors claimed a recession was impossible in Japan; today the same people seem to believe that Southeast Asia cannot experience business downturns. Fortunately, our readers know that investing in rapidly growing economies, like that of the US in the last century, is much trickier than it appears to the casual observer.

A final point about investing in emerging regions: the centres of economic activity change over time. New England experienced a relative decline in manufacturing in the second half of the last century, while the Great Lakes region grew at above average rates. China investors should consider this point: growth could, as we believe, shift from the south to Shanghai and the northeast, and relegate Hong Kong to the status of a Baltimore or New Orleans.

241

Index